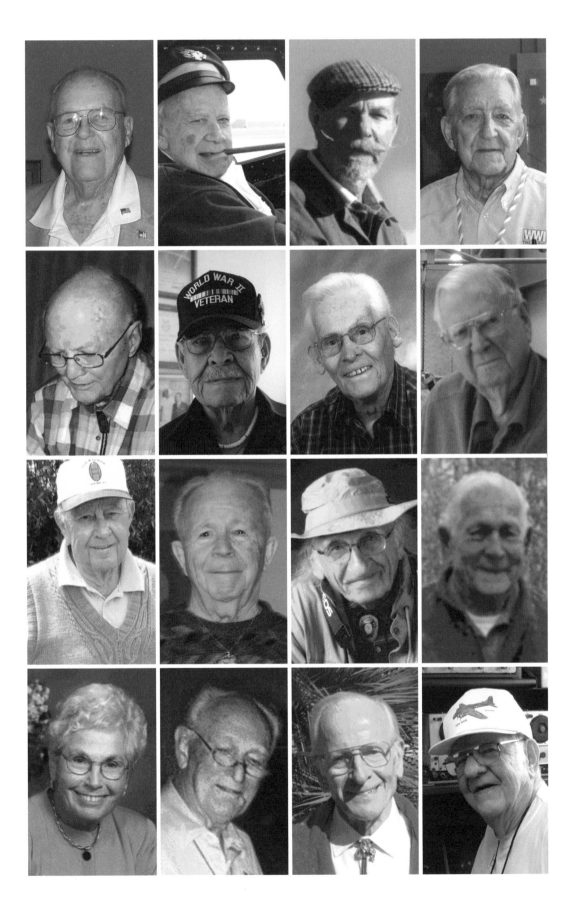

FROM TOP LEFT TO RIGHT

1. John Ervin
2. John Gibbons
3. Vincent "Mike" McKinney
4. George Wichterich
5. Buster Simmons
6. Gilbert Zamorano
7. Jean Rene Champion
8. Thomas Blakey
9. Douglas Jenney
10. Willy Gerstner
11. Ernst Floeter
12. Mike Pachuta
13. Muriel Kappler
14. Frank Towers
15. Hans Eckhardt
16. Frank Buschmeier

WAR
STORIES

WORLD WAR II
FIRST HAND

WEIDER HISTORY
PUBLICATIONS

In this iconic photograph General Dwight D. Eisenhower gives members of E Company, 506 Parachute Infantry Regiment, 101st Airborne Division, the "Full Victory" order of the day as they prepare for their night jump into Normandy.

WAR STORIES

WORLD WAR II FIRSTHAND

D-DAY

THE CAMPAIGN ACROSS FRANCE

JAY WERTZ

WEIDER HISTORY PUBLICATIONS

To John William Finn, James C. Bounds,
Hans Enderle, Raul Garcia, James L. Evans,
John J. Porter, Frank Tuttle, Alan C. Webber
and George Wichterich.

Weider History Publications
An imprint of Weider History Group, Inc.
19300 Promenade Drive
Leesburg, VA 20176
www.HistoryNet.com

ISBN 10: 0-9842127-1-X
ISBN 13: 978-0-9842127-1-2

For more information about this book please visit:
www.HistoryNetShop.com
or call: 1-800-358-6327

TABLE OF CONTENTS

6 Foreword
10 Introduction

CHAPTER ONE
PREPARATION FOR THE ALLIED CROSS-CHANNEL INVASION

12 The Genesis of an Idea
22 The Dieppe Raid
24 Site Selection
24 Landing Craft and Other Materiel Concerns
26 Leadership
30 The Opposition - German Defenses and Organization
35 Allied Personnel
47 Air Operations
55 Amassing the Naval Force
57 Intelligence
60 Final Preparations
68 *Exercise Tiger*

CHAPTER TWO
JUNE 6, 1944

76 The Allied Airborne Operation
95 Air Operations on D-Day
100 Naval Operations Prior to H-Hour
107 The Omaha Beach Landing
132 The Landing at Utah Beach
143 The British and Commonwealth Beaches
150 The End of the Day
152 *The Battle for La Fière Bridge*

CHAPTER THREE
FIGHTING IN THE HEDGEROWS

158 Building the Bridgehead
164 Advances East and West
172 The Caumont Gap

178 Taking Cherbourg
184 The Defense Wears Down
188 The Fall of Cherbourg
194 *American Medical Teams in Normandy*

CHAPTER FOUR
BREAKOUT FROM NORMANDY

202 Plans and Counter Plans
209 Setting Up for the Breakout
232 Patton's Third Army Arrives in France
243 The Falaise Gap Becomes a Pocket
252 *The Plot to Assassinate Hitler*

CHAPTER FIVE
THE ALLIED INVASION OF SOUTHERN FRANCE

258 Anvil Becomes Dragoon
262 The Mediterranean Landings
267 The Allied Push Northward Through Central France
274 *What About the French?*

CHAPTER SIX
THE LIBERATION OF PARIS

278 Patton's Run to the Seine
282 The First Army Advance
284 Movements of the British Second and First Canadian Armies
286 The Paris Uprising
290 Paris Celebrates Liberation
296 *Driving for the Line*

Credits and Acknowledgements
About the Interviewed Veterans
Bibliography • Image Credits • Index

FOREWORD

They are called The Greatest Generation because they fought the greatest war in history. The D-Day landings in Normandy in June 1944 and the subsequent campaign to push the Wehrmacht out of France, the subjects of this book, were one of the key turning points of that war. I knew that generation well.

My parents and most of the adults around me as I grew up in the 1950s and early 1960s were from that generation, of course, but I also had the privilege of knowing many of them as soldiers and of serving with them on the battlefields of a different war. When I enlisted in the U.S. Army in 1966, almost all the senior leaders were World War II veterans. Virtually all the officers above the rank of lieutenant colonel and the NCOs above the rank of master sergeant had served in World War II. Two of the three of the company first sergeants I had in Vietnam were WWII vets. It was their generation that trained me and my generation how to be soldiers and how to survive on the battlefield.

I had the opportunity to pay them back in some small measure in 2004 and 2005, when I was the Department of Defense Executive Director for the World War II 60th Anniversary commemorations in Europe. In June 2004 I had the honor of commanding the 3,300-soldier task force that supported the D-Day 60th Anniversary observances. Preparations for the events started months in advance, and more than a week before the start of the ceremonies we started deploying to Normandy from our bases in Germany. But even before we started that move, it was important for me that all the Young Soldiers I had out in Normandy knew exactly why they were there, just who all those Old Soldiers were, and why this was all such a big deal.

Several weeks before the move I asked Dr. Charles Kirkpatrick, the V Corps Command Historian, to visit all the battalions involved and give the assembled troops a quick history lesson of what D-Day had all been about and why it still mattered 60 years later. A couple weeks after Dr. Kirkpatrick made his rounds, I personally visited the units. I told the troops that although they were going out to Normandy to work on the preparations, to provide the security, and to participate in the ceremonies, they should take every opportunity to talk to the Old Soldiers, to listen to their experiences, to pay attention to what they had to say. It would be an experience they would never forget.

It worked out beautifully. All the Young Soldiers came through. In the days leading up to the ceremonies and during the ceremonies themselves, all my Young Soldiers treated the returning Old Soldiers like rock stars. Often the families of the

---

The New York Times *reports to the nation and the world one of the best-kept secrets in military history – the June 6, 1944 landing of Allied forces on the Calvados coast and Cotentin Peninsula of Normandy, France.*

The New York Times.

6 A.M. EXTRA

"All the News That's Fit to Print"

Partly cloudy and warmer today; moderate to fresh winds. Temperatures Yesterday—Max. 67, Min. 54.

Copyright, 1944, by The New York Times Company.

L. XCIII..No. 31,545.

NEW YORK, TUESDAY, JUNE 6, 1944.

THREE CENTS NEW YORK CITY

LLIED ARMIES LAND IN FRANCE
N THE HAVRE-CHERBOURG AREA;
GREAT INVASION IS UNDER WAY

EVELT SPEAKS

Rome's Fall Marks Up and Two to Go' ng Axis Capitals

S WAY IS HARD

World to Give the ians a Chance r Recovery

Conferees Accept Cabaret Tax Cut

FEDERAL LAW HELD RULING INSURANCE

Supreme Court, 4-3, Decides Business Is Interstate and Subject to Trust Act

PURSUIT ON IN ITALY

Allies Pass Rome, Cross Tiber as Foe Quits Bank Below City

PLANES JOIN IN CHASE

1,200 Vehicles Wrecked —Eighth Army Battles Into More Towns

FIRST ALLIED LANDING MADE ON SHORES OF WESTERN EUROPE

General Eisenhower's armies invaded northern France this morning. While the landing points were not specified, the Germans said that troops had gone ashore near Havre and that fighting raged at Caen (1). The enemy also said that parachutists had descended at the northern tip of the Normandy Peninsula (2) and heavy bombing had been visited on Calais and Dunkerque (3).

EISENHOWER AC

U.S., British, Canad Troops Backed by Sea, Air Forces

MONTGOMERY LEA

Nazis Say Their Sho Units Are Battling O Parachutists

Communique No. On Allied Invasio

By RAYMOND DANIELL

POPE GIVES THANKS ROME WAS SPARED

Voices Appreciation to 'Both Belligerents' in Message to Throng at St. Peter's

Italy's Monarch Yields Rule To Son, but Retains Throne

PARADE OF PLANES CARRIES INVADERS

Witness Says First 'Chutists Met Only Light Fire When They Landed in France

ALLIED WARNING FLASHED TO COAST

People Told to Clear Area 22 Miles Inland as Soon as Instructions Are Given

Eisenhower Instructs Europeans; Gives Battle Order to His Armies

War News Summarized

TUESDAY, JUNE 6, 1944.

Old Soldiers looked on in mild bewilderment, not quite understanding why all these young people were making such a fuss over Old Grandpa. The answer, of course, is that the bond between soldiers transcends any gap across generations. A large percentage of my Young Soldiers then were already combat veterans themselves, having just come back from Iraq. Many would go back again for multiple subsequent tours.

A portion of the Colleville Cemetery on a bluff overlooking Omaha Beach. Here thousands of Americans who fought to free France and the rest of Europe from four years of Nazi rule rest in peace.

80s or older. They are passing fast, but fortunately their voices can still be heard. The critical value of books like this one is to preserve their memories and their voices for future generations. A book like this, however, is a selective sample by its very nature. It is only possible for those who survived the war in the first place to speak and tell their stories. And as the war itself slides farther back into the historical past, the pool of living vets diminishes until all the voices will finally fall silent. I was in grade school when the last Civil War veteran died, and the last World War I veteran died just recently.

About 900 American veterans came back to Normandy in June 2004. There were, of course, many more British and French veterans present, because they had to travel far less distance to get there. Our policy was to treat all World War II vets equally. Even the few German vets who showed up received the same welcome and the same access badges as anyone else. Not a single vet complained about that policy. A fair number of the British veterans attended the ceremonies at Omaha and Utah Beaches, rather than the ceremonies on the British/Canadian landing beaches. Those I had a chance to talk to told me that they had actually come ashore at either Omaha or Utah. They included members of Royal Navy shore control parties, Royal Air Force tactical control parties, and various other British specialists attached to American units to support the landings.

Although I remember them when many were still in their 30s and early 40s, the members of the Greatest Generation are all now in their mid-

For all its value for future generations, a book like this can only go so far. There are so many compelling stories to capture and preserve that it becomes necessary to restrict the reminiscences to the war itself. But for those who survived the war, that experience formed the foundation for the rest of their lives. For some, the Second World War was the high point of their lives. Nothing after that came close to matching it. For others, their experiences in the war so traumatized them that they spent the rest of their lives haunted by its ghosts and shadows, wrestling with private demons few of us could ever comprehend. For others, their wartime experiences fired them with a determination to grasp life and live it to its fullest. The hundreds of thousands of American veterans who took advantage of the

G.I. Bill to get a college education all intended to blaze a trail down that path. For the most part, we do not have the space to consider the post-war

This Robert Capa photograph of a soldier struggling in the surf of Omaha Beach is only one of eleven that survived a darkroom accident after the famed photographer landed with the second wave on an assignment for Life *magazine.*

lives of those whose stories appear in this book. I would, however, like to offer some insights on one of these special veterans, James Milnor Roberts, whom I knew. The aide-de-camp to V Corps commander Major General Leonard Gerow, Lieutenant Roberts landed on Omaha's Easy Red Beach with the 115th Infantry on 6 June. As his landing craft started to disembark, the coxswain was killed by German fire. By the time the war was over Roberts was a major and had served in five campaigns across Europe. Following the war Roberts became the president of the Sykes Advertising Agency in Pittsburgh, but he also remained in the U.S. Army Reserve. On 1 June 1971 he was appointed Chief of the Army Reserve, assigned to the Pentagon. He held that post for four years, finally retiring from the Army as a major general. Upon his military retirement he became the Executive Director of the Reserve Officers' Association, serving in that position until 1984. In June 2004 General Roberts was one of the 100 American D-Day veterans selected to receive the Legion of Honor from the French government in Paris on the day prior to the commemoration events. General Roberts died on 2 January 2009, at the age of 91. He was one of the many junior officers and enlisted soldiers of World War II who in subsequent years left such an indelible mark on their country.

This book is not a comprehensive history of the D-Day landings and the Normandy campaign. That is not its purpose. Its intent, rather, is to offer a selection of foxhole-level views of one of the greatest events in history, as seen by those who occupied those foxholes—and lived to tell about it.

Maj. Gen. (ret) David T. Zabecki, PhD
Shifrin Distinguished Chair of
Military and Naval History, 2012
United States Naval Academy

INTRODUCTION

Most people who are even vaguely familiar with World War II know about D-Day. It has become a two-syllable word to symbolize the key to the Allied defeat of the Axis powers. That is why so much of this volume of *War Stories: World War II Firsthand* is devoted to it.

However, the events leading up to D-Day, the preparation for it and results of it are also vital to a clear understanding of World War II. And because it was truly a world war, events occurring simultaneously in Italy, Russia, the Pacific and elsewhere affected the outcome in France and the war's eventual conclusion. While this volume advances the mission of the project by entering the other major theater of the war, there is much left to do and many stories remaining to tell in communicating one of history's most complex and traumatic periods.

As our distinguished foreword author Dr. David T. Zabecki writes, the purpose of this book is to be neither a comprehensive history of the Normandy campaign nor a chronicle of all the veterans of that campaign. Its purpose is, as he states, to preserve the voices and memories of a sample of veterans – a sample which includes as many veterans as possible from as many forces as possible. I am happy to report that more than seventy-five veterans from all U. S. Armed Forces; from Canada, Britain, Germany and France, have portions of their recollections printed in these pages. And though it is not a comprehensive history, it is a fair overview of what occurred leading up to and beyond that fateful day of June 6, 1944. Many accounts of the campaign have been written; beginning with action reports and official military histories and continuing with academic works and popular histories which have been and will continue to be published. It is hoped that readers of this book will seek out reputable works of history to continue to expand their knowledge on aspects of the campaign that intrigue them.

I have a tremendous staff supporting the research, editing and production of this and every volume of *War Stories: World War II Firsthand.* They are based in eight states and two European countries. However, none of the work we do would be possible without the voluntary cooperation of these World War II veterans, their families and friends. Their stories are the beacons that illuminate and color the history presented here. They provide "foxhole-level views," as General Zabecki has stated, to a war that fortunately few of the rest of us have had to endure. But because they did endure it, embracing the full measure of their assigned duties for the forces in which they served, we live in a world bettered by their sacrifice, learning from their experiences. As always, I invite any World War II veterans or those who hold evidence of their stories to contact us if they would like to participate in this project.

Jay Wertz
Phillips Ranch, California
November 6, 2011

American GIs pose from the deck of a Landing Craft, Tank as part of the preparation for the massive cross-Channel assault.

"Deliver us from evil"

BUY WAR BONDS

OFFICIAL U.S. TREASURY POSTER

CHAPTER 1

PREPARATION FOR THE ALLIED CROSS-CHANNEL INVASION
THE GENESIS OF AN IDEA

n 1944, everyone recognized that it was coming. The "cross-Channel Allied invasion" of Northwest Europe – led by Great Britain and powered by the United States. In late 1940, Adolf Hitler and the Third Reich war machine – discouraged from carrying out the challenging *Operation Seelöwe (Sea Lion)* landing on the British Isles after the Brits put up stubborn resistance in the air and unwavering resolve on the ground – turned their attention to the Eastern Front for what they expected to be a quick and demoralizing victory over Joseph Stalin's Soviet Union. That did not occur and as the war continued it was inevitable that an invasion would occur across the English Channel – going in the other direction. The Allies would be coming ashore in France. The British reluctantly agreed to it. Stalin demanded it. The Americans, upon entering the European war, saw no alternative to it. As time and territory began slipping from their grasp, Hitler and his German commanders fully expected it. The only question remained how, when and exactly where.

These questions and many more were seriously addressed by the Anglo-American allies as early as 1942. In the "defeat Germany first" strategy the United States pursued after America entered the war in December 1941, the imperative to land in force on continental Europe was recognized. President Franklin D. Roosevelt and the U. S. Joint Chiefs of Staff saw the coast of France facing the British Isles – where men and materials would have to be amassed – as the most logical site for an invasion to begin. But America's chief allies, the British, and their inimitable Prime Minister and self-appointed war minister, Winston Churchill, had other ideas about

Rotors

Lampboard

Keyboard

Plugboard

Artists working on the U. S. War Bonds campaign scored a bullseye with this emotional appeal to support America's efforts in the European Theater.

The Enigma machine, seen here in one of its many portable versions, was the basis of German military codes. A series of tumblers were set with a daily key to create readable dispatches from encoded messages. British cryptographers broke the code with a system given the security designation ULTRA.

how the war in Europe should be carried out.

With massive losses in the Spring 1940 Nazi blitzkrieg of Western Europe, Britain had good reason to be apprehensive in returning to the shores at Dunkerque, France or anywhere else along the continental coastline. With his first objective achieved – getting America into the war – Churchill then focused on his second – selling Roosevelt and U. S. military leaders on British ideas of "exploiting

Above: Prime Minister Winston Churchill and other Commonwealth dignitaries visit British soldiers on May 12, 1944. Churchill loved to mingle with the troops and even planned to cross the Channel on D-Day until the supreme commander found a way to scuttle the venture for the prime minister's safety.
Left: Adolf Hitler, accompanied by other German officials, grimly inspects aerial bomb damage in an unknown German city in 1944. The Allied bombing campaign was at its apex at the time this image was made, part of a German film captured by the U.S. Army Signal Corps on the Western Front.

the soft underbelly" of Nazi-occupied Europe to defeat Hitler and Germany. Presented at the Arcadia Conference in Washington just after America's war declaration on Germany, the idea was to find vulnerable spots in the long perimeter of Axis territory and strike them hard and fast. As examples Churchill used places where the British Empire was still hanging on for dear life against the offensive power of the Third Reich – Egypt, Tunisia and the eastern Mediterranean.

American leaders listened to the idea but soon returned to urging a decisive invasion of Western Europe, much to the consternation of the British Chiefs of Staff. They had examined the possibility of a cross-Channel invasion in 1940 in a plan called *Operation Roundup.* As these invasion plans developed in the background of British thinking, American military leaders were already in London monitoring the situation and planning ways to proceed should the U. S. be drawn into the war. The ABC-1 agreement of 1941 and the Arcadia Conference laid out plans for trans-

During the December 29, 1940 bombing of London by Axis planes, one of London's most famous landmarks, St. Paul's Cathedral, stands out from the fires surrounding it. The night terror bombing of London was dubbed the "Blitz."

Atlantic cooperation and Allied command structure, a necessity for launching any large-scale operation by the combined forces of what President Roosevelt was already calling the United Nations.

As the cross-Channel invasion went from a fleeting concept to reality in just over two years, there were a great many factors of strategy, tactics, logistics, manpower, intelligence, combat skill and leadership necessary to tilt the balance in the favor of the Allies. It all began with a five-part strategy developed by the British and expanded

Rescue workers carry out a man who was trapped in his destroyed London house after one of the many air raids carried out on the capital by German twin-engine bombers in 1940.

and refined by military staff work. It predicted the way the Allies ultimately prosecuted the war against Germany. The strategy tenets were: 1) a buildup of war material through the production capabilities of the Allies – primarily the United States; 2) the opening of air and sea lanes across the Atlantic; 3) demoralizing the German army and people, primarily through strategic aerial bombing; 4) containing the territorial expansion of Axis powers in the Mediterranean and Middle East and 5) the invasion of the continent from the Mediterranean or Western Europe. With the full participation of the United States in the war, attempting these objectives would be possible.

In Washington, the Army War Plans Division, headed by assistant chief of staff Brigadier General Dwight D. Eisenhower, was alarmed at German military successes in the Ukraine and the prospect of the Soviet Union falling out of the Allied camp. U. S. Army planners created an elaborate and aggressive Western Europe invasion plan which Army Chief of Staff General George C. Marshall heartily endorsed, and which came to be known as the Marshall Memorandum. In June 1942 Eisenhower was

This photograph is from the first large air raid on London on September 7, 1940, when the Luftwaffe was concentrating on war support targets like the London docks. A scene like this showing the destructive raid, with the iconic Tower Bridge in the background, was a great boost to American sympathy for the plight of the British during the early war.

sent to London to implement the Marshall Memorandum, paving the way for the new U. S. Army European Theater of Operations (ETOUSA), while the British designated a new high level group, the Combined Commanders, to study a possible strike across the Channel in 1942 code-named *Sledgehammer.*

But as the summer of 1942 wore on the Marshall Memorandum and other cross-Channel plans, including *Bolero* (the rapid buildup of American men and materiel in Britain), were giving way to a plan for action in North Africa. General Erwin Rommel was gaining ground there, threatening to overrun the British, and Roosevelt wanted a commitment of American combat forces to hold the interest of the country in the European war. Added to these political reasons for the delay in landing on the continent were practical ones; German U-boats controlling the Atlantic made the buildup in Great Britain slow and dangerous work. Also a lack of landing craft frustrated any large amphibious invasion plan.

Once President Roosevelt made the decision to commit American forces to North Africa, the Marshall Memorandum and *Operation Bolero*

Prime Minister Winston Churchill and President Franklin D. Roosevelt pose for a picture during the January 1943 Casablanca Conference in Morocco. British military leaders continued to complain about the inflexibility of their American counterparts, whose long-range planning required that a date be set for the cross-Channel invasion.

lost steam. General Eisenhower and many of the London-based staff were quickly absorbed into the plans for the combined Allied campaign in North Africa, renamed *Operation Torch.* So were many of the U. S. troops already in the British Isles and those headed there, along with American planes, ships and supplies. The idea of staging a cross-Channel invasion in 1942 or early 1943 appeared doubtful, though planning continued.

When the January 1943 Casablanca Conference commenced, the Allies were feeling much more confident with gains made in the land, sea and air war over the previous six months. The successful North African campaign was in the mop up stages and the invasion of Sicily was next on board for ETOUSA with Eisenhower (a full general since February 1943) in command. However, the American Joint Chiefs, despite Anglo resistance, continued to push for a firm date for a cross-Channel invasion with very good reason – an operation this large needed long term production and logistical planning. The U. S. was also waging a war against Japan, something the British paid scant attention to in 1942 and 1943. British and American leaders did agree to place a firm, if somewhat broad,

General Dwight David Eisenhower was the first choice of the president to be the Allied Supreme Commander in Europe. Ike's boss and mentor, General George C. Marshall, was deemed too valuable in his role in Washington to assume the overseas command.

date range for the operation – sometime in 1944 – and a new organization was established with the idea of planning the invasion in all aspects.

A little-known British general of high integrity and energy, Lieutenant General Frederick E. Morgan, was named Chief of Staff Supreme Allied Commander (designate) – COSSAC. Morgan gave this title to the entire organization made up of staff officers carefully chosen from among American and British candidates. COSSAC set up shop in London in April 1943 and from that time on they were responsible for all planning of the cross-Channel invasion.

While COSSAC began work on a series of diversions the meat of their assignment was planning

Top: Lt. Gen. Frederick E. Morgan conducting a press conference in his role as Chief of Staff to the Allied Supreme Commander (designate). The affable British officer became a top deputy to Eisenhower when the latter was appointed supreme commander.
Bottom: British Churchill tanks languish on the beach at Dieppe, France. German wartime sources claimed to have captured these two tanks and the British Landing Craft, Tank in the background during the operation.

the invasion, which was developed in June and July 1943 between the Washington Trident Conference in May and the August Quadrant Conference in Quebec. The plan, called *Outline Overlord*, was full of important details: weather considerations, deceptions and diversions, troop and air commitments and most importantly, the location of the invasion. Not all of this was mere speculation on empirical data. Events of the previous year did much to give COSSAC planners real data and principles on which to fix their invasion ideas.

THE DIEPPE RAID

By the summer of 1943 there were specific operations for COSSAC planners to study. The Combined Operations Head-

quarters under Commodore Lord Louis Mountbatten had already pierced the French coast with a raid on the port of St. Nazaire, Brittany in March, 1942. This commando action had little impact on either the Germans defending the area or *Roundup* planning at the time, but did challenge the security of Kriegsmarine resources against Allied raids. The vigor of building efforts with reinforced concrete the Germans employed after the raid would have long-term implications.

On August 19, 1942 a designed reconnaissance-in-force at Dieppe, France, was planned as a test run of invasion techniques. The massed amphibious landing of infantry and armor units, backed by air and sea support, would simulate the coordination a cross-Channel invasion would entail. According to the plan, the beachhead would neither be secured nor exploited. The operation was timed to perhaps pull German attention away from the Eastern Front, where Wehrmacht

The aftermath of the August 19, 1942 landing at Dieppe, France on the Channel coast. The bodies of dead Allied soldiers are seen in the foreground. Almost half of those who made the invasion were left behind in the withdrawal.

advances in the Don Basin near Stalingrad were causing serious concern. The one-day invasion was also designed to test new types of equipment.

Elements of the 2nd Canadian Infantry Division under Major General J. H. Roberts landed with British tanks and a handful of U. S. Army Rangers. Two hundred fifty-three vessels were involved in the operation as were 6,100 men and squadrons of planes. But the nine-hour operation met with much heavier than anticipated opposition. German deception had led the Allies to believe the garrison at the port was 1,400 when in fact it was 5,000 men. The new British Churchill tank, rushed into production, was too slow and heavy to support an amphibious landing. Extraction of the force under fire was difficult. The Dieppe landing cost the Allied force nearly 1,000 dead and 2,000 men from the Canadian 2nd Division were taken prisoner. The lessons of this tactical failure would immediately affect planning on both sides of the conflict.

SITE SELECTION

The most important lesson the Allies learned from the Dieppe reconnaissance-in-force was that a concentrated point of attack would be necessary for the invasion. Hitler's reaction to the Dieppe engagement was to ramp up construction of fixed fortifications, making for slim odds of success in attacking reinforced port areas. Even if air and sea bombardment succeeded in driving out the garrisons, the damage and sabotage done to port facilities could render them useless. A beach landing would be necessary at any location, though proximity to a navigable port would be an important consideration.

After considering and eliminating possible landing beaches from Antwerp to Brest, one location remained encouraging. It was the Calvados coast of Normandy. Cherbourg to the west of the landing area would ultimately be the designated port facility. The Calvados coast beaches were protected from the harshest Channel weather and core samples secretly taken by British commandos revealed a composition firm enough to support tanks. The location was nearly equidistant from debarkation ports on the east and west coasts of southern England. However this landing site placed the Allies west of the important Seine River and lengthened the lines of communication in moving eastward toward Germany.

The selection of the Calvados coast was the key item in the presentation of *Outline Overlord* (a name selected from a long list of possibilities) to Allied military and political leaders. The job that Morgan and COSSAC accomplished in researching the landing site and other considerations charged to their assignment was so thorough there was barely any discussion of the results of their planning. At Quebec the outline,

and therefore the operation, was accepted as firmly as the British were willing to do and turned into *Operation Overlord.*

LANDING CRAFT AND OTHER MATERIEL CONCERNS

In one of many famous Winston Churchill quotes from World War II, the subject of landing craft was addressed with appropriate sarcasm: "The destinies of two great empires [Britain and the U. S.], seemed to be tied by some goddamned things called LSTs..." The Prime Minister was bemoaning the fact that landing craft inventories were vexing planning strategies in the cross-Channel invasion and other operations including those in the Pacific Theater. The U. S. Navy was not prioritizing landing craft when there were hundreds of warships to build in the two-front war. However, U. S. Marines had been thinking about the problem for some time and took the lead in landing craft development and use.

Design, construction and delivery of sufficient landing craft to accomplish a large invasion in Western Europe were problems that continually appeared in planning the cross-Channel operation. Innovations like the wood-hulled Landing Craft, Vehicle and Personnel (LCVP), designed and built by the Andrew Higgins Boat Company of New Orleans and additional contractors, were crucial in creating the landing armada. The LCVP, which GIs often called the "Higgins boat" during and after the war, possessed a small turning radius so it could quickly drop its cargo (a 36-man platoon of soldiers or a 12-man squad and a Jeep) through a steel drop-down bow ramp and return for subsequent loads.

A solution also had to be found to get vehicles and small craft through harsh Channel weather conditions and ashore in France. Attention

The Landing Ship, Tank was the workhorse of the cross-Channel invasion. Here LST-543 unloads a DUKW (nicknamed "Duck") on a metal pier of the Mulberry system artificial dock.

turned to Venezuela, where shallow draft drilling rigs glided across the country's oil-rich lakes. Two of the boats were brought to England and adapted with huge vertical doors that could open up facing a beach to provide vehicles a drive-off ramp in shallow water. Production then began on these ships (a ship was a vessel over 200 feet long in navy parlance) designated Landing Ship, Tank (LST). Capable of carrying 44 tanks, a company of men and LCVPs on deck, the LST was the workhorse of the invasion. A similar but smaller vessel developed was the Landing Craft, Tank (LCT), which could hold four tanks or other vehicles, rocket launchers or artillery pieces. At Dieppe the LCTs were successfully tested in combat for the first time. The various types of landing craft were already in use in Tunisia, Italy and the Pacific Islands where they proved their reliability and usefulness. Navy and Coast Guard coxswains and mechanics ran and serviced the landing craft.

Planners realized that in the first days or possibly weeks of initial landing reinforcement LSTs would have to shoulder the load. But with changing tidal conditions, wave action, long voyages across the Channel and other challenges, would beaching LSTs be enough? As planning continued engineers worked up a multi-stage artificial harbor system called Mulberry, which could be towed across the Channel and assembled at a secured beach. Two Mulberries were designated for *Operation Overlord*; one for the eventual American beach near Colleville-sur-Mer and one for the British-Canadian beach near Caen.

While landing craft and artificial harbors pointed to the specialized needs of this giant amphibious operation, there were many other materiel details to attend to. Manufacturing of war materiel in the United States, greatly aided by a large influx of women into the workforce, the "Rosie the Riveters," and in British and Commonwealth countries needed unprecedented output to keep up. By the time *Operation Overlord* was expanded with a Churchill suggestion to add a landing on the east Cotentin peninsula, planners predicted it would take 25,000 uniformed noncombat personnel to support a 15,000-man division-sized force. They focused on the logistics necessary to keep the forces ashore in Normandy supplied via landing craft on the beaches or through the Mulberries.

After the men operating them, weapons were the most important consideration for the success or failure of what would happen on the beaches. Every conceivable type of armament was available, and factories of America and her allies were turning out incredible numbers of them. Although the infantry would have to secure the beaches and beach exits, armor would lead the campaign; therefore, tanks and other mechanized weapons were given the utmost attention. Beyond the selection of the most reliable front line tanks, led by the American Sherman M-4 medium tank, other specialized weapons were needed.

Plans called for tanks to begin the campaign as infantry support, providing immediate artillery cover on the beach. British General Percy Hobart was put in charge of a task force that developed an M-4 with a collapsible float and duplex-drive propulsion system for beach landings and other specialized vehicles dubbed "Hobart's Funnies." For the airborne units that were an integral part of *Operation Overlord*, experience in the Mediterranean showed the Douglas-built C-47 *Dakota* to be the best jump plane. British-made *Horsa* and the American-built CG-4 *Waco* gliders would carry Allied glider troops in the operation. Planes from the United States, including transports and combat war birds, were ferried across the Atlantic by the Air Transport Command (ATC) or flown by partial or complete crews of newly trained U. S. Army Air Force personnel.

LEADERSHIP

Of all the Americans involved in the operation, one had a unique position and title – but the Supreme Allied Commander was as yet unnamed. This was a great concern to another Supreme Commander, Marshal Joseph Stalin of the Soviet Union, who met Roosevelt and Churchill in the first "Big Three" Allied summit at Tehran, Iran in November, 1943. The Soviet premier, with typical Stalin candor, made it clear he wanted the invasion of Northwest Europe – the much-awaited Allied "Second Front" – a top priority and pushed for the naming of a Supreme Commander. As a result, at the conclusion of the Tehran Eureka summit Roosevelt, on December 3,

Three women work on a vessel at an American shipyard in 1942. The wartime employment of "Rosie the Riveters" filled the void in manufacturing employment when millions of American men went to war, and also gave the women new skills and income opportunities.

appointed General Dwight David Eisenhower as Supreme Commander Allied Expeditionary Force (SHAEF).

Eisenhower executed a transfer of power in the Mediterranean, took a short leave home and arrived in London on January 14, 1944. He retained his personal chief-of-staff, General Walter Bedell "Beetle" Smith, and welcomed Morgan's invitation to remain at HQ as assistant chief-of-staff. Eisenhower selected Air Marshal Arthur Tedder as his second in command. Senior British officers were designated to lead the air, ground and naval forces in *Overlord*. Eisenhower felt the hubbub of London with its distractions and politicians was not the ideal place to make the crucial decisions for this monumental operation. He moved to a cottage in the suburbs at Bushy Park and tackled the directive that had been issued to him by the Combined Chiefs of Staff on February 12, 1944: "You will enter the continent of Europe, and, in conjunction with the other United Nations, undertake operations aimed at the heart of Germany and the destruction of her armed forces."

Eisenhower worked superhuman hours, was out in the field often, ate on the run, drank gallons of coffee and smoked four packs of cigarettes a day. A family man, he communicated often with his wife, Mamie. For his companion during the long ordeal in England, he requested a dog and received a Scottish Terrier puppy.

Called "The Big Three," Soviet Premier Joseph V. Stalin, U. S. President Franklin D. Roosevelt and British Prime Minister Winston Churchill pose with military leaders at the Tehran Summit. The two western leaders were well aware that the common enemy did not erase their differences with the Soviet leader over issues such as Poland's future as an independent nation.

THE OPPOSITION – GERMAN DEFENSES AND ORGANIZATION

Across the Channel in France, Erwin Rommel also had a puppy at his headquarters, a dachshund. The former "Desert Fox" had other commonalities with Ike, the man who helped defeat Rommel in North Africa. Rommel, extracted by Hitler from that situation, winless once the Americans arrived, was initially designated to take over the fight in Italy. The Führer then changed his mind and gave the new field marshal command of the first reserve army group formed to react to situations that might develop. By late 1943, German reversals and Soviet-Anglo-American cooperation indicated that the reserve army group would probably be most needed in the West. Rommel would become the key player in defending against the cross-Channel invasion, yet a convoluted command structure, logistics and manpower problems, and differing strategic ideas among the German military leadership left Rommel with a compromised command as he prepared to face the largest Allied offensive operation west of the Ukraine.

The cross-Channel invasion was not going to arrive in front of a demoralized Wehrmacht as early planners had hoped; they were arriving opposite a well-organized, combat experienced force ready to contest the

By many accounts, the German commander most revered by the men who fought under him was general, later field marshal, Erwin Rommel. His early success against the British in North Africa earned him huge popularity at home in Germany and the moniker "The Desert Fox."

landing to the best of its ability. But in 1944 the problems facing the German armed forces in France, Belgium and Holland were great and diverse. Despite the Axis commitment – the appointment of a fighter like Rommel was designed to bolster moral in this theater – the defense was not solid enough to succeed against an overwhelming Allied force that could land at any of a number of strategic points along the Channel coast.

As early as 1942 Hitler had recognized the danger posed by an Allied invasion along the vulnerable coastline of "Festung Europa" and issued Führer Directive 40, a general plan to defend the coastal areas, particularly those abutting the Western front. Although the directive placed an emphasis on inter-service cooperation in a defense that would use all three branches – land, air and sea – to beat the enemy back before or immediately after landing, the structure of German leadership prevented more than voluntary local cooperation. Despite this obvious shortcoming, the directive called for building and manning fortifications, guarding airfields and ports, patrolling undefended areas, maximizing local intelligence and fighting to the last man.

But work on the Atlantic Wall, as the series of Channel-facing casemates, obstacles and armed positions was called, moved along slowly and always in the shadow of events on the vast Eastern Front. The commander who oversaw this theater called OB West from 1942, Field Marshal Gerd von Rundstedt, was one of the top soldiers in the army and

Upper Left: *Grossadmiral Karl Dönitz (right), who brilliantly led the U-boat force that dominated the Atlantic in the early war, assumed command of the German Navy in January 1943. He was later Adolf Hitler's hand-picked successor.* **Upper right:** *A German battery of large caliber guns in a bunker at Crisbecq on the Cotentin Peninsula.* **Middle right:** *This German bunker was one of many protecting Cherbourg.* **Bottom:** *Field Marshal Rommel inspecting the German position near Fécamp, north of Le Havre, on January 17, 1944 during his tour of Atlantic Wall defenses.*

although not a Nazi, had Hitler's respect. Rundstedt battled with shrinking German resources, mostly in air defense and sea patrols, in his command which extended from Norway to the Pyrenees. Yet, his major concern was the quality and quantity of combat troops in the theater and their lack of adequate transportation.

As the war raged on the Eastern Front, the best units in France and elsewhere in the OB West command were constantly being swapped with worn-out units from the East. These Eastern Front veterans were, at best, wounded and war-weary survivors of the brutal struggle against the Red Army. Of lesser quality were new recruits; some previously classified unfit for service, others who had held critical jobs on the home front, and many just very young or old. When these sources began to dry up, the Wehrmacht augmented them with Russians and Eastern Europeans (*Ost* battalions) as well as other foreign nationals – many of them prisoners-of-war – who were drafted into service without the commitment and esprit-de-corps of their German counterparts. They lacked training in the basic fundamentals of combat.

The East-West swap of units and men affected these two German military veterans in different ways. Hans Eckhardt, a 17-year-old from the Sudetenland, volunteered and received admission into the very competitive Luftwaffe flying personnel program. He was placed on active duty in the fall of 1942.

"We spent a short time in Germany then we were shipped out to France near the west coast for Luftwaffe training regiment. So we did what was called in America boot camp. We were trained with guns, machine guns and mortars and we were also kind of manning the Atlantic defenses. There were three battalions and every

third night we were on the alert. We slept in our uniforms, with our boots on, and we practiced that within three minutes we were down out of the barracks and into trucks where we were ready to go to the coast where there were fortifications. This was an early response in preparation for D-Day. It was in late 1942.

"[The Canadian attempt to land at Dieppe] was far away from us, but we heard about it in the newspapers. It was a flop. The Canadians were ill-prepared. One thing that I recall from the reports was the tanks were not prepared for the gravel on the beaches. They got stuck. It was very poor intelligence, they expected sand, but it was gravel."

Before long Eckhardt was reassigned to the Eastern Front and put on a train that took him through Germany and to the Ukraine. Fritz Baresel from Stuttgart volunteered for the army in April 1942 to ensure that he was selected for panzer training. His father, a veteran officer, and brother were already in the German armed services. Fritz trained near Stuttgart, had tours of duty in Russia, Hungary and Potsdam, and received the Panzerkampfabzeichen, which means Tank Battle Badge, the Iron Cross Second Class and the Verwundeten-Abzeichen which means Wound Badge for a small wound received in the Ukraine. By April 1944, he was just 20 years old and had already served two years. He was attached to the prestigious Panzer Lehr Division. Like many of those he served with, Baresel had been wounded on the Eastern front.

"It is a story few will believe. After a tank battle in the Ukraine in 1943, we returned to a safe place and stationed the tanks in a circle, cannons facing out. All not on guard duty were allowed to sleep. I crawled under my tank, but the ground was uneven and my legs stuck out.

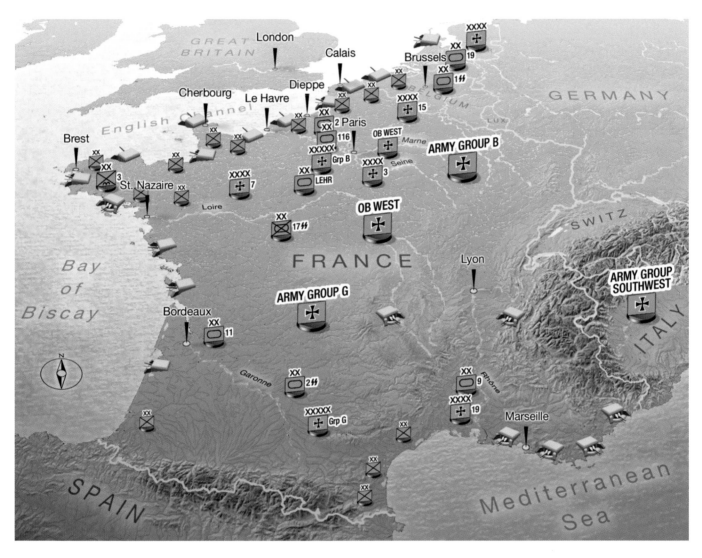

During the night a Russian plane dropped a bomb right in the middle of the assembled tanks and a fragment lodged itself under my left knee cap. As a 20-year-old, I was so tired and slept so well that I didn't wake up when the fragment hit me. I saw in the morning a hole in my pants and after investigating I realized I was wounded. My [envious] crew members drove me to a first aid station, from there [I went] to a hospital in Poland and from

By the Spring of 1944 with the Allied invasion of Northwest Europe imminent, the German leadership amassed 58 divisions in France and the Low Countries, divided into two army groups. However Hitler kept personal control of the Panzer divisions, thus diluting the effectiveness of that sizable force, already compromised by the differing tactical views of the local commanders. The army group HQs are located with the smaller Grp. tokens. Two of the region's three coastlines would ultimately carry Allied invasions.

there in a long train ride to a hospital in Loerrach at the Swiss border."

His wound eventually gained him a ticket to the Western front, which nearly all German veterans say was much better than going East.

"We stayed in Hungary 'til April 1944, when we were transported by train to France in preparation of the expected invasion. We camped near Chartres."

The Eastern Front was like a sponge that soaked up men and materiel and the personnel situation became critical in 1943. Reverses in Russia and the need to take over defense of Italy after the September capitulation of the Mussolini regime there put even more pressure on the situation. Recognizing that this vulnerability might encourage the Allies to invade France, Hitler issued a second directive for the West. Führer Directive 51 started to improve the situation in 1944 and among its provisions was a strict prohibition on raiding units in the West without the expressed permission of the Supreme Armed Forces Commander. However, the temptation to borrow from the West to stave off the Russian advance in the East continued.

About the time Führer Directive 51 was issued, Erwin Rommel was setting up his headquarters in a chateau northwest of Paris. His tour of the Atlantic Wall in November 1943 greatly alarmed him about its vulnerable condition. Rommel now embraced the concept of a static defense and he was convinced that the coming Allied invasion must be stopped at the beaches. If not, Allied air superiority would pounce on any counterattack and crush it. As the only senior commander in the West to have experienced the overwhelming

Members of an anti-aircraft unit in the defense of Le Havre operate their equipment. The man to the left is using an optical rangefinder while the other turns hand wheels to set direction and elevation.

effects of Allied air superiority (the North Africa campaign), Rommel was being a realist in doubting that a massed armor reserve could succeed in counterattacks against the Allied forces once the beachhead was established. He geared his tactics to defeat the Allied forces on the coast within 48 hours of landing.

There were command issues that worked against Rommel. His jurisdiction extended only about twenty miles inland from the coast. Beyond that most of the panzer divisions were stationed under the local command of General Leo Geyr von Schweppenburg and ultimately under Hitler's personal control. The inter-service cooperation was done in by scant resources and proud commanders. Kriegsmarine, in 1944 commanded by Grossadmiral Karl Dönitz, had few surface ships in the Channel region and U-boat numbers were dwindling fast, with only a few snorkel-types available for attacking harbors. Commander in the Channel region, Admiral Theodor Krancke, could only manage limited patrolling. Reichsmarschall Hermann Göring's Luftwaffe was in better shape than the Kriegsmarine, but fighter and fighter-bomber inventories in France had been significantly reduced by June 1944 and were not very effective as offensive or defensive weapons.

Meanwhile, Rommel threw himself into the work of planning and building fixed fortifications of the Atlantic Wall. He pressed combat forces into the construction effort to augment the German paramilitary Organization Todt and forced or paid foreign labor. It was a daunting task but one that proceeded steadily, as concrete was one of the more plentiful resources available to Germany by that stage of the war. While Rommel was accused of spending the short months he exercised his command pouring concrete, mines were really his signature item in strengthening the Atlantic Wall. His soldiers planted mines of every size, shape and purpose – anti-personnel mines, underwater mines, anti-tank mines. In addition, he called for obstacles to foul Allied landing craft on the way to the beach. The obstacles were studded with mines to blow up the enemy vessels upon landing; and mines and obstacles to be laid in the beach and access roads to impede or destroy every living and mechanical thing that reached the shore. The Normandy portion of the defense line was formidable by the beginning of June 1944. One area where the mine and obstacle work was nearly complete was in the region designated by the Allies as Omaha Beach.

Colonel Ernst Goth who, according to his grandson, dreamed of becoming a mathematics teacher, was in command of Grenadier Regiment 916 of the 352nd Infantry Division in Normandy. A third of the regiment was made up of veterans of the Eastern Front and the rest were young conscripts who had just finished basic training. His regiment was to hold the sector between Vierville-sur-Mer and Colleville-sur-Mer, in front of what would become Omaha Beach.

"At the beginning of the year [1944] Field Marshal Rommel, whom I had already met before, came to visit me. His first words were, 'Goth, they'll be arriving here, where you are...this looks just like the bay at Salerno.' After the field marshal had made his inspection, I received a lot of equipment from various sources, including thousands of mines and stakes, for reinforcing the sector with my men."

German field artillery in Normandy. At the beginning of the war German field guns were moved by horse teams exclusively. Gradually as the war continued some of the more mobile units used trucks for their towed guns.

ALLIED PERSONNEL

From all states and U. S. territories they came, even expatriates who were drafted through consulates in countries like Mexico. These were the more than a million and a half men and women who would perform every combat and combat-support function, along with their allies, in *Operation Overlord*.

Over an eighteen month period before D-Day the Yanks would be a familiar sight in the hamlets, towns and cities of England, Scotland, Wales and Northern Ireland. The buildup, *Bolero*, began with those first American units assigned to Iceland and Northern Ireland in 1942 and continued in a thousand different ways until the United Kingdom was teeming with Americans in every nook and cranny. For most this was their first experience in a foreign land. The one comforting thing was that the people where they were headed spoke English, or at least that's what they called the strange and heavily dialected language the Americans encountered.

Sam Hobson had drawn a low draft number in his home state of South Carolina. By the beginning of 1942 he was in boot camp.

"They said they'd make a man, a soldier, out of us and that would be all we'd need. Well, I went to Fort Jackson and joined the 118th Infantry Regiment, and I stayed with them until the end of the war. We were part of the 30th [Infantry] Division. We were separated from them and left the states in August of '42. And we went to Iceland and took over for the British there. We were to keep the Germans from coming into a strategic port for them to have shipping and everything. So we did our service there and in fifteen months we went to England. We got to England and were scattered over England and Ireland."

Jackie Volkl was a member of the Women's Army Corps (WAC) in 1944. Prior to joining the WACs in the summer of 1942 she was working for the Civilian Air Administration in Dutch Harbor, Alaska but was evacuated when the Japanese first bombed that Aleutian Islands out-

post. After basic training and several assignments in the U. S. she volunteered for duty overseas.

"We went on the *Isle de France*, which was a cruise ship, all by ourselves. There were no other ships around. No escort. Cruise ships could go faster than any submarine and that was why cruise ships like the *Isle de France* and the *Queen Mary* always went alone. In the spring of '44 we landed in Scotland where all the ships landed, and it took us nine days to cross the ocean. One time we stopped dead in the water and everybody was scared to death, because they knew there had to be a submarine around some place but nothing ever bothered us. We got to England and were sent down to southern England and I was assigned as secretary to the commanding officer of the base. It was a base of supplies for the GIs getting ready to go across to Normandy. Of course we didn't know it was Normandy at the time."

Charles Norman Shay was a Penobscot Native American from Maine drafted into the Army. Two brothers, both of whom enlisted, preceded him into the U. S. armed services. After training stateside, he shipped out to the British Isles.

"I traveled on the *Queen Elizabeth*, which had been converted to a transport ship, and the *Queen Elizabeth* was a very fast ship. [She] traveled back and forth, to my knowledge…traveled back and forth.

"When I landed in England, I was sent to a replacement depot where I stayed ten days or maybe two weeks and then I eventually received

Mary Josephine Farley, age 20, had gained the mechanical skills required to rebuild the engine on this Curtiss Seagull in her job at an American naval base. The "Rosie the Riveters" like Mary were fearless in facing whatever challenges were given to them in order to keep the war production effort going.

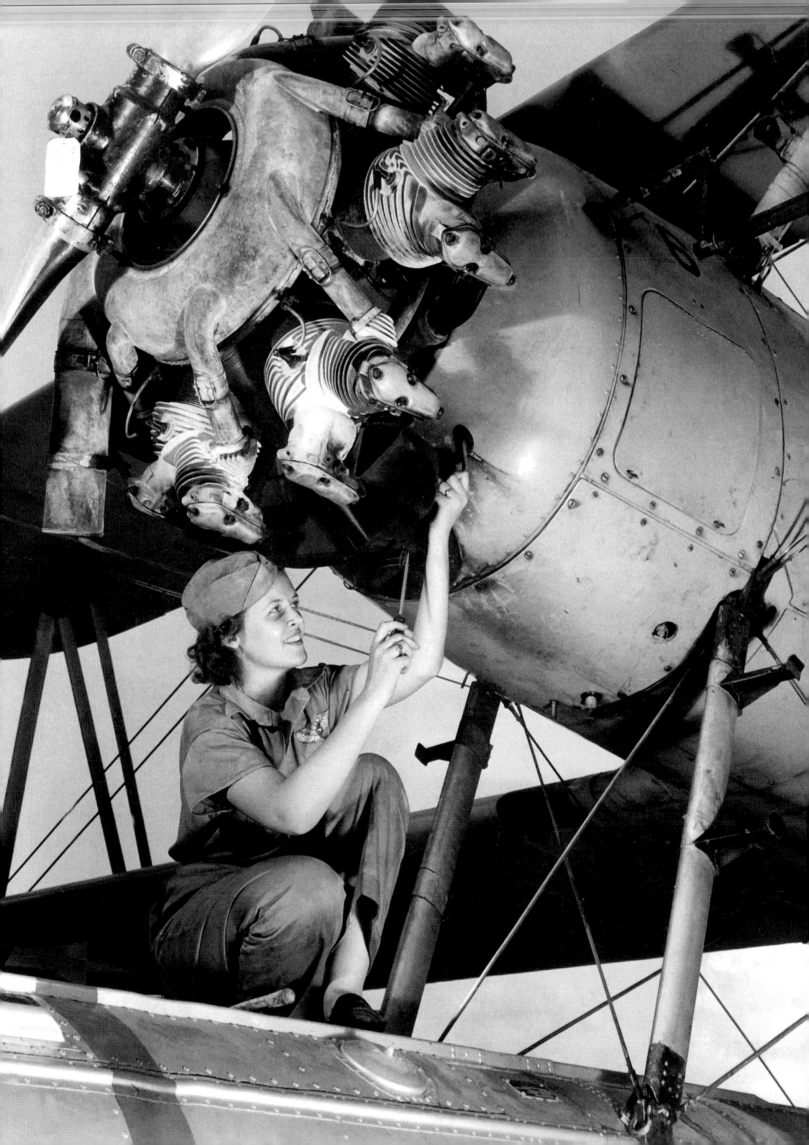

an assignment to the 1st Infantry Division, 16th Infantry Regiment, the medical detachment, which was stationed in Dorset County, a little village by the name of Bridgeport, which is near the English Channel coast."

Fred Purdy of Alabama also crossed on the *Queen Elizabeth*. He was trained at the Signal Corps school at Fort Monmouth in northern New Jersey.

"We were going to take cryptographic [courses]. And I went to school there until early in 1944... January. I was called out to replace a soldier that was in the signal corps, and he was onboard the *Queen Elizabeth*, New York harbor. We were not in an escorted convoy because the *Queen Elizabeth* was one of the fastest ships afloat at the time, and it cannot hardly be lined up by a submarine. We did have two anti-aircraft crews manning aircraft guns, the blue watch and the red watch I believe was what they were called, but we had no incidents of any kind, went straight through up the Firth of [the] Clyde to Glasgow."

J. J. Witmeyer, infantryman from New Orleans, describes his journey across "the Pond."

"We went over on the S.S. *Strathmore*. That was a British ship. I think it came out of Indian service or Mediterranean service. By that time I was in charge of the company as an enlisted man. This guy [in the company was] telling the story that they used him up in the crow's nest which was a lie, but we did station people on the rail in case there was a torpedo. It's a psychological thing...you weren't supposed to fire at the torpedo, there's a chance you could hit it and explode it. But over the years in drinkin' and what not, he told them he was in the crow's nest and he shot a torpedo one time, and it happened to be a whale. And I told him that's all untruth. I said you got that out [of] the bottle."

Buster Simmons joined the North Carolina National Guard in 1940. His unit, part of the 105th Medical Detachment, became the medical detachment for the 120th Infantry Regiment. After assisting with thousands of induction medical examinations and serving in various U. S. training camps, Simmons' unit was sent in the beginning of 1944 to Camp Miles Standish in Massachusetts, a major staging area for trans-Atlantic convoys.

"So we stayed there just a couple of weeks until they put us on the S.S. *Argentina*, and we come across the Atlantic in the largest convoy of ships to ever leave the United States. There were 52 destroyers around that and it was our anti-submarine shield. We left on Lincoln's Birthday and landed on Washington's Birthday in Gourock, Scotland. I had some great experiences on that ship, it was like a Caribbean cruiser, but not like a Princess Line cruise, it was nothing like that. They had taken the ballroom of that thing and put 1,000 sleeping areas in there, not cots. They were welded to a steel post from the floor up to the ceiling, with ten men stacked on top of each other. There were 1,000 men in that ballroom, and the whole 120th Infantry Regiment[al] Combat Team, field artillery, and supporting units were on that ship."

Surgical technician Eddie Sutton of Pocahontas, Arkansas crossed the Atlantic on the *Queen Mary*.

"I went into the service February the 8th, 1943 and I had my training in Camp Barkley, Texas. After my eleven weeks of basic, I went to advanced training in San Antonio to become a surgical technician, and after that, we shipped out to England and I went to England on the *Queen Mary*. That's one of the bigger ships that was owned by the British, by England."

Hal Baumgarten from New York City was attending New York University and taking compulsory ROTC classes there when he was drafted into the army in June, 1943. At Camp Croft, South Carolina he was convinced to forgo the continuation of officer training and sign up for the Army Specialized Training Program (ASTP) at Clemson University. The ASTP sent promising young soldiers to pursue college degrees with the reward of an officer's commission upon graduation. However, as was the case with many recruits at that time, Baumgarten saw his ASTP participation cancelled and he was designated to go to Europe as an enlisted soldier.

"They transferred us to Camp Shanks, New York to be shipped overseas. So one night, in the middle of the night, we went across the Hudson

These technical huts and airfield at Reykjavik, Iceland, are pictured during a lull in a blizzard which hit the island February 21-27, 1945. One of the early tasks of the U. S. Army during the war was to replace British soldiers in Iceland to free the "Tommies" for duty in Europe. Before America entered the war, a small force of U. S. Marines also had a tour of duty here.

River to the pier. We boarded the *Ile de France*, which was the third largest ship in the world at the time, and we zigzagged across the Atlantic with no escort, 'cause the ship was that fast. Took us five days and seasickness to get to Gourock, Scotland. And we took a train there, and went down to southern England. They kept us in what they called a repo depot, which was a replacement place. And this was all the guys that were cancelled out of ASTP."

It was vital to get the planned number of American service people abroad in a very short time in *Operation Bolero* so ships were acquired in many ways. Though many GIs crossed the Atlantic on the *Queen Mary*, *Queen Elizabeth* and other fast cruise ships, many others crossed on Allied navy transport ships including the so-

called "Liberty ships." These were transports built to a common specification and turned out by U. S. shipyards in four days, 15 ½ hours, keel-laying to launch. Al Webber was drafted in the summer of 1943 and was also sent to Camp Croft in Spartanburg, the "country club" of the infantry he called it, for basic training as an infantry replacement. He was then sent to Camp Shanks in New York to await overseas orders.

"We left April 5th of '44 in a blinding snowstorm. We left from New York, Staten Island. Liberty [ship], actually it was just a hulk, it was an old tub. I don't think it qualified as a Liberty, it was just a tank that floated. We went over and when daylight came the storm eased up…looked out on the horizon all we could see were ships, ships, ships for miles and miles. Our convoy pooled with a convoy coming from Boston and the whole bunch of us went together. All the ships got there safely in Prestwick, Scotland on the 14th of April. We spent the night in Glasgow, I believe, and we hopped on a train going south and we rode and rode down into the west of England and came to rest in a little town in Somerset County in England, the southwest of England by Bristol Channel."

Besides U. S. Army personnel, including WACS, every other branch of the armed forces was represented in the buildup for D-Day. There were U. S. Army Air Force flight crews and their support personnel. The navy had staff officers, yeomen and Shore Patrolmen in England as well as the crews of a vast armada of ships including U. S. Marines on shipboard duty. The U. S. Merchant Marine worked the busy ports of the

This U. S. War Bonds poster is illustrated with an American GI about to lob a hand grenade. By the time this war bond series was issued the United States was heavily engaged in the European war.

British Isles and towed the Mulberries across the Channel. And members of the United States Coast Guard, like Tommy Harbour of Mud River, West Virginia, ran many of the landing craft in the combat zones.

"I had just finished one semester down at Marshall College, gettin' ready for another semester. And the draft board told my father, 'As soon as your son gets eighteen he's leavin' town.' And so my cousin, Tom Snyder, called me and said, 'Harbour, let's go down and join the Coast Guard.' And I said, 'Well suits me all right.'"

After Harbour went through basic training at Manhattan Beach, New York, he turned down an opportunity to get an officer's commission at the New London, Connecticut Coast Guard Academy and instead learned landing craft tactics with the Marines at Camp Lejeune. That experience led him to become an LCVP mechanic with his ticket punched to England.

"So finally, the next thing I know I was at Hampton Roads. Our main thing was to learn how to run, operate [and] how to disperse the troops from the Higgins boats. So, there was over a 100 of us standin' out on the dock there at Hampton Roads, and this lieutenant jg [junior grade] came out there and now here's all them new LCVPs was out there tied together and he said, 'Now I want a coxswain and a motor mac and a seaman in every one of these boats.' So we all made a dash.

"We went to Pier 97 in New York, and it was a rainin'. Bad night. And I never will forget [the] Salvation Army. There was two or three elderly women and men out there, givin' out donuts and coffee, on the dock. And I been a givin' to them for sixty-five years, 'cause I never tasted anything so good in all my life as them donuts. We was two or three weeks goin' across, zigzagging. And that's

The Queen Mary, *the largest luxury liner in the world, stands in New York harbor in 1945. During the buildup for* Operation Overlord *the vessel made many trans-Atlantic crossings, bringing American troops to the British Isles.*

when we went in at Glasgow, Scotland, and we had a lot of maneuvers on the Firth of the Clyde."

While Harbour, Webber, Simmons and these other American GIs were boarding ships and going abroad for their first duty, some of their countrymen had already served in North Africa and Italy. These soldiers would join the cross-Channel invasion with the combat experience they shared with some of the British and other Commonwealth forces.

Pete Chavez from Alameda, New Mexico served in an anti-tank battalion that saw action in North Africa and Sicily. The 65th Armored Field Artillery was then assigned to accompany the newly formed 4th Infantry Division in training in England.

"We came through Gibraltar there. We were kinda by ourselves, just one destroyer was with us. And we sailed from Palermo and went through Gibraltar and landed in Liverpool. Then from there they sent us to Banbury [Cross], England, you know, and that's where we spent most of our time training. From there, we used to go to train on the coast there. And then we got ready for D-Day."

Jim Weller had similar experiences in the 62nd Armored Field Artillery. After seeing combat in North Africa and Sicily, the unit got a break.

"We was brought back again to Palermo and we had a few opportunities to go to Palermo and see the city. So finally we had orders, line all your things up, all your equipment, all you guys are lucky…you're going to the States. Well, they don't tell the truth about the war you're in so we ended up in Glasgow, Scotland. Right before Christmas we took the train out of Glasgow, Scotland. We went into England in Leicester and

Oxford, and then they put us in some kind of camp down there at Banbury Cross."

Though Americans made up the bulk of the attacking force, they were joined by those native to the Isles; the British soldiers who would comprise two ground divisions and one airborne division on D-Day and, like the Americans, a population to provide a continuing supply of manpower to follow up the initial beach assault. Unlike most of the Americans in *Overlord*, these were by and large combat veterans of France, North Africa and the Balkan state battles.

But not all were veterans. As the American draft was adding new recruits every month in the States, at the end of 1942 the British Parliament lowered the age of recruitment to eighteen to augment their manpower. Bob Littlar was an 18-year-old in the beginning of 1943 and, although he requested service in the Royal Air Force, he was told the need was for infantrymen. After basic training he was sent to join the 2nd Battalion of the King's Shropshire Light Infantry stationed at Lockerbie, Scotland.

"There were about thirty-eight of us in this group, all kids like myself, and we all arrived there and were allocated to the best company in the battalion, X Company, John Roberts' company. They'd put the colonel there to sort the battalion out, to get us into a state fit for action. We did a lot of training, and I should think we were very well trained, but we hadn't met an enemy! Even the old regulars put us kids right. I remember my old sergeant saying to me, 'You think you know all about weapons, don't you? You don't know a damn thing. I'll show you.' Because you don't just use the weapon for what it's allocated for, you know, you use them for all sorts of things. It was an education.

"I got made a lance-corporal at Lockerbie and I don't know what happened when we got down to what they called J-5 near Lewes, but I was made a corporal there. I was given a new section then, and a new platoon commander, who was later killed in Square Wood. He was another public-school boy, a gentleman, by the name of Dai Rees, a ruddy good officer actually. He got killed on D-Day night."

Added to the British and American contingents of the *Overlord* force were Commonwealth soldiers, principally the 3rd Canadian Division, and soldiers from other countries in the United Nations who had reason to fight the Nazis – they were displaced from their homes or they were expatriates who were joining their countrymen forming units in England to oppose the Axis powers.

In June 1940, Brig. Gen. Charles de Gaulle, an ambitious tank commander and minor French minister, escaped to England where he declared that the Vichy French government under Marshal Pétain, who negotiated an armistice with and supported Germany, did not represent the surrender of France. Under the patronage of

Soldiers of the 2nd Ranger Battalion load onto British LCAs in preparation for their landing below Pointe du Hoc. The LCA was similar to the LCVP but lacked the drop down ramp at the bow.

Churchill and with British money, he founded the Free French movement to resist Third Reich domination of his home country. De Gaulle put out a call worldwide for Frenchmen to come to the aid of their homeland. He intended to form Free French combat units to join the invasion.

Jean Rene Champion was born in Paris but left France at an early age when his mother, who was then living in the United States, sent for him.

"My mother and I really never got along. And as soon as I graduated from high school at age sixteen, I hit the road. I hoboed and rode freight trains all over the United States for the next four years. I worked on cattle ranches, I chauffeured for a millionaire in Florida for five or six months. I just worked wherever I could find some work. Anyway, one day I was sitting in somebody's car and the radio indicated that the general by the name of de Gaulle was forming an army to drive the Germans out of France. De Gaulle, who was based in England, was appealing to Frenchmen the world over to rally to him. That sounded like a great new adventure to me. Anyway, to make a story short, I called the telephone number that was given. I didn't really expect to ever hear from them again, but by golly a couple days later I got a telephone call telling me that they wanted me to come and join them in England and they gave me instructions for where I should take the ship, and they paid for it."

Airborne troops were among the best trained personnel required to execute *Operation Overlord*. They were the largest of many specialized disciplines that were to enter combat in the operation. Since the development of paratrooper operations by the Germans (based on a 1922 Soviet experiment), Allied armies were quick to adopt the concept. The British began training airborne units with much resistance from both army and RAF top commanders. Volunteers flocked to the new branch however, and after successful operations in the Mediterranean, the paratrooper concept won out over those resisting it.

American paratrooper units began in 1942. The

excitement of this branch appealed to Tom Blakey of New Orleans, who went on to serve in the 82nd Airborne Division. There was something at the time that drew Blakey's interest to the paratroopers.

"The reason we wanted to be paratroopers was in the middle of 1941 *Life* Magazine did about an eight or nine page spread on the 'new' army. The new army was paratroops. Now we looked at that and read it; you know the draft was going on in 1941, it had been going on for several months and we had a draft number and we knew we were going to be drafted at some time. We knew we would have to volunteer for the paratroops. When we got through with that 90 days [basic training] we were sent to Fort Benning and went to parachute school, that's how I got into the paratroopers."

James Libaudais was a Cajun from the bayou country who was drafted in the army in March of 1942.

American soldiers aboard LCVPs in a training exercise. In the foreground is PA13-22. The first number in the series on LCVPs denoted the transport ship from which the landing craft was launched.

"I went to Camp Beauregard in Louisiana and from there I went to Camp Claiborne. At Camp Claiborne they were starting, do you remember the picture *Sgt. York*? We was going to draft troops from the entire nation, out of every state, to make an all-American division. By the way our general was Omar Bradley. We trained probably for a few months and then somebody came up with the idea that we need airborne troops. They took our division which was probably sixteen or eighteen thousand troops, cut right in half to make the 101st and 82nd because you can only get about eight thousand troops in an airborne operation. After training we finally went to Ft. Bragg.

"I went overseas in the 101st and we landed in Liverpool. We went to a place in England called Reading and it was a barracks right in the town, an old English brick barracks and we stayed there for a while, then they sent us to Lancaster, England."

While the first two American airborne divisions were assembling

Troops of the 325th Glider Infantry, of which James Libaudais was a member, await the command to board on the morning of June 6, 1944. On the glider fuselage are the three white and two black stripes painted on all Allied invasion aircraft to protect them from friendly fire.

for the operation (the 82nd having already fought in the Mediterranean), the British 6th Airborne Division was preparing for its D-Day mission to land behind the lines on the eastern flank of the invasion area. With the three airborne divisions identified for *Operation Overlord* a total of nine Allied divisions were now committed to the operation. Also, for increased security and clarification, the amphibious portion of *Overlord* was given its own code name – *Neptune*.

AIR OPERATIONS

If the Allies were going to succeed in the cross-Channel operation the air war would have to tilt significantly in their favor. By 1944 the Luftwaffe lost its air dominance in the West through attrition primarily as a result of British ground and fighter action in the Battle of Britain. The majority of German fighters were withdrawn to the interior of Germany to fight off

the commencement of strategic bombing of the Reich homeland by the British. In the fall of 1942 the U. S. Army Air Forces (USAAF) arrived in England and the VIII Bomber Command was formed to carry out missions of daylight precision bombing. With their techniques and equipment the Americans felt this bombing concept would crush military and industrial targets in the war to defeat Germany.

Precision daylight bombing had proven costly and ineffective for RAF bombing missions for the first two years of the war. In response, they switched more than three-quarters of their air missions to nighttime area bombing – essentially "carpet bombing" of a broad area with no effort to pinpoint specific targets. As a result, RAF targets were the heavily-populated areas that held enemy war production factories. These missions saturated the cities of Cologne, Hamburg and other war production centers in 1942-43. The effort was aided by the "Gee" navigational aid as well as bombers dropping tin foil strips to confound German radar. But the cities were heavily protected by flak guns up to 88mm and ringed with searchlights to illuminate attacking bombers. German gunners still brought down large numbers of RAF

planes. The Luftwaffe also developed squadrons of night fighters to add further misery to RAF flight crews.

Meanwhile the Eighth Air Force, formed from VIII Bomber Command, depended on close formations to concentrate the defensive firepower of the formidable air-to-air .50-cal. machine guns that bristled from B-17 Flying Fortress and B-24 Liberator bombers. And while these armaments and tactics were fairly effective against Luftwaffe fighters, they couldn't lessen anti-aircraft fire. Also, although the sophisticated Norden bombsight was excellent in clear weather, it was not so good in the cloud cover often found over German targets. Losses for the Eighth Air Force precision daylight bombing began to mount in 1943 while mission effectiveness was uneven.

Flying Fortresses wait in line at an English airfield in preparation for a bombing mission. Once airborne the pilots would maneuver the planes to create their box formations for the attack.

Robert Wolff was the son of a Union Oil executive and World War I veteran who was recalled to the U. S. Naval Reserve in World War II to manage American oil resources in the Pacific. But young Robert's interests were elsewhere.

"I've always had an interest in flying, building model airplanes and so forth when I was a kid. And when the war came along I decided I wanted

to ride to work rather than walk to work. So I applied to get into the [Air] Cadets in March of '42 and joined the army as a buck private. Six weeks later I was appointed as an aviation cadet and went to Santa Ana [California]. That was where the training base was. I got to the 100th Bomb Group toward the end of July [1943]."

Army Air Force Lt. Gen. Ira C. Eaker (right) and Lt. Gen. Jacob L. Devers observe as pilot and Medal of Honor recipient Lt. Col. Leon W. Johnson points out the scoreboard of a B-24 Liberator that participated in the August 1, 1943 low-level mission to bomb the oil refineries in Ploesti, Romania. Eaker, along with Lt. Gen. Carl Spaatz, developed U. S. bombing assets in Britain before he was assigned to the Mediterranean. Devers would command an army group later in Northern Europe.

bomb the Messerschmitt fighter aircraft manufacturing facility at Regensburg, Germany.

"Our 3rd mission was to Regensburg which is in southeastern Germany. That was August 17th, 1943. That's a date I'll always remember. [We were in the air] approximately ten hours and it was pretty hellish on that one. We crossed the Channel and entered Holland or Belgium, I can't remember which, about 10:00 o'clock and for the next two hours there were planes dropping all the way around us. It was pretty rough, a lot of flak and fighters. The fighters are the thing that I remembered most. I

Wolff came into the 100th Bomb Group, 13th Combat Wing, 3rd Air Division of the Eighth Air Force at a time when the American flyers were getting their feet wet in dangerous daylight missions. One of the most ambitious was to

saw planes falling apart, burning. Flames coming out of everything in the cockpit, it was pretty bad.

An American B-17G in flight. The Boeing-built bomber, along with the Consolidated B-24, made up the heavy strategic bombing fleet of the U. S. Army Air Force.

field we came to, a place called Bone. It was an RAF field. Just iron mats laid on the sand there. And they wanted us to go around once because there'd been a crack-up on the ground, but we were committed, the lights were flashing on the gas gauges and we were just about out [of fuel]. We landed and taxied off to one side and the engines stopped, stopping one at a time, so we were out of gas...we just barely made it.

"We took a hit on the left life raft door. Something popped the latch on it and out it came and hit the horizontal stabilizer on the left side and put a huge dent in it which slowed us down, put us into a dive; but we managed to get back up in the formation. Then what I assumed to be a 20mm shell from one of the fighters hit the leading edge of the vertical stabilizer and put a big hole in that, and that was sucking air and slowing us down so we were using an awful lot of gas to keep up with the group.

"And that was the end of that mission as far as that was concerned. We stayed there overnight and were picked up by a transport, taken to Marrakech. Spent two or three days there and then we had arrangements made to fly back in a transport to England. That was an exciting mission. That was the one that sticks in my mind most of all."

"Just about two or three minutes before we dropped our bombs, everything stopped. And there was no fighters, no flak, no nothing. We dropped the bombs successfully and then turned toward Italy and the Mediterranean. We were all through and then it was just trying to get to our landing field in North Africa before we ran out of gas. We had to leave the group at the first air-

Eventually it was proposed that a strategic air force would also operate from the Mediterranean to aid in striking German targets that were being moved southeast to escape the England-based bombers. But the coordination proved elusive, and finally the U. S. Joint Chiefs of Staff proposed an overhaul, forming the U. S. Strategic Air Forces in January, 1944. With this reorganization came an increased number of bombers and fighters, the latter equipped with external gas tanks for increased range. A series of missions to Berlin was designed to not only knock out German production assets, but to expressly draw Luftwaffe fighters into combat with the U. S. fighter escorts. The 100th Bomb Group was one of the Eighth Air Force units that participated in these operations. Pilot John Gibbons from Spokane, Washington was accepted into the Air Cadet program of the Army Air Corps in January 1942 (the U. S. Army Air Corps was renamed U. S. Army Air Force in March 1942).

"I went to basic flying [training] in South Carolina, and then they, out of basic they assigned me to twin-engine training, which was the forerunner of bombers. And I graduated in May 1943 and I was automatically...I guess automatically...assigned to B-17 training in Sebring, Florida. I wasn't really supposed to go to combat in the bombers. They assigned me to learn to fly the C-54 and fly supplies over to China. [But] somebody some place along the line put me back in B-17s and sent me up to pick up a crew in Moses Lake, Washington, and from there to Sioux City [Iowa] and then over to England.

"Well, we flew across the ocean and you turn [in] your airplane in Prestwick, Scotland. I was assigned immediately to the 100th Bomb Group, with the 350th Squadron, and I arrived at the 100th Bomb Group a few days later in January '44. We were [based] up in what they called the triangle of Ipswich, Dulwich, and a place called Thorpe Abbotts.

"I was green, you know, 22 years old. Oh, we heard a lot about the 100th Bomb Group along the way, and as soon as we got there we heard all the horror stories...rumors were that your chances of completing twenty-five missions was less than 50-50. Back in those days, you flew your 1st mission as a co-pilot, and my 1st mission was to Regensburg, and we saw the fighters and flak. And naturally you were scared, things like that. But we got back from the 1st mission, and then my crew and I were to fly the 2nd mission together.

"I really didn't consider myself captain of the crew, but I guess I was the commander, I was the pilot of the airplane. That week was the week of the massive raids into Germany. So my 1st mission, my 2nd mission, and my 3rd mission and my 4th mission were all to Berlin. So the 1st mission, I was flying a composite squadron to the 95th [Bomb Group] and the Eighth Air Force [mission] was aborted, but the major that was leading the 95th decided to take 31 of us into Berlin, and I was one of 31 or 32 that went to Berlin on that 1st mission. On the 2nd mission the 100th Group suffered some of the greatest losses. I think we lost 16 or 17 airplanes. We were under attack for, I'd say, for 20 or 30 minutes. It was a massive attack by fighters. And of course, over Berlin we saw layers of flak. And as I said, we lost, it was the biggest loss the 100th Bomb Group had on that mission. The 4th mission, I went back to Berlin again, and flew under the same stuff. It was a pretty miserable week."

The Berlin missions from March 3 to 8, 1944 shifted the balance of power in the air to the Allies. The Luftwaffe lost between 5,000 and 6,000 planes in the air through attrition and denial of production from Allied bombing in early 1944. The American fighter escorts were part of the Ninth Air Force, designed as the air arm of SHAEF, called the Allied Expeditionary

Air Force (AEAF). Besides providing air cover for the strategic bombers, the Ninth Air Force operated medium bombers, reconnaissance and transport operations to support the cross-Channel invasion. The RAF also had a tactical air force based in the British Isles.

Just as things were improving for this thrust, called the Combined Bomber Offensive, all of these air assets were called into play against a new set of targets that would not only threaten staging of the cross-Channel invasion, but turn the tables once again on British terror bombing in Germany.

German scientists were rapidly advancing their technology in jet and rocket propulsion and this led to two unmanned aircraft models, the V-1 pilotless aircraft and the V-2 rocket. Most of the launch sites were in the Pas de Calais area where both weapons could set a course and range for London. Hitler believed that the renewed use of terror weapons on England, in conjunction with pushing the Allied offensive back into the sea, would so demoralize the Allies that they would be unable to recover.

On his 5th mission, John Gibbons' B-17 was part of a group ordered to bomb a suspected V-2 site on the French coast. Frank Buschmeier was an Ohio native who was a waist gunner – manning one of the two .50-cal. machine guns in the aft quarter of the bomber called the waist guns – in Gibbons' regular crew. He recalls the mission.

"On the 19th of March we were going to go in late in the afternoon and bomb rocket sites on the French coast, and we were gonna be over the target in eighteen minutes, something like that, at about 26,000 feet. We were on the bomb run and still out over the water, and the anti-aircraft shells are coming up busting all around us and then all of a sudden there was like a *whomp*. Like a shell exploded on the nose of the plane, and then another one, and then the tail after that; and I said to myself, 'The next one is going to be dead center,' and it was. It hit right in the radio room, blew out the bottom right side and part of the ceiling on the airplane. And I called [pilot] John Gibbons, and I told him, I said, 'The whole radio room's been blown away.'

A British Lancaster bomber, built by Avro. The other two British strategic bombers were the Short Stirling and the Handley Page Halifax.

"He dropped down to 10,000 feet and traveling down the French coast we had two bombs hung up in the bomb bay and that was supposed to be my job to go up there and drop them…loosen them…drop them…but with the radio room floor gone, I couldn't get to the bomb bay.

So he had Arnold, the top gunner, and Red, the bombardier, go back there and they finally worked the bombs loose...dropped them...and then we headed back to England. And [when we] got over to the coast of England, white cliffs of Dover, he asked the navigator how long to get to the base, and he said about forty minutes, something like that. And so John decided to land at the first air base he saw, which was the 353rd Fighter Squadron, and he touched down there, very soft landing.

Waist gunners inside a B-17 Flying Fortress bomber. They were part of a crew of ten and were in a very effective position to use their .50-cal. machine guns in defending the plane from fighter attacks.

left the parachute on the ledge behind me. And so I turned, snapped on the parachute and Walker was gone...radio man was gone...and the ball turret gunner said he saw him fall through the hole.

"Well, John told everybody to get rid of the [machine] guns, anything we had, to lighten the load. So we were throwing things out and [Roy] Arnold, the top turret gunner, in taking his guns out and throwing them out through the bomb bay, he popped the rip cord on his parachute, and now the parachute was billowing out alongside the plane...which [was] putting stress on the tail, the rear section. And so our ball turret gunner, Sprague, popped out of his ball turret and went through the right waist gun window and pulled the chute in tight against the fuselage and held it 'til Roy could form it back.

"Everybody from there, pilots and the engineers, said it was impossible for that plane to fly but it did. John landed it safely...very good pilot. On that first hit, too, I called John...I stayed in contact with him...told him about the radio room. I noticed that the radio man had been killed; it looked like he had been through two or three shotgun blasts. His clothes were shredded and he was slumped over on the radio table. I thought...instinct told me to go back, go put my parachute on, reach up there, grab him and pull him back in the waist. Well, I don't know if I could have reached across the opening there, even, but I never wore my parachute. I had a chest pack, and it was in the way of firing the gun, so I had the harness on and I

"And then I noticed that the control cables were hanging down, so I thought we've got to do something with them, and so I was trying to tie them together as best I could. And to this day, I don't know if I completed that or not, but John Gibbons later said for a while he had no control, and suddenly he had control again, so maybe I did do something with that, but anyway, it was a kind of a hairy day."

U. S. Navy PT boats race through the open waters of the English Channel. Famous for their service in the Pacific, the wooden-hulled patrol boats also performed many important functions in the cross-Channel invasion.

As important as the Combined Bomber Offensive had become in the war, *Operation Overlord* was about to change the focus of strategic air missions in April 1944. The *Transportation Plan,* concentrating on railroad marshalling yards (where the repair facilities were), bridges, rail lines and rolling stock, was designed to create as much havoc as possible behind the front lines of the invasion beaches in order to prevent the movement of German armored reserves to the battle area. The strategic air chiefs didn't see the value in this idea and offered as an alternative, the *Oil Plan*; increased focus on Germany's oil refineries and synthetic fuel plants. No gas, no counterattacks. The *Oil Plan* would be useful later, SHAEF insisted, but only the *Transportation Plan* would effectively utilize the Allies' new-found air superiority in the tactical D-Day situation.

Some ninety-three targets were identified and more than 76,000 tons of bombs were dropped between the April start of the *Transportation Plan* and D-Day. Targets were scattered and random so as not to focus attention on the invasion area. The U. S. B-26 Marauder, a medium bomber, was the most effective plane in this operation, but American Flying Fortresses and British Lancasters participated as well.

"Oh yeah, we bombed quite a few railroads," recalls pilot John Gibbons. "I really don't know how many. And we bombed the airfields too, the fighter bases, because they wanted to get rid of the fighter bases. We bombed quite a few prior to D-Day. And of course, we bombed the [railroad] marshalling yards."

Despite high hopes for the *Transportation Plan,* SHAEF intelligence reported in May that the operation had not done as much damage to German logistics as SHAEF had expected. The Germans commandeered French railway cars to replace the more than 25,000 destroyed by the

Allied bombers and made repairs quickly to damaged rail lines, yards and turntables. However, the Allies destroyed bridges over the Seine River, giving a key segment of German reinforcements a great challenge in reaching Normandy.

USS Nevada, *followed by USS* Texas, *sailing the English Channel. By America's entry into World War II the mammoth battlewagons were hardly used in ship to ship sea battles but their firepower against shore batteries was a major component of the Normandy campaign.*

Force O (TF-124 – Omaha Beach) was commanded by Rear Admiral John L. Hall, who also was in charge of amphibious training.

The fire support ships – those expected to blast German shore batteries – did not include U. S. Navy vessels until planning discovered a shortage. As a result of a February 1944 "landing craft" conference in London, the U. S. committed three battleships, three cruisers and thirty-one destroyers to D-Day fire support. Many other U. S. Navy vessels – minesweepers, supply ships, PT boats, destroyer escorts, even sixty Coast Guard cutters for search and rescue – joined the landing craft and fighting ships in the operation.

AMASSING THE NAVAL FORCE

While much of the U. S. Navy's function, and that of the British Admiralty, leading up to D-Day was procuring, equipping, maintaining and operating landing craft, there were other operations as well. An entire organizational arm of the U. S. Navy was set up in England to manage the bases, ships and crews that would, added to those of the other Allies, put more than 5,000 vessels in the Channel waters for *Operation Overlord*.

Two task forces were set up to handle the crossing based on the location of the landing beaches. Rear Admiral Alan G. Kirk was placed in charge of the Western Naval Task Force (American beachhead) and Royal Navy Rear Admiral Sir Philip Vian, the Eastern Naval Task Force (British/Canadian beachhead). Under Kirk the command of Force U (TF-125 – Utah Beach) was assigned to Rear Admiral Don P. Moon and

The three American battleships assigned to fire support at Normandy were USS *Texas*, USS *Arkansas* and the Pearl Harbor veteran, USS *Nevada*. As a dispersing clerk assigned to *Nevada's* paymaster, Woodrow Derby was in combat on two of the war's most significant dates – December 7, 1941 and June 6, 1944. He recalls the big ship's activities after she left the Pacific Fleet.

"[From] Boston and New York we escorted three or four large convoys and turned them over to the British at Belfast, Ireland. Now

these convoys, we were right square in the middle, we're the big defense and it must have been one hundred ships around us. Hard to believe but there were destroyers and destroyer escorts all around the outer edge protecting us with no problem. After the last trip up to Belfast we went down the Irish Sea around southern England."

Throughout the first years of the war the British navy mined the English Channel. The process continued leading up to the cross-Channel invasion but the Bay of the Seine, facing the invasion beaches, was avoided. This fact was observed by several German navy officers, but their observations went unheeded at the higher command levels.

The German navy did patrol the coastal waters, but their E-boats (similar to USN PT boats) were the largest Kriegsmarine craft in the immediate area. With so few ships, they rarely ventured near English ports or the coast except at night or in fog; and they didn't attack. The notable exception was the night of April 27-28, 1944 during *Exercise Tiger* (see page 69). Thanks to diligent patrolling by U. S. Navy and Royal Navy ships and planes, German U-boats were kept from discovering or disrupting the intense naval activity leading up to D-Day.

Thirty RN, Commonwealth and USN warships, as well as three ships contributed by the French and Dutch, were included in Admiral Kirk's Western Naval Task Force 122. The balance of seventy-three warships accompanied the Eastern Naval Task Force. Along with vessels involved in the Mulberry harbor project, fire and salvage operations, the warships, landing craft, transports, patrol boats, minesweepers and other

Trucks and Jeeps for the Normandy invasion are combat loaded into an LCT at an English port facility.

ships and boats created the largest naval force ever used in a military operation.

INTELLIGENCE

As technology took steps forward with wireless communications in World War II, the enemy's ability to compromise that form of communication posed greater risks to operational security. The advantage of a wireless system, that it could be instantaneous and communicate anywhere, could also prove its downfall when it came to security.

Though the Nazis developed and used the Enigma encoder/decoder for all their coded military communications, certain aspects of the system of identifying code ciphers were given greater security than those employed by the Japanese. Of course British and American code breakers were able to duplicate Enigma quickly, but not all messages were decoded with the same ease and speed as were Japanese messages. One of the things that greatly aided the Allies' successful decoding of German military messages was the state of the human intelligence situation in the European Theater.

As early as 1940, the British were able to compromise German agents in the British Isles. By identifying and forcibly turning German agents, they controlled what information could be leaked to the enemy and what would not. This ability to manipulate what information the Germans received was of great help to Allied intelligence and verification of their code-breaking efforts.

Knowing that some information of what was transpiring in the British Isles would make its way to the Abwehr, OB West, Armed Forces High Command (OKW) and other top German commanders including the Führer, deception schemes became the most elaborate of all Allied counter-intelligence efforts. Since the greatest secrets of the cross-Channel invasion were its date, time and location, deception played an enormous part in hiding the truth from the enemy.

Lt. Gen. George S. Patton, already known in Germany for his exploits in the Mediterranean (and his superb skill in mobile warfare), was placed in charge of the First U. S. Army Group, an entirely fictitious entity portrayed as being based in the area of Dover, the famous English city across the Channel from Pas de Calais. By feeding the press, radio communications and double agents messages about Patton's fake army – information that would make its way to Nazi commanders – the hoax could be pulled off. Though Patton wasn't happy about being excluded from the greatest Allied undertaking of the war, he agreed to participate in the plan, but was also promised a major post-D-Day command.

There were fake maneuvers by the First U. S. Army Group and camps were kept "alive" for the benefit of German aerial reconnaissance. The plan worked by confirming the best guess of Hitler and German military leaders about the location of the invasion, the Kanalküste, across from Dover in the Pas de Calais region of France. Activities lasted through June 6 and even continued after D-Day, making the Germans hesitant to move forces from the Pas de Calais for fear that Patton and his army would still cross there.

Many other security measures were implemented to insure the secrecy of the invasion. A level of security within Top Secret called Bigot was instituted to give the closest guarded details of the mission access to only a few select commanders. English citizens were often inconvenienced by security measures, especially in regard to activities near the coast. As noted, bombing and mining missions were purposely designed to keep the Channel crossing location unknown to the enemy. Charts and maps were passed without incident despite the great number needed for commanders of the many operations.

As far as intelligence coming from the Continent, the Allies had a distinct advantage in what they knew about their enemy. Active intelligence came from three basic sources: surveillance (mainly aerial reconnaissance), spies – both active and captured enemy spies or deserters (of which there were few in the initial stages), and civilians living in German-occupied countries. Aerial reconnaissance had been going on for years along with the occasional gunboat and commando raids across the Channel. But many things could be hidden from the prying eyes of aircraft and even the occasional trek to the beaches of Normandy. Unlike the Germans, the Allies had many thousands of potential, if not entirely reliable, eyes and ears on site to deliver information.

Most of the population in occupied France (by November 1942 there were German troops in all parts of the country, including the Vichy region), and the Low Countries went about their normal business between 1940 and 1944; but a large segment was unhappy about the circumstances they were in and resolved to do something about it. These French men and women were sometimes politically motivated but were mostly patriotically motivated to rid themselves of the Nazi occupiers. In fits and starts the Forces Françaises de l'Intérieur (FFI) became a regionally organized network of informants, guerilla bands and amateur saboteurs under the guidance and supply of the British Special Operations Executive

General Bernard L. Montgomery, General Dwight D. Eisenhower and Air Chief Marshal Arthur Tedder watch American troops practice for the Normandy invasion.

(SOE) and U. S. Office of Strategic Services, Special Operations (OSS/SO). They planned and executed sabotage operations but mainly were an active form of reconnaissance before and during the invasion.

FINAL PREPARATIONS

More Planning

By February 1, 1944 with the publication of the *Neptune* Initial Joint Plan, planning was passed down through the lower levels of combat organizations in 21st Army Group and naval, air and support forces. The time had arrived to set an exact date for D-Day (although the term is general in military parlance, after June 6, 1944 it has come to mean the Allied landing in Normandy). D-Day had already been postponed a month to allow time to build more landing craft. Consulting the almanac for June conditions in the invasion area, Allied planners identified only two periods with the desired combination of tides, moonlight and weather windows; June 5-7 and 18-20. Ike selected Monday, June 5, 1944 as D-Day.

Near the end of April, Admiral Ramsay relocated his headquarters to the sprawling country mansion of Southwick House seven

miles inland from Portsmouth. Eisenhower soon moved his headquarters into a trailer camp on the spacious and wooded grounds. Montgomery, overall ground commander for the invasion, had a motor trailer there as well. Southwick House would be the seat of all important command meetings until D-Day save one grand spectacle at 21st Army Group headquarters. Meanwhile, activity in the British Isles continued at all levels by military units of every type in preparation to accomplish their *Overlord/Neptune* assignments.

Training and Quarantine

In bases and camps all over the United Kingdom the routine training of military personnel involved in the operation was segueing into the particularities of amphibious assault. An assault training center for GIs at Woolacombe, in operation since August 1943, prepared the Americans for the invasion under Lt. Col. Paul Thompson's leadership. Elsewhere, specialty units such as engineers and tankers practiced debarking their equipment from beaching craft. The American airborne units moved their camps to places where the access to aircraft and landing sites was suitable for jump training.

"We were assigned to the 505 PIR [Parachute Infantry Regiment]," explains

As part of Operation Fortitude, *decoys such as this inflatable rubber tank which these soldiers are moving to a new location were massed along the coast of England to give credence to Lt. Gen. George S. Patton's fictious First U. S. Army Group.*

Tom Blakey. "I went with an advance group and we drove down to Nottingham. We started making [parachute] drops. I didn't know what they we aiming for and neither did anyone else. It could have been a crossroads, a bridge as far as I was concerned. I never was told we gotta take that bridge. I was told after we got in quarantine; then we found out what we were supposed to do. Up to that time we just jumped and did things."

Charles Norman Shay was receiving extended training in field medicine.

"We knew that we were training for something big because we were training in the field, learning how to treat wounded…apply splints, apply tourniquets to stop heavy bleeding, to apply

The headquarters of the Allied air commands were based throughout southern England. There were also dozens of American and British air bases, with the home base of the U. S. 100th Bomb Group of the Eighth Air force shown here as an example. Also illustrated are the debarkation ports for the Normandy landings and German E-boat attack on the Slapton Sands Force "U" rehearsal the night of April 27-28.

more pressure if necessary. We knew that we were training for the invasion of Normandy…or the invasion of Europe. We didn't know where it was gonna take place. We broke up our medical aid station and I had been assigned as a medic to F Company…[an] infantry company…one of the platoons of the F Company."

Buster Simmons was also continuing his training as a medic in an infantry company.

"We got on a train and rode the train to the tip of the English isle and down to the Channel coast. We went to a town called Bonder Regis, which was a seashore resort town, and this was in February [1944]. The people who owned the places weren't there, we just took over the homes that the people had there, the United States had paid for them. We stayed there and we were training the whole time there. You can't get too much training. We were there until we moved back kind of northeast of there to about thirty miles northwest of London, at a town called Hillsbury."

Fred Purdy was still getting acclimated to army life in the U. S. Army Signal Corps.

"From Glasgow, we got on the train and went all the way down to the Salisbury Plains near Salisbury, England, and within sight of Stonehenge, which is the old rock formation known as one of the antiquities of England. I met a Lieutenant Hicks, Earl Hicks. He called me and about six or seven other guys and told us that, 'Fellas, I've been watchin' y'all, and I'm gonna have a mission to do some special work, and I'd like to have you guys come with me.' We didn't particularly like the outfit we were training with at the time, so we joined up with Lt. Earl Hicks for training."

New Jersey native Joe Sorrentino was assigned to the U. S. Army Quartermaster Corps after basic and went overseas in a convoy. He arrived in the British Isles in 1943 where the Quartermaster Corps was busy preparing all the material needs for the forces in the cross-Channel invasion.

"Went to Plymouth. Marsh Mills was the name of the little town, suburb of Plymouth. And we stayed there…in fact they had the big quartermaster depot there, I mean gigantic, gigantic thing. And about eight of us, we were stationed at the gate, we had to check all cars comin' in and out. And we went to fireman's school while we were there, we learned how to train, how to put out incendiary bombs.

"Well, while we were there, we did have one air raid in Plymouth, and it was late at night, and where our gate was, right off to the railroad. They had spotted a plane, and the anti-aircraft were firin' at it, and

These tractor trailer cabs were among thousands of motor vehicles stockpiled for the invasion of France. They sit in an English farmer's field converted to a vehicle park in May 1944.

An anti-aircraft unit guards gliders and Dakota C-47 transport planes assembled in preparation for Operation Overlord.

it come down towards us. So I jumped in a foxhole; we had a foxhole there. One guy didn't wanna jump in no foxhole. His name was Gruber. I says, 'Get in the foxhole, they're comin' right this way!' So he says, 'If the bomb has got your name on it, it's gonna hit ya, no matter where you are.' Believe me that's the first time I ever heard this expression. So I told him, 'If a bomb's got my name on it, he's gonna have to look for me.' And I heard that all around the camp after, 'cause most got a kick out of it."

Hal Baumgarten went through rigorous infantry training beginning on Colonel Thompson's course.

"Now, our training was excellent. I was sent to Company A of the 116th Infantry, 29th Infantry Division, with a lot of the guys that were with me at Camp Croft. We had a guy from Bedford, Virginia training us, 'cause they were the 'Boys from Bedford.' Company A was the leader of the whole pack there. So finally they let us join the group and they broke up into boat teams. Twenty-nine men and one officer to each boat team. We lived, slept and ate in boat teams and we trained on the moors with mock-up assault boats. And we were trained to go out in these assault boats and fan out and attack pill boxes. And they did it so many times that it became rote, you could do it in your sleep.

"We were all pretty rugged, good shape. We attacked pill boxes on the beach with bazookas. Then in April, we landed on Woolacombe Beach with the British Navy, in LCAs, which is the British version of the Higgins boat. So you're crowded in, twenty-nine men and one officer, and three British sailors. We had pill boxes on the beach itself, and we attacked it with the tactics that we were taught. Then later in April we had two maneuvers from a British ship. It was called the *Empire Javelin*, which was a Liberty ship, built in the Kaiser shipyard in San Francisco."

When it came time for training the larger units in concert, the British provided a coastal strip at Slapton Sands (South Devonshire) that approximated the terrain of the Normandy landing sites. Almost 3,000 civilians were relocated from the village and nearby farms. The area was large enough to accommodate air and sea units into the training exercises, and live firing would be part of the rehearsals. Thompson and his staff designed the drills at Slapton Sands and eight other locations for all types of units that would be hitting the beach. The British had similar sites for British and Commonwealth forces east of Portsmouth.

As the training exercises were winding down, the next challenge was to direct the five assault divisions, their support units and follow-up divisions to the debarkation ports in southern England. The movements of men and material needed to be closely coordinated and as a result staff work continued day and night in the months just before D-Day.

When she was settled in England, WAC Sgt. Jackie Volkl received an assignment to be secretary at one of the American supply bases. In May, a number of WACs were gathered to form a large secretarial pool.

"Just about six weeks before D-Day we were sent down to Portsmouth, England and there we worked on manifests for the ships that were going to take the guys across and all that bit. There were oodles and oodles of gals who were typing and we were in all different locations. That's where I was when D-Day occurred. The reason we knew it had really occurred was we were wakened about 1:00 o'clock in the morning by planes going overhead, going out, and we looked outside and they were the planes dragging the gliders. Those were the first ones to go across and we saw them go so we knew then that

D-Day had occurred. Then we saw the bigger planes going out with the paratroopers and of course they had bad things happen like at Ste.-Mère-Église and we didn't know it would be so bad for those guys."

As the historic day approached, the ground units were marched or transported into a series of temporary tent camps near the coastal debarkation points. An entire regiment was assigned to each of these temporary camps which were located beside roads on the way to the debarkation ports. Everything was camouflaged to hide the true nature of these troop marshalling areas and blackout conditions were enforced. The GIs called these barbed wire surrounded camps "sausages" because of their shape.

Jim Weller observed what happened when his tank destroyer unit was ordered to the marshalling area.

"So finally we moved down [to the coast] about a week before the 4th [of June] and we stayed at this camp. It was a sealed camp and they give us all kind of different training and they showed us maps and nomenclature, how the beach was going to look. We was around doing all that to get prepared for the invasion, we was going to go on the 5th."

Albert Piper was in the headquarters staff of the 32nd Field Artillery, attached to 1st Infantry Division, nicknamed "The Big Red One." He describes life in the "sausage."

"I don't remember too much training. I guess they figured we knew what the hell we were doing. But I know that they put us in a fenced area and put English guards on us, which nobody cared quite for that one. And of course, as you know it was the first day of June or whatever it was, and they wouldn't let us out. We were there for that."

Every soldier was issued a new uniform and a new weapon. The uniform contained a substance that was supposed to retard chemicals in warfare, but all it did was prevent the fabric from breathing and made it too cold. They were issued French guidebooks and condoms. The latter many soldiers put to good use before the invasion by covering the muzzles of their rifles with them to keep the bores of the weapons dry. And special precautions were taken with the equipment to be used in the amphibious assault.

"We got the order one day to waterproof all our equipment," says Joe Sorrentino, "and we had to seal up all the windows of the trailers, and the motors in the trucks. Had to put this gluey stuff they called Bostik that makes everything waterproof."

Loading

On May 23, General Eisenhower made the final decision to proceed so that all ships had sufficient time to get underway from their remote berths and keep to schedule. On May 28 the order went out to get underway, and all naval crews were sealed in

American troops and vehicles crowd a dock during the loading phase of Operation Neptune. *Anti-aircraft battalion soldiers are trying on their newly issued lifebelts as they stand in and around their halftracks armed with quad .50-cal. machine guns.*

their ships as a quarantine measure. The first ground units began boarding ships on May 30, and loading was complete on June 3 when all loaded ships awaited convoy formation in the assembly ports on the southeastern and southwestern English coast.

David Troyer was in the 3207 Quartermaster Service Company. He had witnessed first-hand the tragedy during *Exercise Tiger* when much of his unit's equipment and a sister company perished in the attack. But he was prepared to go in with the first wave at Utah Beach.

"We were boarded ship the 4th and at midnight of the 4th our ship's crew gave us a steak dinner, cherry pie, and ice cream. We figured this was to some of us, this would be our last supper."

Weather patterns were monitored making use of all Allied reporting stations. Since abandoning their base in Greenland, the Germans had no advanced weather station reports to keep pace with SHAEF resources. That would work to their disadvantage when the weather turned sour in the Channel.

General Eisenhower and his staff, beginning on June 1, met

twice daily with the SHAEF Meteorological Committee. And the weather began to look bad for the operation on Saturday, June 3. At a Southwick House meeting at 0400 on Sunday Eisenhower polled the operation leaders. All but Montgomery wanted to postpone. Eisenhower pondered the decision between 0500 and 0600 and decided to delay the assault for twenty-four hours.

"We were prepared to go the first night, the night of the 4th," explains paratrooper Blakey. "D-Day was originally scheduled for the 5th so that meant we had to go on the 4th because we had [to go] from Nottingham clear down to the ocean, assemble, and then come across around the peninsula that juts between Jersey and Guernsey so we had a pretty good flight. I'm not sure I remember exactly how long it was, maybe 3 or 3½ hours from Nottingham around all of that.

"We started to leave the night of the 4th but we got called back and then went the night of the 5th. The night of the 4th everybody was just as happy as they could be. We knew this was coming...we knew when we got to the aerodrome and were quarantined that we were there for a reason and we were going. Everybody I knew was glad about it because there was two ways of getting home, a bad wound or a trip through France and Germany. And this was the first step."

"OK, Let's Go!"

The postponement of D-Day to June 6 would be a one shot option. The ships in Task Force 122 would have to refuel after that target date and *Operation Neptune* would then have to wait until the second window of opportunity later in June. It rained all day on June 4. The mood was somber when the senior commanders met at Southwick House on Sunday evening. Then Group Capt. J. M. Stagg, RAF, who made the predictions on behalf of the Meteorological Committee, brought some news to the gathering. He predicted a break in the weather for June 6. Eisenhower decided to have the operation resumed and the convoys began forming through the night.

When the Supreme Commander and senior commanders gathered again at 0400 on June 5, Stagg was reporting more evidence that the weather break would occur on Tuesday, June 6, but the window of favorable conditions would be small. Once again, the military leaders offered their opinions, but only Eisenhower could decide. The ships would have to be recalled quickly if there was to be another delay. He paced, expressed his concern for the men, thought and paced some more; and then turned to face the group, saying, "OK, let's go."

"Come near June, seemed one night these planes come over pullin' gliders, you know," recalls Joe Sorrentino. "Every night for about a week they'd go over...over one direction. About an hour later they'd come back. So one night, they come over and they had all these white stripes on 'em. We didn't know what they [the stripes] were, what they meant. Anyway, they didn't come back like they usually do. So during the early morning, we heard this rumble, rumble and we didn't know what was goin' on. And we find out later on that the invasion started."

"The second night there wasn't any gaiety going around," says Blakey. "We were all so scared it would be canceled. But it wasn't. We got on with it on the 5th. They got that little clear spot and Eisenhower said 'let's go' and we did."

Joe Sorrentino from New Jersey. "I was inducted December 7th 1942, exactly one year after Pearl Harbor. They called us the 'Pearl Harbor Avengers.'"

Jackie Volkl, whose maiden name was Orlene M. Ijas, was known to her friends as "Jackie" when she was a Master Sergeant in the WACs.

A minor wound got Fritz Baresel away from the tank war on the Eastern Front and into the famous Panzer Lehr Division which fought the Allies from D-Day on.

Al Webber fought with the 90th Infantry Division in France. Post-war he played great Dixieland trombone and worked as an editor with the Weider History Group for 16 years.

Ernest "Andy" Andrews came from Chattanooga, Tennessee and was drafted into the army in June of 1943.

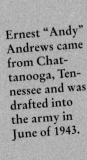

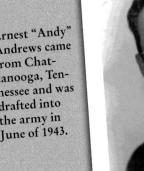

Robert Wolff had an interest in flying all his life and flew a B-17G in Europe. He was shot down and became a POW for a time.

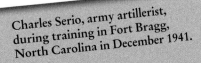

Charles Serio, army artillerist, during training in Fort Bragg, North Carolina in December 1941.

Exercise Tiger

At the end of April 1944, the "dress rehearsal" for the 4th Infantry Division landing on Utah Beach, code named *Tiger*, was scheduled at Slapton Sands, off Portland, England at Lyme Bay. These advanced landing maneuvers, of which *Exercise Tiger* was one, involved all operational aspects of the proposed landing: land, sea and air. A simulated air bombardment preceded the convoy on the night of April 26-27, 1944, which crossed Lyme Bay, then cast off loaded landing craft for a morning assault by 4th Infantry Division soldiers. The exercise was beset by problems and misfortune almost from the beginning with the landing of the first convoy on the morning of April 27.

"When we left Falmouth," says the Coast Guard's Tommy Harbour, "We loaded up probably four or five hundred Army [soldiers]. They all was out on deck. So, we went up around the coast of England, the ship [USS *Bayfield*] never did anchor. We had about fifteen or twenty Army guys in our boat. Now this was at Slapton Sands and we was supposed to take those guys in and let 'em off. They said, 'Take 'em in to the beach.' There was no beach. You know how them swamps is down in Georgia that's got all moss hangin' down? That's what we run into.

"So [boatman] Harold went up there and I let the ramp down a little bit, and he took a boat hook and got to checkin' the depths, 'cause I didn't wanna let them boys out in water over their head, you know. And when water got down to about a foot deep or so, why I let the ramp down and they jumped out in the water. Hated to do that 'cause we was taught to land 'em dry, up on the beach, see. So then we found our way back to the *Bayfield* and they hoisted us aboard. I don't know what happened to them guys, 'cause it was almost dark whenever we got back there to the *Bayfield*."

David Troyer also landed with the first convoy on April 27.

"*Exercise Tiger*...this exercise was the real McCoy, and we...I don't know how many times we dismantled our bags, put it back together, waiting to be taken to the port and we finally did. We were already ahead of the LSTs and we sit there and we made the landing and slept in sands. I was in 3207 QM Service Company, and we sit there and waited. There were British machine gunners on the beach supposed to be shooting over our heads and they blew some of us down when we came in. The other part of the beach, our own big artillery firing on the beach, troops were coming in there also. There's more casualties there. And later in the afternoon of the 28th, we knew something had happened because our sister company, 3206, was supposed to be in."

The Commander in Chief-Plymouth was in charge of the all-British patrol of motor torpedo boats (MTBs) and motor gunboats along with two destroyers which guarded the mouth of Lyme Bay. Another patrol of MTBs watched activity off Cherbourg, France. Eight more LSTs were due in for the landing exercise on the night of April 27-28.

About midnight a group of nine German "E" boats, which the Germans called S-boats, slipped

Soldiers disembark from Landing Craft, Infantry (LCI) 84 during an invasion dress rehearsal at Slapton Sands, England.

into Lyme Bay and fired torpedoes at targets of opportunity. Only one destroyer, HMS *Azalea*, was on post that night; her partner had developed problems and was not replaced. *Azalea* misinterpreted a flare shot about 0130 from a distressed LST as part of the exercise; by then guns on the LSTs were engaging the enemy. The MTBs and gunboats also joined the fight but were unable to destroy any of the German attackers.

LST-507 was the first ship hit, struck by one torpedo at 0204. *LST-531* took two torpedoes, rolled over and sank in six minutes. *LST-289* also took a hit while engaging in a firefight with the E-boats, but remained under power and eventually made it back to port. Though pursued by the British ships, the S-boats fled within an hour under a smoke screen and outran their foe.

Dr. Eugene Eckstam of Wisconsin was a U. S. Navy medical officer attached to *LST-507*. The ship came from Brixham with infantry and support troops on board. What was supposed to be a mock "General Quarters" alarm in which Eckstam treated simulated casualties turned into something very different in the early morning hours.

"Well, we hit the sack in the evening and we had 'General Quarters' about one-thirty in the morning; and we'd had 'General Quarters' four or five times a day anyway because of the air raids and we thought, oh, just another drill. Submarine alerts were another cause for 'General Quarters' and we reported to our station…mine was in the wardroom of the top[side] and nothing was happening. I heard gunfire and I remember saying that somebody better watch out what they're doing or somebody's going to get hurt. What a remark, in hindsight!

"We got hit around 0203 and, as it was, I was just raised up inside and fell down on my knees. I probably would have fallen overboard had I been on the deck to watch what was going on. We didn't know for sure until the next day what hit us.

"I went into the wardroom to wait for casualties and they were just minor little things…scratches and stuff…nothing major. So I went down below deck just to see if there was anybody hurt down there. I went as far forward on the sides as I could and the sleeping compartments and there weren't any people there dead or alive that I could see and then I opened the door into the tank deck, the hatch, and there was a raging inferno there. The force of the fire just about knocked me back on my heels. So I could hear the guys screaming and hollering [in there]."

Patsy Giacchi came from northern New Jersey where many of Sicilian heritage like his family resided. He was also on *LST-507* for *Exercise Tiger*. Giacchi was nervous as he waited on the ship for the landing in the morning.

"You look around, you see guys talking, some guys are sleeping. I was scared. I didn't sleep that night. I lay down on the stretcher. Patty Moreno was writing a letter to his grandfather, and I was looking at the two big doors, and I could see little puddles of water where the big doors open up. Then I looked around and I said, 'Let me see now, the steps are over there, just in case,' and then, *boom, boom, boom!* I don't know what it was, the guns were shooting, other LSTs were shooting. I waited a while, and then the second time I heard something, and it jarred the ship. I said, 'Patty, I'm going.'

"I put my helmet on. I put my life belt on, and I checked it. And I started to go up the stairs.

An LCVP carries soldiers to a rehearsal landing at Slapton Sands. While the dress rehearsal for Force "O" took place with few problems, the attack on LSTs of Force "U" disrupted the entire event.

As I got to the top, I couldn't believe it. I saw the ocean was on fire. It was the real thing! I said, 'This can't be a joke!' Behind me comes another guy, his name was Bradshaw, and we look around. He said, 'Oh my God! What's this?' Then we got a direct hit. *Boom!* I flew up, ten, fifteen feet...I came down. Bradshaw landed on the side of me. We turn and look and we can see the ship, the *[LST-]507*, was in half.

"I had a gash in my forehead and I was bleeding. I lost my helmet. I had it with the strap loose, and when I went up and came down, it fell off. Then we went over the side. When I came up, I saw a navy man; they had gray helmets, we had green ones. He was wrapped around a gun, dead. He must have been firing the gun when the torpedo hit. He was wrapped around the gun and there was blood all over him.

"I hit that water and never gave up. And I was not a good swimmer. I feared water. That belt saved me. When we hit the water I swallowed so much salt water, because I wasn't prepared for that part. We start to drift away. And as we're pulling away, we held hands, and we could see other guys in the water. The water was on fire, there was a gasoline smell, but the worst thing was the death cry of the sailors and the soldiers, 'Help! Help! Help!' And there's nobody to help. The blood was coming down my forehead, but I didn't care, I knew what I was doing. We held on together, Bradshaw and I, and we started to

LCVPs of transport PA-13 land soldiers during a training exercise at Slapton Sands. In the background an LST prepares to beach and open its huge bow doors. The soldiers wear gas detection bands on the left sleeves of their uniforms as gas warfare was still considered a threat.

drift. He looked at me and said, 'Patsy, hold on, we're doing fine.'

"As we drifted, every now and then you'd see something like a shadow off in the distance; it could have been an E-boat going back. But the four or five hours we were in the water seemed like four or five days. Bradshaw was a year or two older than me, about 22 or 23, and you know how the Southern boys speak very softly. 'Patsy,' he says, 'we're gonna beat this thing.'"

Paul Gerolstein, USN, was a Gunner's Mate 2nd Class on one of the LSTs in the second convoy. Like the other LSTs in the convoy, *LST-515* was loaded to the gunwales with tanks, trucks and troops.

"We never unloaded because when we got to Lyme Bay, it was too dark, I guess. It was in the middle of the night, and we were in the middle of a channel. *LST-515* was the

lead ship. We had a commander on board. Commander [B. J.] Skahill, he was in charge of the whole convoy, of the whole flotilla there. And then around two in the morning, we were called…we had 'General Quarters,' and we were attacked by the German E-boats.

"Well, when they got torpedoed, the commander gave the orders for all the LSTs to scatter, to all go different ways and my captain, [Lieutenant Commander] John Doyle, God bless him, he says, 'We're going back.' The commander was telling him, you know, to head for shore or something, but Doyle went back to the scene, where the ships were torpedoed, and we rescued over 100…I don't know, 117…something like that…of people that were in the water. And that water was cold. It was in the forty degrees."

"My company commander told me first-hand the things that had happened," says Troyer. "The first thing he told me was that

An M-10 tank destroyer in the foreground of a rehearsal landing at Slapton Sands. Behind the tank an LCT and the larger LST are arriving at water's edge. Already unloaded in the foreground are rolls of Sommerfeld wire mesh tracking used to aid trucks and other wheeled vehicles to cross the sand.

our big gunship that was to bring up the rear of the convoy rammed another ship [on its] way out of port, bore a big hole in the bow and had to go back into port. This left one small gunship to take care of the eight LSTs in this convoy.

"The next thing that took place was the British Navy, American Navy was on two different wavelengths…did not correspond with each other and when these nine E-boats came out of Cherbourg looking for something, they aimed for the convoy with one small gunship for protection. They started in and they hit the *LST-507*, which contained infantrymen. The next LST was the *531* and the 3206 Quartermaster Service Company, all their equipment, all of 3207's company trucks and equipment. One Jeep, the commander's Jeep, had one mile on it. [*LST-531*] took a double torpedo and sank in six minutes. The next LST that was hit was the *289*, but it did not sink. It was towed back into port and some of the things my commander told me is some of the infantrymen from *LST-507* had jumped in the water with full packs, the life preserver around their waist and they struggled trying to keep upright."

Exercise Tiger has become controversial for the atmosphere of secrecy Allied leaders immediately clamped over the disaster. Fearing negative consequences that could jeopardize *Operation Overlord* if the scope of the disaster became known, participants and witnesses were sworn to secrecy and threatened with heavy penalties for breaking their silence.

"We were enlisted men and, you know, they didn't tell us anything," recalls Gerolstein. "And when this all happened, we took it as just the war, that's just what it was. And when we came back, all the survivors that went to the hospital, the doctors and the nurses, everybody in that hospital was told to keep their mouths shut and don't ask any questions, and if they do, it's a court martial offense because it was so close to the invasion, and they didn't want it to get out, you know, so it was total hush-hush."

After spending many hours in the bay, Giacchi and Bradshaw were picked out of the water by a British corvette.

"Before you know it, it's the next morning," remembers Giacchi. "Me and Bradshaw are in this room, and they've got a tremendous table set up. And on the table there's all wallets that they've picked up, because they had two colored companies going out, graves registration, with grappling hooks to pick up bodies. Now we're on land. They had sent an LST out to pick up some bodies, and they came back and opened up the two big doors. You looked in and you could see piles of soldiers and sailors, dead. They closed the doors right away because the port was loaded with English police and civilians, and they didn't want everybody to see what was going on because it was supposed to be hush-hush. This was a tragedy. It never should have happened, especially with D-Day five or six weeks away."

"That evening [April 28]…we didn't even pitch up tents," says Troyer. "We were told we would be taken out of the area early the next morning and we were whisked out of the area. My company commander was in charge of identification…Slapton Sands…with the deceased, and he stopped counting at 1,200. And I have asked generals, colonels, even an admiral where the difference was…the 749 [killed] that were supposed to be at Slapton Sands…they stopped counting at 1,200. We know it was estimated between 1,200 and 1,600 lost on *Exercise Tiger*. I've been told by many officers that if it wasn't for the changes that were made after *Exercise Tiger*, D-Day would not have been a success."

CHAPTER 2

JUNE 6, 1944
THE ALLIED AIRBORNE OPERATION

One hundred five minutes before midnight, June 5-6, 1944, American paratroopers of the 101st Airborne Division took off in 432 Dakota C-47 transports – displaying an unmistakable pattern of three white and two black stripes on the wings and fuselage of the planes – to carry them across the Channel in a partly cloudy moonlit sky. Further east, troopers of the 82nd Airborne Division boarded another 439 C-47s, while members of the British 6th Airborne Division loaded up or felt tow ropes began to stiffen between their Horsa gliders and the transports towing them into the air. Once the C-47s carrying serials of the 501, 502, 506, 505, 507 and 508 Parachute Infantry Regiments (PIR) took off into the sky, the tarmacs would be readied for the first group of American glider troops to take off at dawn on D-Day. The roughly three and a half hour flight across the Channel was not particularly pleasant – the sketchy weather and bundled nerves caused some of the

paratroopers to hope the jump would come quickly and release them from the cramped confines of the transports.

"First the mood was very quiet and subtle," says Tom Blakey of the 505 PIR. "Some of the fellows were resting their heads back…they were either asleep or they were acting asleep. Some were wired and smoking. Some were doing the [rosary] beads that they had and it was no big deal then because it still could be called back and nobody wanted that, they wanted to get on with it.

"The ride wasn't bad…we didn't get up into it [the cloud bank], we were underneath it. We had already gotten our instructions with visits to the sand table before we got on the plane. In the ride, I don't know how far but the pilot told us to look down and, my God, you never saw so many boats in your life. You could have walked from England to France ship to ship. It was amazing how many boats were in the water."

The largest airborne operation to date involved 7,000 British and Commonwealth and 13,400 American paratroopers in the first wave plus 4,000 follow-up infantry, engineer, medical and signal corps paratroopers with heavy equipment. Dean McCan-

Left: The parachute memorial at the town church in the center of Ste.-Mère-Église symbolizes the landing of Private John M. Steele of the 82nd Airborne, whose chute became ensnared by the church's steeple.
***Right:** Maj. Gen Matthew Ridgway in a photograph at the time he commanded the XVIII Airborne Corps.*

dless was a 2nd Lieutenant in the 505 PIR. He was a graduate of Kansas State College, ROTC student and commissioned officer before the war started. A veteran of North Africa and Sicily, Mc-Candless was communications officer for the 1st Battalion, and was responsible for setting up headquarters communication.

Maj. Gen. Maxwell Taylor, commander of the 101st Airborne Division, was chief of staff of the 82nd Airborne when it was established and served with the division in the Sicilian and Italian campaigns. He became commander of the 101st in March 1944.

"The night before, they fed us really good and they encouraged us to lay down and take a nap 'cause we would be jumping at night. As we were loading the plane, one of the guys in our company had a grenade in his pocket go off. It killed him and several guys and damaged the plane. And that stunned us but they told us, 'Go on, go on. The ground crew can take care of him. Go, go.' So we went."

At 2215, June 5, when the C-47s carrying the 101st were powering into the sky, the first warnings to German defenders of an imminent invasion were being laid on desks at the northern France headquarters of Army Group B and Fifteenth Army. German agents who had infiltrated the French Resistance had been logging the preparatory messages broadcast over the BBC which put regional FFI leaders on alert. A confirming message "B" would then trigger coded messages within 48 hours, related to sabotage targets to be carried out in sync with the invasion. SS intelligence in Berlin reported the initial intercepts to Admiral Dönitz's Kriegsmarine headquarters where they were interpreted as an exercise.

The news of the confirming message "B" was met with little alarm at the headquarters of German armed forces commands in France. For one thing, the intelligence supposition was highly speculative and lacked corroboration. The sea patrols in the channel, as well as mine laying operations, were cancelled in the high-running seas and storm that gripped the Channel on June 5. Luftwaffe reconnaissance had not flown a patrol since the beginning of the month. The German flying weather patrol, which could only range as far west as the Irish Sea, did not detect the break in the weather seen by SHAEF's meteorologists. Even if they had, the weather break probably would have been discounted because Admiral Theodore Krancke's assessment of a cross-Channel invasion was that it would require five days of clear weather with calmer seas to pull off.

The ground units were equally uninspired by the intelligence report. As in the children's story, the boy had cried wolf so often, many thought this was just another false alarm of an invasion that had been anticipated for a month. Though Fifteenth Army raised the alert status to the highest level, Seventh Army was less prepared – General Friedrich Dollmann and most senior officers were preparing for a map exercise in Rennes on the morning of June 6. Army Group B was similarly wary. Field Marshal Rommel was already in Germany with his wife for her birthday on June 6 and preparing to meet Hitler at Ober-salzburg to lobby for reinforcements for his command. OB West was still predicting that the invasion would be coming over from Dover and even when reports came in of parachutists on the ground, they considered this a diversion to the anticipated Pas de Calais region landing.

There were diversions on D-Day at Pas de Calais and elsewhere, but nothing of the scope of what was going on at Normandy. This was the real thing, as noted by Lieutenant Colonel Hoffmann, a battalion commander in the 709th Division. It began at 0130 when he observed transports roaring

This group of C-47 transports, part of the 96th Troop Carrier Squadron, 440th Troop Carrier Group, is on a refueling mission to U. S. airborne forces on Normandy's Cotentin Peninsula. Earlier on D-Day they carried men of the 3rd Battalion, 506 PIR of the 101st Airborne Division to their drop zones inland from Utah Beach.

These airborne soldiers are pathfinders, men who jump first and mark drop zones for the rest of the airborne forces. The marking equipment they carry adds to their already heavy packs. They pose prior to boarding their jump plane with the pilots and crew who will transport them.

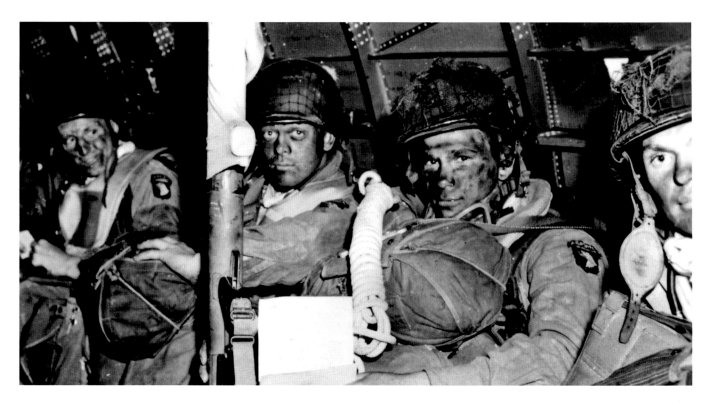

over the west Cotentin Peninsula from his headquarters near Montebourg. In the skies above, in the first wave of the 82nd

Inside a Dakota transport plane with members of F Company, 506 PIR of the 101st Airborne Division, the "Screaming Eagles." Their shoulder patches display the division logo.

airlift was 1st Lieutenant John M. Marr, rifle platoon leader in the 2nd Battalion, 507 PIR.

"Well, we were in the marshalling area at Martlesham Heath Airfield in England and that's the airfield from which we took off to go into Normandy. And we took off shortly after midnight...well it was very close to midnight... and formed up the sky train and flew down by the Channel Islands off of the coast of France. And then [we] made our turn and progressed southeastward across the Cotentin Peninsula to a drop zone which was right near Amfreville, France."

The objectives of the American units were all on the Cotentin Peninsula and aimed at securing exits for the U. S. VII Corps from Utah Beach and slowing any German counterattack there.

The land behind the beach area drained the Douve and Merderet rivers and was flooded on Rommel's orders, leaving nine causeways to carry all traffic from the beach. The drop area for the 101st was planned north of the hub city of Carentan, inland from Utah Beach, and the 82nd drop zones were to the west, straddling the Merderet River near the town of Ste.-Mère-Église.

In his 91st Air Landing Division camp not far from Cherbourg, Ernst Floeter was in his tent. His nighttime watch was cancelled. But Floeter soon observed that this would not be like any other day he had in the army up to that point.

"So on that night, on the [5th-]6th they told us, no watch tonight, the weather's so bad, they are not coming tonight. So that was a watch-free night and we slept in tents and about 10:30 at night I woke up...was a horrible noise in the air. And I look out, and there came the American airplanes by hundreds, lots of them. And they released the paratroops just outside of our line, near Ste.-Mère-Église. So at 12:00 o'clock [0200 GMT] our commander told us the invasion has started. So we were happy. Finally, something happens [laugh]. It got pretty boring.

"So on the next morning we had to cut, we had to destroy our telephone lines and watch out for the American and British fighters because they came down and chased a single soldier. We heard them all…they come down and then they shot the machine gun. And so we heard it all day long. But we were not accosted, we were pretty safe."

To the west, Colonel Ernst Goth was also becoming aware that the invasion his 916th Regiment was preparing for was about to begin.

"In the evening of June the 5th the regiment was combat ready and in position. The soldiers were in different positions around the beach. Observation posts, strong points [Widerstandsnester – WN], underground shelters and trenches. Most of the men were at a far distance from the beach as we assumed that there would be a big aerial bombardment before the Allied troops would storm the beach. At about 0200, we were put on maximum alert. Incoming messages from other units told us about paratroopers and glider landings in the sectors around Carentan."

By 0215 June 6, the German LXXXIV Corps headquarters was alerted. Anti-aircraft fire peppered the American transport planes. That was inevitable, but the paratroopers had another complaint about the night jump in the early hours of June 6; the pilots, anxious

Shown here on a piece of nylon parachute material are some of the items carried by D-Day parachutists: the 101st Airborne shoulder insignia; a scale map of Carentan, France marked Secret; the M2 "Presto" switchblade jump knife which was carried in a special pocket of the M42 jacket; the famous cricket signaling device; the dog tags of Garland Doan, D Co., 2nd Battalion, 502PIR, with chain and lucky coins; a luminous disc containing radium, which was worn in darkness on the back of troop leaders' collars or helmets; and a French to English phrase book.

to avoid the flak and confounded by the weather, approached the drop zones often too high or low and at too high a rate of speed. The pathfinder jumpers, who were dispatched first to mark drop zones, also had a difficult time marking zones for the 82nd landings because they were amidst German ground units. As a result, the pilots couldn't locate the drop markers. Many of the sticks (a stick is one planeload) of paratroopers landed off-target and spread out.

"On May the 28th," recalls Marr, "they changed the mission and decided to drop us closer to Utah Beach than they had previously planned. And so, they dropped us... our regiment and the 508th Regiment were dropped to the west of the Merderet River, which flows north and south at that point at Amfreville and Ste.-Mère-Église. And we and the 505th regiment and the glider troops of the 325th landed on the east side of the Merderet River. Our focus was on Amfreville and establishing an airhead line that went in a sort of a half-moon shape, anchored on the Merderet River on the north side and joining with the 508, who continued the airhead to the southwards, and anchored on the Douve River, to which the Merderet River flowed.

"But the big surprise was the huge inundated area about a mile wide at its widest point. We didn't know that it was underwater and indeed, as we approached the area, and the red light came on, it looked as though we were flying over a very wet meadow because of the high water grass that was growing in the inundated area. Our drop zone was to the north and slightly west of Amfreville, but we overshot [to the east] and dropped into the inundated area.

"Where I dropped, the water was armpit-level deep, and of course it read from very shallow to well over the head particularly the closer to the river that we dropped. I was all alone. I was the jump master on my airplane and the last two of my platoon to get out of the airplane were immediately captured on Utah Beach. So we were strung out in a long drop, and it would be five days before I saw what I knew to be my platoon again. I was therefore sort of, well, fighting with people from several different organizations."

"Well I hit the ground pretty quick," remembers Blakey. "There wasn't any time to have anything going on in my mind then. We were dropped pretty low and some of the guys carried a leg bag, these wonderful leg bags and they lost those. We were going too fast and we were going low. When the chute opened I got a terrible jolt and I'm sure everybody else did too because they were all in the same condition. I got on the ground in a little town called St.-Marcouf, beautiful little town. Just outside the town I could see the Germans and they knew I was there. I heard rifle fire over there so I went over there and there wasn't anybody there, heard it someplace else and I went there. I didn't have any idea where I was going. I could just tell an M1 rifle by the sound, and I was going for the sound, but when I got there I couldn't find anybody.

"Very few lights were on, it was still raining, not heavy but it was raining and you got wet. I guess they [the village residents] stayed inside. I don't remember seeing a civilian at all. I wasn't routing around to find anybody but jumpers. You never know whether a civilian is a friend or not,

Top: Brigadier General James Gavin, assistant division commander of the 82nd Airborne Division, briefs pathfinders prior to the D-Day jump. Bottom: Troop carriers and gliders approach France as they take the 325th Glider Infantry to Normandy on June 6. This photo, taken from a Waco CG-4A glider cockpit clearly shows the tow rope to the Dakota "tug."

An infantry squad of the 101st Airborne Division rides in a Waco glider during a training mission.

but it turned out all of them were [friendly]. But you didn't know that to start with. So I didn't fool with civilians or their houses or where they were living. I was just trying to find a few guys to find out where I was.

"Finally I said, 'Hell let somebody find me.' I didn't want to get messed up out there and get captured by myself. We were up to our ass in Germans. About 4:30 or 5:00 o'clock in the morning we had got together seven of us. The other guys were from the 507 and most of them knew each other so they probably came out of the same plane. We were then looking for a place to find out where we were. If we could find where we were then we would know where to go, and we finally found a road junction sign that said Ste.-Mère-Église with an arrow pointing. So we got off the side of the road. The Germans were coming in with trucks and movement all around, but not where we were. We stayed a safe distance from the road. We had no problem getting to the railroad and down the railroad to

around the water. Then we knew where the bridge was so we went there. It was maybe 7:30 or maybe as late as 8:00 o'clock. I don't remember if I looked at my watch. I know we got there early in the morning, so we took positions at the bridge and that's where we were for the next 3 ½ days."

"I was lucky enough that I landed close to the drop zone," explains McCandless. "They scattered the guys all over. As I came down I saw what looked like a transformer and I was slipping like hell to avoid it and I landed in a barnyard. General Ridgway [Major General Matthew B. Ridgway, 82nd Airborne Division Commander] jumped that night. He [also] landed in a barnyard with some cattle. He said when he saw that cow he coulda kissed her [laugh].

"That's a big relief 'cause there were no mines or anything to worry about. I'm sure that's what Ridgway had in his mind too. We did get together. Our battalion commander then was Major [Frederick A.] Kellem. He was just a dif-

Soldiers of the 82nd Airborne Division en route to Normandy in a British-built Horsa glider.

ferent kind of guy. I remember him singing 'Rye whiskey, rye whiskey, rye whiskey, I cry. I'll be drinking rye whiskey the day that I die.' And it was he that called us the Jack of Diamonds battalion. And on our helmets we had a red diamond with a 'J' in it and then like, cannonball crowns. Anyway, we set up our command post.

"A few people [were in the area]. But the battalion commander [determined that]…we would take anybody who had a gun and could use 'em. One battalion was charged with taking Ste.-Mère-Église and our battalion was supposed to take that bridge over the Merderet River."

Some sticks of the two U. S. airborne divisions ended up as far as 35 miles north or south of their designated drop zones and most of these paratroopers quickly ended up in German hands. The plan was for the three regiments of the 101st (501, 502 and 506) to establish a line from Pouppeville on the south end of the flooded area inland from Utah Beach to St.-Mar-

tin-de-Varreville in the north and secure four beach exits. The left flank at St.-Martin was to meet the right flank of the 82nd. Though scattered about, a large group of 101st troopers landed in the vicinity of St.-Côme-du-Mont on the southern flank. This was fortuitous because the 101st also was ordered to seize the lock at la Barquette to control the flood plain of the river along with two bridges at le Port. They were also ordered to destroy a road bridge near Carentan and a railroad bridge north of St.-Côme-du-Mont to prevent German forces from crossing the Douve River from Carentan.

Further north, the 377th Parachute Field Artillery Battalion supported the 502 PIR. They were to overwhelm the battery at St.-Martin-de-Varreville quickly with the 2nd Battalion remaining there and the 1st Battalion establishing contact with the units from the 82nd to the west. But the 502nd came down far from the proposed drop zone. Indeed, the entire division in the north was scattered. The 3rd Battalion of the

502nd landed near Ste.-Mère-Église. The 501st had similar difficulties assembling.

One of the 101st paratroopers who landed out of place and had to improvise was Captain Sam Gibbons. The officer in the 3rd Battalion went on after the war to become a long-serving congressman from Florida and chairman, Committee on Ways and Means. He recalled his jump on the 50th anniversary of D-Day at the commemorative ceremony in Normandy.

"Fifty years ago I was a captain in the 501st Parachute Infantry and I landed about eight hours before the invasion over south of Ste.-Mère-Église. [In the first hours] it was scary and it was lonesome. I was by myself except that I had about fifteen Germans firing at the planes about 70 yards away from me. I finally got out of their range and picked up some more parachutists and we went ahead and did our job."

Many of the American jumpers were in similar circumstances. Using the toy cricket clickers they were issued to facilitate making contact with fellow Americans, they searched in the dark for comrades, no matter what their unit. Though it seems like an odd expedient, the cricket clickers worked just fine in most cases.

"Everybody that I know of had one," says Tom Blakey. "They got that thing in the hangar and they started clicking, I thought the world was coming to an end. Everybody was clicking it."

Passwords were also used and the classic baseball challenge questions. Though about sixty percent of the equipment dropped from the planes was destroyed, the paratroopers had their personal arms. Some commanders encouraged the use of knives and bayonets in any early interaction with the enemy. But mostly the GIs were concentrating on finding friends and avoiding the Germans in the early going. The 101st commander, General Maxwell D. Taylor, jumped with the first wave even though the

This glider landed at Landing Zone "W" at 2120 on D-Day carrying nine soldiers of the 82nd Airborne Division's NCR platoon. While awaiting salvage the Waco glider shares a French field with its original inhabitants.

This aerial view of Ste.-Mère-Église shows in the foreground the town church, city hall and other buildings in the center square where early morning fighting resulted in the town being liberated by members of the 505 PIR.

day before he had torn a ligament in his knee playing squash. He assembled a small group of American paratroopers in the 101ˢᵗ sector. In addition to his aide, a lieutenant, Taylor's group soon included Brigadier General Anthony McAuliffe, a colonel, three lieutenant colonels, three other lieutenants, a few non-commissioned officer (NCO) radiomen and about a dozen privates. Taylor observed, "Never in the annals of warfare have so few been commanded by so many." Taylor then led this unique patrol toward the objective at Pouppeville.

Another paratrooper from the 101ˢᵗ was 18-year-old Eugene Cook from Ohio who tells of his experience landing near Ravenoville, about four miles northeast of Ste.-Mère-Église.

"Well, just on the trip over, we were singing for awhile, and then everybody got a little apprehensive and quiet. Coming over we had a lot of flak, and of course the airplanes scattered. Then finally, the green light came on. We

jumped at about 275 feet, we were pretty low. We had a hard landing. I broke an ankle when I landed. Fought on it for fourteen days after that.

"I didn't know [about the broken ankle] for a couple of minutes until I got out of my parachute, stood up, and fell over. The result of that was that I could not meet up with anyone in my stick…I was all by myself for a couple of hours. I was on a farm. You could hear gunshots, probably aerial fire, things like that. It was not very close.

"Well I first found a guy from the 502nd, then we eventually linked up with seven or eight other guys, and one of them had talked to a girl or something. This was at about 4:00 o'clock in the morning. We got on the road and went to Ravenoville. We had two point-men, but when we got up to them they were both gone. One had been captured, and we don't know what the hell happened to the other.

"We got to the town and surveyed it a bit. I think

An American soldier sprints for the entrance to the church in Ste.-Mère-Église.

there were twenty-two of us actually in the town. That was early in the morning. It took about two hours to capture it. I don't know, but I think there were about two hundred Germans in that town.

"It was more house-to-house fighting, it was a small town. You would throw a grenade in this window then walk in. We were fighting individually, or in groups of two or three. That took about two hours and then we took some prisoners and took them back to the church. This was at about 7:00 o'clock in the morning. We just settled into the town and had some skirmishes with some people coming up from the beach at that time. And that lasted all of D-Day, into the night. The next morning we headed for our drop zone, where we were supposed to be. So that was D-Day."

The widely scattered air drops served to confuse Allied intentions in the minds of the Germans. By 0400, however, German commanders estimated that the intention was to cut off the Cotentin Peninsula at the narrowest point on its neck. Few German commanders realized that a beach invasion was not far off. The general actions of the German units in the vicinity of the drop areas, the 709 (static) Infantry Division, 91st Air Landing Division and the 6th Paratrooper Regiment, were to stay in their prepared defensive positions, making only small local ventures outside them to counterattack. Communication between headquarters units was hampered by telephone lines put out of commission by the French Resistance.

Gradually, larger groups of American jumpers began to form. Advancing eastward, a mixed unit patrol under the command of Lieutenant Colonel Robert G. Cole, 3rd Battalion commander in the 502nd, eventually arrived at St.-Martin and found the battery destroyed and

Members of the 2nd Platoon mortar squad, F Company, 505 PIR who were dropped by error in the town square of Ste.-Mère-Église early on the morning of June 6. From the left are John P. Ray, Philip M. Lynch, John M. Steele and Vernon L. Francisco. All but Steele were killed in action.

abandoned, so they continued eastward. After liberating the village of Carquibut (not their objective) Captain Gibbons pushed his patrol toward the assigned objective on the Douve River. In the 82nd Airborne Division sector, Lieutenant Colonel Edward C. Krause took the 3rd Battalion of the 505th to his objective, Ste.-Mère-Église, and forced the surrender of the German garrison with little effort. The American flag was raised over the first liberated French town.

The 507th and the 508th regiments of the 82nd did not have well-placed landing zones in their efforts to straddle the Merderet River and protect the left flank of the invasion. Some commanders, including assistant division commander Brigadier General James M. Gavin, were able to form groups of men along a railroad embankment – to which the men naturally gravitated – but the bridges over the causeways had to be secured intact and this proved to be quite a challenge.

By this time, as dawn and the sea invasion were about two hours away, the American gliders began coming in bringing artillery, heavy equipment and reinforcing infantry. Among those coming in on D-Day in CG-4 Waco gliders was James Libaudais.

"We flew from England over the Channel and I later found out there were 5,000 ships out in the Channel. I said if I fall out of the sky I'll land on one of the ships. One of them ships shot a cannon and our glider went up about forty feet in the air from the concussion and all of a sudden we leveled off. [I was in the] 325th Infantry Regiment. They said they needed an 81mm mortar platoon and a machine gun and I was a squad leader in 81mm mortars."

The Germans had a special surprise for the Allied gliders. Already the paratroopers were en-

countering the scourge of mechanized warfare in Normandy – the hedgerows. These were formidable earthen embankments, often topped with trees or bushes that surrounded Norman fields. Landing a glider within the confines of one of these boxes was difficult at best. To make matters worse, anticipating glider operations Rommel had installed anti-air-landing obstacles. These were stakes topped with mines and connected by barbed wire called "Rommel's asparagus." The hedgerow country in Normandy and Brittany received top priority in this effort. Fortunately for the American glider units, most of these obstacles were installed further inland. The Germans had expected the Allies would drop paratroopers far behind the lines. That would have been General Marshall's plan if carried out but SHAEF wanted them used in close tactical support of the beach landings.

"Ste.-Mère-Église, that's where we landed," states Libaudais. "In Normandy the hedgerows were this high, and then the trees, so when we come in we had to go in quick. We landed and hit a hedgerow about 110 miles an hour. You shake; you get up because machine gun fire, *Tick, Tick*. We only have canvas, you know, to guard us but they are a strong thing. There's tubular steel and you could stand a pretty good crash with 'em. We were in the hedgerow and there was some artillery firing and some machine gun fire comin' and one of our boys started, 'I'm hit…call the medics!' Of course that's what you hear all day long, 'Medic! Call the medics!' I crawled up to him and I said, 'Okay hold on, where ya hit?' and he said, 'I'm hit in my leg.' We took a pouch and tied it on our leg and in there was a little brush, swab thing you know, to clean your gun, and a can of oil. Well, don't you know a bullet or shrapnel or somethin' hit that pouch, cut that can in half, and the oil's running down his leg. I turned him over and I said,

'You're not hit pardner, that's oil going down your leg.'"

Some of the objectives of the two American airborne divisions were secured easily and others would be contested objectives throughout the day. But the paratroopers were astride the main road from Paris to Cherbourg; they were slowly gaining control of the Utah Beach exits and had a foothold along the strategic Douve and Merderet rivers.

An altogether different scenario occurred to the east where the British 6th Airborne Division landed along the Orne River and Orne Canal without detection initially. They came on a direct route south across the Channel to land in the area northeast of the city of Caen. Individual parachutists and Horsa gliders landed on both sides of the Orne and moved to seize or destroy key bridges over the Orne and Dives rivers.

Landing shortly after midnight, many of the units suffered through the turbulent flying that put them down outside their landing zones. One pathfinder unit landed on the front lawn of the German 711th Division headquarters. But six gliders pinpointed their objectives – the bridges over the Dives and Orne rivers that were to be destroyed. These volunteer patrols went about their business and were successful in wrecking the bridges that would bring German Fifteenth Army forces to the invasion site. Meanwhile a bridge spanning the Orne River and the lifting bridge at Bénouville over the Orne Canal, vital to hold, were captured in a *coup de main* operation by Major John Howard's D Company of the Oxfordshire and Buckinghamshire "Ox and Bucks" Light Infantry. The canal bridge was renamed Pegasus Bridge after the emblem of the 6th Airborne Division.

Another important objective was the battery at Merville which threatened enfilading fire on Sword Beach. In an operation which Lieutenant Colonel T. B. H. Otway had to improvise because gliders landed in the wrong places, the battery was neutralized. The signal went out that it was secured and naval gunfire, which would have to have been extremely lucky to deal a death blow to the guns casemated in six feet of concrete, could move onto other targets.

The British 6th Airborne Division had secured its basic objectives prior to the beach landings and held the flank positions throughout the day. They would be on the leading edge of the first major German counterattack in the afternoon.

In the pre-dawn hours of June 6 German high commanders were piecing together what was happening. Was all the noise and confusion made by bomber crews bailing out, sabotage by FFI operatives or an airborne invasion? It was all three, but with the appearance of the paratroopers on the Orne River and sightings of a vast armada on the water, Field Marshal Gerd von Rundstedt finally concluded the Allies were landing between the Orne and the Cotentin Peninsula. He still considered the Normandy invasion a precursor to a larger action in the Pas de Calais. But he knew the Allies must be engaged. He requested permission from OKW to use the panzer divisions in the area, specifically the 21st and Panzer Lehr Divisions. However, OKW would not release Panzer Lehr and Rundstedt was reluctant to ask Hitler directly.

Fritz Baresel, assigned to Panzer Aufklärungs Lehr Abteilung 130 (ALA 130) in the Panzer Lehr Division, knew that it was only a matter of time until they would engage the Allies in France.

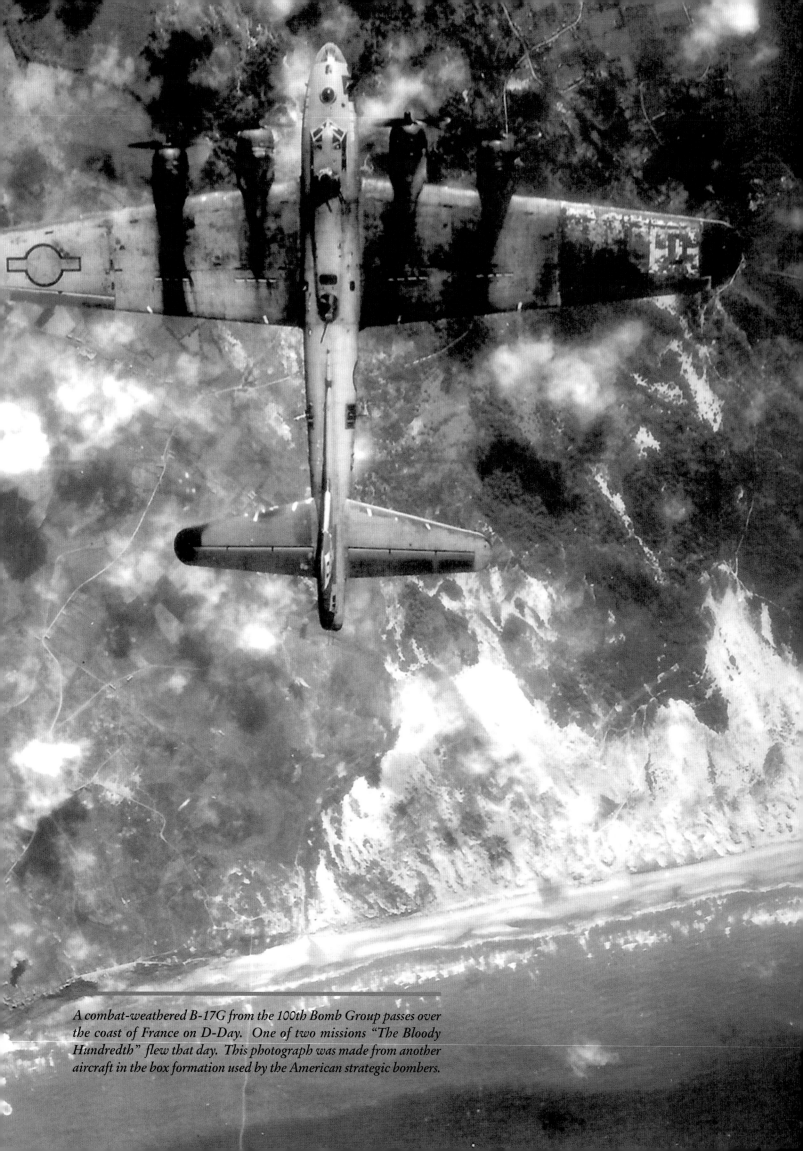

A combat-weathered B-17G from the 100th Bomb Group passes over the coast of France on D-Day. One of two missions "The Bloody Hundredth" flew that day. This photograph was made from another aircraft in the box formation used by the American strategic bombers.

"We were camped near Rouen since middle of May 1944 expecting an invasion closer to the English Channel. On June 7, 1944 we moved towards the landing beaches. Everything was fluid and I cannot recall seeing any defense line set up in the early part of the battle."

Baresel's unit would begin a cat and mouse game with Allied bombers. The fear of losing the battle between Allied air and German armor that so concerned Rommel was about to begin; but first those bombers would concentrate on the static batteries of the Atlantic Wall in a last pre-invasion effort to neutralize as many guns as possible opposing the sea invasion.

AIR OPERATIONS ON D-DAY

Most battles in World War II were fought in three dimensions, and the Normandy invasion was no exception. If one considers the German line of defense in cube form, their most effective defense came from the bottom side; land and sea mines that were responsible for the majority of Allied personnel killed on D-Day. The other five sides of the cube were controlled by the Allies; the frontal assault on the beaches, the enfilading fire from the sea on two sides and the operations of the airborne units and FFI in the rear. What remains of the cube is the top – where the Allies dominated the air.

Between the American Eighth and Ninth Air Forces and the British Bomber Command and RAF Second Tactical Air Force the Allies put an incredible 10,521 planes in the air on June 6. How that many planes could be in the air at once without incident is unfathomable, and there indeed were collisions. Many of the air crews flew multiple missions that day. If D-Day ended in failure, the air forces could not take the blame for lack of maximum effort. The 1,200 heavy bombers, B-17s and B-24s, of the Eighth Air Force, had initial targets over Omaha Beach and British and Commonwealth beaches. Preceding them, the RAF Halifax and Lancaster heavies worked specific targets, including the Caen railroad station.

Among the many Eighth Air Force airmen at work that day were those in the 100th Bomb Group. And while most of the effort of the strategic bombers was done in the months leading up to the invasion, they were proud to be a part of the June 6 attack. From diaries of ground and air crewmen, a revealing snapshot of the activities of that day comes to life. William R. Fogle, a radio maintenance technician in the 418th Bomb Squadron, recorded the events of D-Day in his journal at 2100 on June 6.

"Well it finally happened! The invasion is on. The tip-off came last night when we were ordered to safety wire the I.F.F. [tracking device] in the 'off' position. We were told over a month ago to be prepared to do this, and we had the handles drilled already. The radio boys had to safety the U.H.F. in the 'receive' position. Last night, we had all the ships ready to go by midnight and had all the Defense Crews alerted. The machine gun nests all around the perimeter [of the air base] were manned, and all the guards were on the alert. I worked 'till nearly midnight and then pulled guard 'till 5:00 a.m. The first mission took off at 0330, the next at about 0600 and the latest, which we are 'sweating out' now, took off at 1730. Their mission was scrubbed this afternoon for a little while. Reason: The infantry had taken their target already. They were re-briefed and took off. We expect them back around 2300. It looks like another all night affair. Hope it's quiet.

"The rumors are really flying thick and fast again. According to the radio and rumor, things are going good. We are listening to an address by King George. I guess they are listening in at home now. That's a favorite hobby right now, wondering how they are taking the news there. I'll bet Dad has been glued to the radio all day."

Major Marvin Bowman, one of the S2 (Intelligence) officers for the group told of the pre-flight briefings in his diary entry for June 6.

"The invasion began this morning. Briefing at 2300 hours last night, 1215 hours, and 1415 hours today. Captain Bowman had first three main briefings, Captain Mackesey the gunners. Captain Hutchinson briefed the afternoon mission. Crews' morale bounced up 100%. First take off at 0230 hours. First two waves bombed coast using PFF [radar guided]; third wave had Falaise for a target but returned with bombs when no PFF could be found. Last wave of the day left at 1700 hours, returned at 2315 hours. Had a good view of the invasion, the undercast having broken away. Told of hundreds of ships unmolested off the coast, indicating that shore batteries have been silenced. Hundreds of gliders going in; no air opposition at all. German radio is something to hear; are reporting the invasion a complete flop; a few parachutists who were quickly eliminated. Whom do they think they are kidding? Figures indicate that between 0300 and 0800 hours the 8th AF dropped 10,000 tons of bombs, flew 7,500 sorties and put 31,000 fliers over targets. Jersey and Guernsey attacked, according to reports. Standing down tonight. We have temporarily run out of bombs."

Ed Wolf made short notations in his diary at the end of D-Day.

"After arising at 0300 the day before, we were alerted at 2200 – no sleep – briefing for officers at 2300 – lead crews were briefed from 1800 to 2400 the previous night – No briefing for gunners. First takeoff about 0230 hours – 20th mission to Caen, France – flew 6:15 hours – returned to base – had lunch and left at 1700 for mission 21 to Falaise, France – Bridge. Second trip – what a sight of gliders going in. Late arrivals at base in darkness and rain, thank God for the uppers that kept us going – flew 7:00 hours – a total of 13:15 hours today. Howard had a younger brother making the beaches in one of the first waves with the engineers. Kennedy remarked 'What a display of ships off the coast of France.' He felt that we were really part of something! Impossible to sleep after we got back. Always bragged that the area we bombed was the best operation Ike had going during the initial period."

Even though the strategic bombers of the Eighth Air Force and RAF Bomber Command flew thousands of missions on D-Day, it was the medium bombers of the tactical air commands that had the greatest impact on the beach defenses. For the American squadrons of the IX Tactical Air Command, the M-26 Marauder and A-20 Havoc aircraft were used. The British tactical squadrons flew Hawker Typhoons and engaged in dive bombing of targets. The sorties by the medium bombers of the IX TAC were low level runs at 500 feet over Utah Beach. These proved to be effective in stunning, and sometimes knocking out, the coastal garrisons there. But flak was heavy and the medium bomber commands sustained some combat losses.

Rounding out the air armada, which flew a total of more than 14,000 sorties on D-Day, were the fighter squadrons. For these missions, the USAAF used primarily P-47 Thunderbolts and

P-38 Lightnings, the twin engine Lockheed fighter with a fuselage resembling a catamaran. The Lightning was fast and maneuverable, but its in-line engines could be damaged more easily than the P-47 radial Pratt & Whitney 2000 engine. The P-51 Mustangs were held out of the D-Day flight plans. They were more important to the long bombing missions that would soon commence again. The British relied on the venerable Spitfire.

Bruce MacKenzie enlisted in the Royal Canadian Air Force in 1941. After distinguishing himself in flying U-boat patrols off Eastern Canada, he was assigned to a squadron of Spitfire fighter-bombers with the RAF Second Tactical Air Force based in England. In addition to cannons and machine guns, Mackenzie's Spitfire carried three bombs.

"On the actual invasion day, our squadron was assigned to cover the landings of the British Army units on the beaches of Normandy. We did two sorties that day, one at dawn and then later in the afternoon of June 6, 1944. It was a harrowing experience. We had a bird's eye view of the tremendous fleets and heavy bombardments from the Navy. We could also view the landings and the fierce tank battles inland towards the city of Caen. Interestingly enough,

Flying Fortress bombers pass over the D-Day armada on their way to Normandy targets. Although the impact of these bombing runs was not immediately felt by the invading ground troops they pinned down German armor and squelched Wehrmacht counterattacks on D-Day.

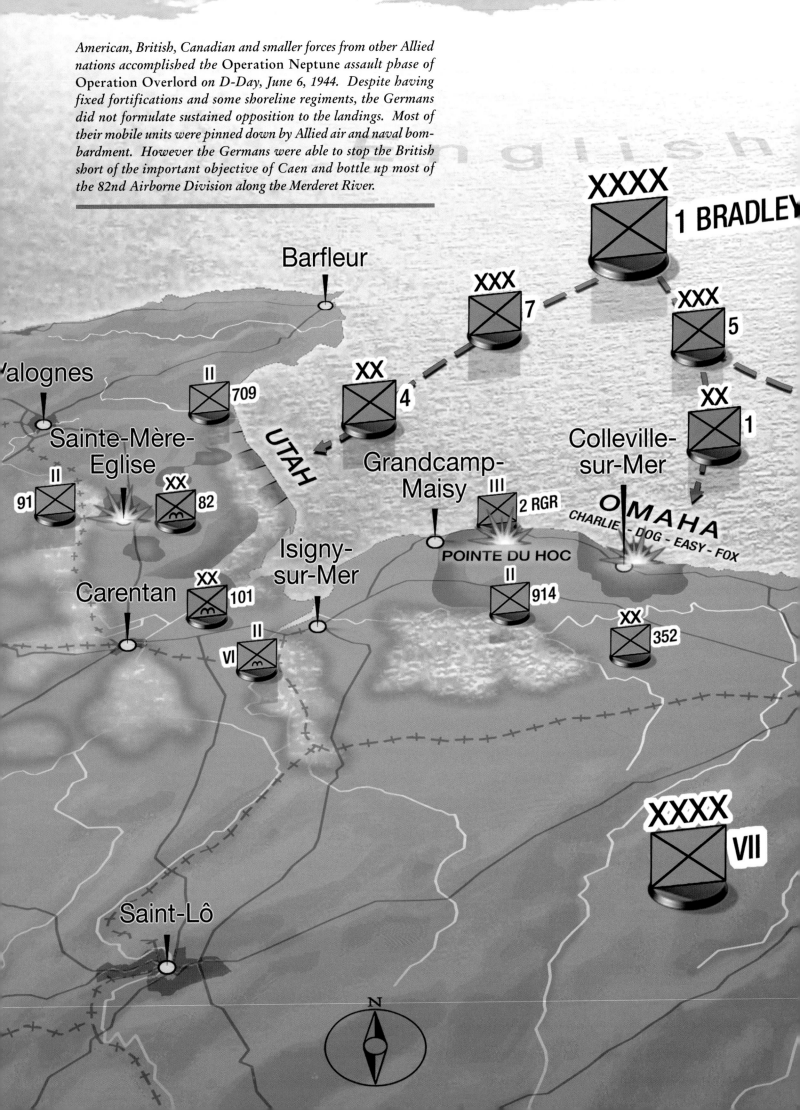

American, British, Canadian and smaller forces from other Allied nations accomplished the **Operation Neptune** assault phase of Operation Overlord on *D-Day, June 6, 1944. Despite having fixed fortifications and some shoreline regiments, the Germans did not formulate sustained opposition to the landings. Most of their mobile units were pinned down by Allied air and naval bombardment. However the Germans were able to stop the British short of the important objective of Caen and bottle up most of the 82nd Airborne Division along the Merderet River.*

Barfleur

1 BRADLEY

7

5

Valognes

709

4

Sainte-Mère-Eglise

91

82

Grandcamp-Maisy

Colleville-sur-Mer

2 RGR

O M A H A

CHARLIE - DOG - EASY - FOX

1

UTAH

Isigny-sur-Mer

POINTE DU HOC

Carentan

101

914

352

VI

Saint-Lô

VII

N

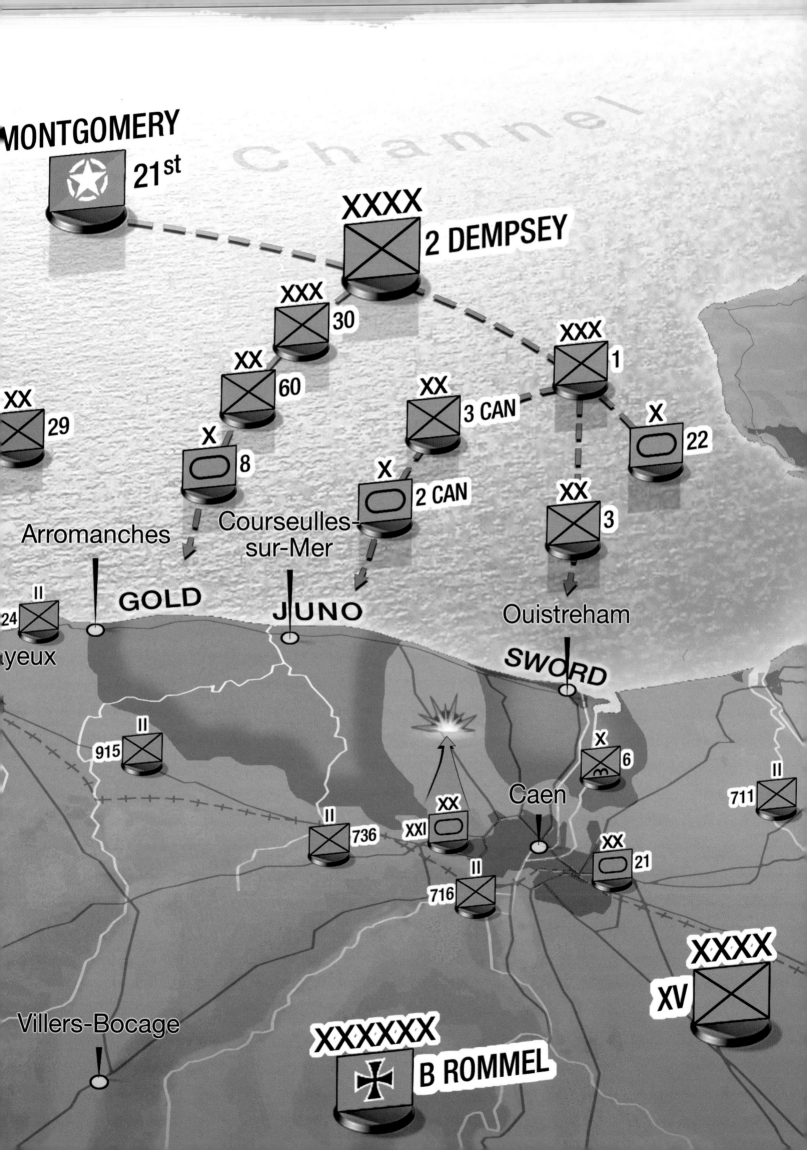

MONTGOMERY 21st

XXXX 2 DEMPSEY

XXX 30

XX 60

XX 29

X 8

XX 3 CAN

X 2 CAN

XXX 1

X 22

XX 3

Arromanches

Courseulles-sur-Mer

Ouistreham

GOLD

JUNO

SWORD

II 24

Bayeux

II 915

II 736

XXI

XX

X 6

Caen

XX 21

II 711

II 716

Villers-Bocage

XXXXXX B ROMMEL

XXXX XV

no German fighters or bombers appeared to challenge our airspace. We provided air coverage daily until we established an airstrip on the Beach Head [beachhead]."

Nearly all fighter pilots on D-Day, like Mackenzie, noted the lack of opposing German fighters. That's because the success of nearly wiping out the Luftwaffe presence in France eliminated fighter-to-fighter combat on June 6. Only a few Allied fighter pilots saw Luftwaffe planes on D-Day; those that flew perimeter patrols looking for U-boats or other potential hazards on the flanks of the Channel crossing. The cross-Channel convoys were screened by a constant umbrella of fighter squadrons flying 3,000 to 5,000 feet above the water. Fighter squadrons also accompanied gliders and performed other reconnaissance and patrol missions. The P-38s were the only fighters used across the Channel because their shape could be easily identified by shipboard gunners. Despite this, several P-38s were victims of friendly fire as they flew over the task forces in the Channel.

Often airmen remarked afterwards that even if they couldn't locate their targets or missed them because of weather or timing issues, they hoped that their exploding bombs made some good foxholes for the invading forces. Though the strategic bombers did little damage to the Atlantic Wall on D-Day, they did make some foxholes and hit other targets inland. An unintended but practical advantage provided by the strategic bombers releasing their payloads late was the number of land mines exploded inland from the beaches. This would be tremendously helpful in the days to come. The tactical bombers had good success on the beaches and the fighters kept watch over it all. With only 113 planes lost on D-Day, and only one Luftwaffe mission over the landing area – carried out late in the day – the Allies truly commanded the skies on D-Day.

NAVAL OPERATIONS PRIOR TO H-HOUR

As impressive as was the showing in the air, the display on the water was truly historic. There were actually 6,939 Allied ships and craft involved in the D-Day sealift. The finely-tuned naval order of battle began with days of maneuvering around the coast of the British Isles. Even with the one-day delay, all vessels got in the right place at the right time. Late on June 5, most of the ships were heading through a mine-cleared channel south of the Isle of Wight and toward Area "Z" thirteen miles to the southeast. Here a circular set of lanes was designated, nicknamed "Piccadilly Circus," through which most of the Normandy-bound convoys passed.

First in line were the costal minesweepers (YMS) which began working through the wide belt of the main German mine field which extended from the Cotentin Peninsula to the Dover Strait. The YMS boats had a head start on the operation on June 4 before the invasion was postponed. However, one mine eluded that sweep in the stormy weather on the fourth and in the early evening of the fifth as USN Mine Squadron 7 was working the area minesweeper USS *Osprey* fell prey to the floater and went down with six killed, the first U. S. Navy personnel killed in *Operation Neptune*. There were no other incidents at that stage of the operation and five lanes, one for each task force (Forces U, O, G, J and S) were opened across the Channel and buoy marked.

Hal Baumgarten recalls the trip across the Channel on a transport carrying part of the 29th Infantry Division.

"I got up in front of the bow with a few other 29th Infantry Division guys, and we started steaming

At sea, a convoy of Landing Craft, Infantry steams in two rows toward the landing zone at Utah Beach, a barrage balloon above each craft. One LCI flotilla commander had the cables cut when the barrage balloons were helping shore batteries find range on his boats.

out of the harbor with all these ships, part of the armada. When we went out of the harbor, we turned left, or east, and we joined a tremendous armada of ships, with barrage balloons over it. We were guarded by PT boats. The mine sweepers were in front, to clear the path. So, it was the greatest armada, there was something like 5,000 ships."

As the convoy lanes crossed the middle of the Channel and approached the Bay of the Seine, they were split in two; one for fast ships such as destroyers and one for slow vessels such as Landing Craft, Tank (LCTs). The fire support ships arrived at their designated lanes. The battleship USS *Nevada*, for example, in the bombardment group of Force U, entered channel No. 2, the fast lane closest to the Cotentin Peninsula. Following her were cruisers USS *Quincy* and *Tuscaloosa* and HMS *Black Prince*. *Quincy* had the distinction, later in the day, of providing fire support for an objective of the 101st. The coordinates were called in by a naval spotter who jumped with the parachute division. It was a rare instance of naval guns supporting airborne operations.

As the fire support ships moved into position in the Bay of the Seine and the transports awaited the command "Away all boats!," Allied observers were surprised to see the beacon from the Barfleur lighthouse on the northeast tip of the Cotentin Peninsula working normally. Nowhere was there an indication that the Germans were reacting to the pre-invasion maneuvers. As mentioned, Admiral Krancke had cancelled water patrols because of weather concerns and his conviction that the conditions were not right for an invasion. Luftwaffe reconnaissance also remained on the ground that night. The first indication that an invasion was in progress came when ships appeared on German radar at 0309 and the C-47s began rattling the windows in Lieutenant Colonel Hoffman's headquarters.

The thundering, flame-belching naval bombardment such as the world had never seen was about to add to the misery of the German garrisons occupying the Atlantic Wall. Bud Taylor, who was on USS *Pennsylvania* during the Pearl Harbor attack was on board USS *Thompson*, DD-627, one of 12 destroyers of Force O Bombardment Group under Rear Admiral C. F. Bryant.

"We trained for D-Day. We was about the third destroyer in on D-day. We arrived first before the troops ever got there. At daylight we was right against the beach [at] Omaha. On the *Thompson* I was gun captain of a port quad 40mm. We just had two, one on each side. That was my side, the port side, and that was the way we was going, we was facing land.

"We'd spot and then we'd fire where them cliffs was. At one time I put down I think it was 1,000 rounds, strafing. The soldiers couldn't get up over these cliffs. As soon as they'd stick their heads up they'd shoot. So they told us to put 1,000 rounds about level with the ground. I tried to scare 'em off until we could get some soldiers up there. We'd fire a little bit here and a little bit there, but that was most of my firing, for the 40mm.

"We used the 5-inch .38s. We fired at a pillbox over there and Shoot! We would not knock these things off with that 5-inch. And this battleship [was sitting] way off out there…and asked them to give us a hand on this pillbox. They said they would. That was the *Texas*, I believe it was. And this crew I had they had never seen battleship fire or nothing like that. And I told them I says, 'Soon as that thing fires, we right between them and that pillbox…you all look right up there you gonna see these 16-inch shells.' They said, 'Aw, you're crazy.' I said, 'Okay.' About that time they started coming down. Well, these guys went running. They said, 'It's gonna hit us.' 'Naw,

they ain't gonna hit us, it goes right over.' [laugh] It was sort of comical really 'cause they'd never seen anything like that. Of course, I'd been on a battleship and I knew what they was going to do.

Small boats equipped with cannon or rocket launchers prepare to launch from USS Bayfield. *Dozens of specialized armed and unarmed small craft participated in* Operation Neptune *including command and control boats, rocket launchers, water carriers and kitchens.*

that. But when they hit that pillbox there wasn't nothing left of it. They hit that right the first time. I mean, that's it."

Woodrow Derby was on USS *Nevada*.

"They didn't make no noise hardly 'cause you had all this other gunfire. You'd just happen to see these three big old balls, they just *sssshhh* like

"At midnight on the 5th of June and the morning of the 6th of June I was up on deck. I heard the damnedest noise you ever heard in your life. I looked up and the sky was full of big planes…many of them were towing gliders they would drop behind the German lines at Normandy and the paratroopers dropped out of these big planes. It was the darnedest thing you ever saw but we kept going and anchored off Utah Beach about 5 miles at sea and we went to 'General Quarters.' We were at 'General Quarters' for 80 straight hours, that's 24, 48, 72 plus 8 hours, bombarding for the troops to go in. I thought it would never stop but it finally did."

Frank Haigler, an officer in a shipboard Marine detachment was also on *Nevada*. His impression of what took place in the early morning hours of D-Day was similar.

"That was really something, to hear all the planes going over. Just hundreds and hundreds of planes. Too dark, but we could hear them. And then off to port and starboard, we'd see so many ships…small, large…and I have all those records. I saved all the diagrams of all the ships and all, which are interesting.

"The landing instructions there at Omaha were very, very complicated, and that's just one little section of the whole Normandy operation. But I have pages, and pages, and pages of that stuff. The organization, the tidal, the currents, you know, at specific times that various ships were involved, the targets on the shore, how they were all numbered, the number of rounds expended for each gun on each target. The identification signals for each of the different ships. Really, very involved to make an amphibious landing.

"I have lists of all those targets [for USS *Nevada*] and the number of rounds for each gun fired at each time on different targets. I was a little surprised that it [the concussion of firing] wasn't more, because I was topside all the time. My one battery

spot was right next to a 15-inch when they'd go off. But the more noticeable ones were the 5-inch that went off. They had a very severe, crashing sound, whereas the 15-inch didn't. But, interestingly, we could see the projectiles as they left the gun.

"After we'd expended our allotted amount of ammunition, the third day, we had to go back to Portsmouth and rearm. And then, went back again."

While the pre-invasion bombardment of the Atlantic Wall was being carried out by the battleships, cruisers, destroyers and other fire support ships, the other critical operation at sea was taking place as well. Assault units were filling up the LCVPs and other landing craft bobbing up and down in the water while lashed to transports and LSTs. The wind was blowing and the swells were 4 to 5 feet where the transports dropped anchor 22,000 to 23,000 yards off shore. Men climbed down the rope ladders into the landing craft lying well below the main decks of the transports. A few men ended up in the sea and had to be retrieved. Despite the precarious process, none of the landing craft floundered before or during loading.

Charles Norman Shay, the medic with the 1st Infantry Division, remembers the process.

"It did not take us very long to travel the few miles across the Channel, and about 1:00 or 2:00 o'clock in the morning, we anchored about 12 miles off the coast of France. And then the order came to debark; that we were going over the side on net ladders and we would be loading into landing craft. And when the order was given to start loading, that's what we did.

"The seas were still very strong, the landing craft were bobbing up and down beside the transport

D·DAY

ships, and when we went over the side on the net ladders, we had to be very precise when we left the ladders to jump into the landing craft. We had to time it because…to avoid injury when landing in the landing craft, or to avoid missing the landing craft and perhaps landing in the water between the land-

ing craft and the transport ship. If that happened we were launched anyway."

And Albert Piper, the radio operator with the 57th Field Artillery headquarters, was transferring from a Landing Craft, Infantry to an LVCP.

The 14" guns of the battleship USS Nevada *(BB-36) fire on the Azeville battery north of Utah Beach on the morning of June 6, 1944. Their initial targets were spotted by air reconnaissance. Later shore control parties called in targets of opportunity.*

"The boat I got on, which is just a regular landing infantry deal, was one that you went down the side of the ship. You know one bad deal was sea sickness. There was a lot of guys sea sick. At the time we went down on the side of the ship, battleships were firing, which make a lot of noise, really. Well that [getting off] was a little tricky because of the swaying of it, you know. And I'm afraid to get caught in between it, or fall, 'cause you have a heavy packet, have a lot of stuff on us. But then, when I got on the boat I was all right."

Hal Baumgarten describes his personal preparations for entering the Normandy invasion in the first wave as a member of the 116th Infantry Regiment.

"Now when we got close to the French coast, the *Empire Javelin* peeled off to the west and anchored 11 miles off Dog Green sector [of Omaha Beach]. We had our so-called last meal. I ate some Cadbury chocolate bars…I didn't like the British food. I took my shower with salt water and Lava soap. And I, oh, I had my head shaved in Blansford, for hand-to-hand combat. And I had my bayonet, razor-sharp, both ends, and balanced for throwing. I had metal cleats on my shoes to use as a weapon, believe it or not, to mash somebody's face in, and stuff like that.

Crew members of an LCI are pulled from oily water off the Normandy beaches. Eighty-three foot U. S. Coast Guard cutters dominated the Sea Rescue Group.

"We all chose our own ammunition. I had two bandoliers of armor-piercing ammunition, .30-caliber. Two bandoliers is 96 bullets. I carried BAR [Browning Automatic Rifle] ammunition for the guy in front of me, which was Clarence Riggs of Pennsylvania. He was the BAR man, I was his assistant.

"I had a headache so I went looking for a Company A aid man, fella named Mullens, and I asked him for some APCs, which is two aspirins and he gave it to me. I didn't know that aspirins…you know, I'm a physician now…I didn't know that aspirins made you bleed. So I bled like mad when I got wounded.

"So anyway, at 3:30 in the morning we started getting off the ship. The weather was horrible and they hadda lower us over the sides, already in the boats. So I said my goodbyes to the Company A guys that were in my old boat team. The minute we were lowered over the side, the boats hit the water, we were thrown around like matchsticks. Every man was immediately soaked with the icy-cold English Channel water. The water got up to our knees, and the lieutenant said, 'What are you waiting for? Start bailing out with your helmets.' The bilge pumps weren't working in the LCAs. Had we landed in an LCVP, Higgins boat, we wouldn't of had that problem…sides are higher, the water wouldn't of come in. So in order to stay afloat for three hours, we hadda be bailin' out with the helmets, and we were all freezing."

Jim Weller's self-propelled gun, an M-7 105mm howitzer, came in with Force O as part of the 62nd Field Artillery Battalion.

"We finally got on our LCTs, landing craft tanks. It held four tanks, or three tanks and a half-track or a Jeep or something. So, they told us in the meantime that we would be in the first wave and that was going to be at Fox Green and we was supposed to be supporting the 16th Infantry [Regiment] of the 1st Division. So we finally took off on the 6th about, I'd say about 1:30, 2:00 in the morning, and we started on in. The weather was bad. It was grey, a lot of people were sick on the boat and we were told not to eat too much spaghetti and cheese because you're gonna upchuck. Well, the captain told us, he said, 'Eat as much as you can because you won't eat for three or four days.' So we let them do whatever they wanted, the new guys, so they had to find out the hard way."

Coast Guard mechanic Tommy Harbour's LCVP was finally underway and headed to shore with dozens of others.

"We took the troops on 'bout 4:00 o'clock in the mornin'. It was dark and the water was pretty rough. We was about 10 or 12 miles out. So, we circled in the rendezvous area, and then we followed the cabin boat from the *Bayfield*. We was supposed to hit Utah Beach. Admiral [Don P.] Moon was in charge of the landings at Utah Beach, and he was on the ship with the staff. Six hundred ship's crew, 200 boat division, and we had some high-ranking Army officers on there, too, 'cause everthin' went through us at Utah.

"Well, we was goin' in. Everything was workin' fine. Soldiers was all right. Gettin' some spray up over the front, a little bit wet. And here come a cabin boat by, and I never did see the number on it. It wasn't our cabin boat. Told old Jones, the coxswain, said, 'Follow us.' So we pulled outta line, 'cause he was a lieutenant. So we got behind him. And it's not very far from Utah to Omaha, just a few minutes. So we left the Utah bunch and we followed that cabin boat, and we got down there pretty close to Omaha Beach, and that cabin boat turned and waved us on in. I don't know why they done that, but anyhow, we done what we was ordered to do."

THE OMAHA BEACH LANDING

Omaha Beach was a crescent-shaped beach about 7,000 yards wide. At low tide the beach would run for 300 yards up to a shingle, which was an angled plane of flat, baseball-size rocks where fishing boats beached. By high tide the waves would be lapping this shingle. Beyond that was a sea wall from four to twelve feet high on the right and a sand dune line on the left. A beach road, partially paved, that the Germans strung concertina wire across, was behind the wall and sand dune line. Beyond those features the beach extended for an uneven width and contained beach villas inland from the road, many of which had been destroyed as part of the German defensive preparations. A tiny village, Les Moulins, lay on the beach toward the west end where the beach was sandy, but elsewhere marshy pockets punctuated the flat terrain. Behind this sea level area, steep cliffs averaging 100 feet and topping out at 170 feet supported a high ridge that overlooked Omaha Beach. The cliff had folds and scrub vegetation.

The ridge was punctured by five draws (gullies) that supported one paved and three unpaved roads as well as a trail at the east end. These draws were the principal objectives of the first wave. They were also the most heavily defended areas at Omaha Beach. At the top of the ridge three villages were located within a half-mile of the ridgeline – Vierville, St.-Laurent and Colleville, all with the suffix "-sur-Mer" added, meaning "by the sea." The suffixes are typically dropped in wartime accounts. To the west of Omaha Beach was Pointe de la Percée and then Pointe du Hoc (Pointe du Hoe) where the Germans had located a major battery of large caliber, partially casemated guns. East of Omaha Beach the ridge continued in steep cliffs past Port-en-Bessin to the area where the British and Canadian divisions landed on the beach flats. Omaha Beach was the most opportune section between the British beaches and the Cotentin Peninsula to land. Without the landing here, the assault's wings would have been widely separated, unconnected and subject to defeat in detail by the enemy. The Germans, of course, recognized the value of Omaha Beach and sited guns to cover it from every possible angle with overlapping fire.

In the carefully drawn plans made by USA V Corps commander Major General Leonard T. Gerow and his staff officers, battalions of two infantry regiments, the 16th of the Big Red One and the 116th of the 29th Infantry Division (attached to the 1st Infantry Division for D-Day), would assault Omaha Beach in companies in the first wave. They were to be preceded by 32 Duplex Drive tanks of the 741st and 743rd

Soldiers of the 1st Infantry Division head toward Omaha Beach on the morning of June 6 aboard a Landing Craft, Vehicles and Personnel (LCVP).

Members of the 2nd Battalion, 16th Infantry Regiment of the 1st Infantry Division disembark their landing craft at 0630 on D-Day at Easy Red Sector of Omaha Beach.

Tank Battalions and covered by the close support fire of tanks and guns firing from LCTs, along with rocket barrages from LCT-Rs.

In the early hours of June 6, the 116th Infantry Regiment of the 29th Infantry Division, the old Stonewall Brigade of Virginia, found itself in the heat of the bloodiest D-Day fighting against the German defenses protecting les Moulins and Vierville draw, a key exit from the beach.

The beach was divided into eight parts, code named from west to east: Charlie; Dog Green; White and Red; Easy Green and Red; Fox Green and Red. On the right, the 2nd Ranger Battalion was to land simultaneously and scale the high cliffs of Pointe du Hoc to overwhelm the battery there. What looked neat and logical on paper was about to come apart at H-Hour, 0630, and require intelligence, training and improvisation to prevent disaster.

"At Omaha Beach there was the 62nd and the 58th [Armored Field Artillery Battalions]," says Jim Weller. "We went in to a thousand yards to the beach, firin' on targets the navy had selected. What we was doing is we were firing high explosives, white phosphorus shells and yellow smoke, and we was marking the targets actually for the battleship *Texas*, *Arkansas*, the cruiser *Augusta*. We was the first ground unit to go in and fire on the fortress of Europe. In fact, they give us a Presidential [Unit] Citation."

The first problem was the Duplex Drive tanks. Nearly all were lost in heavy swells immediately after being launched at H-Hour minus 50 minutes. Although the landing was timed to avoid as many of the underwater obstacles as

A bangalore torpedo explodes a gap in the barbed wire separating the beach from the beach road at Omaha.

possible and this generally worked out well, the current carried most of the units of the 116th and the 16th too far to the east. Hence many of the initial assault companies ended up in other beach zones, bunched together.

The air bombardment did nothing to impede the German beach defenses and the naval barrage did not put the guns facing Omaha Beach out of commission. So the German defense system of nests and strong points on the ridge were training their guns on the landing craft coming to shore. Fearing the gunfire, some coxswains in the first wave stopped their craft far out when they hit sandbars. Those that did come the whole way in were very anxious to drop their loads and take off again.

Another major problem was one of the largest intelligence miscalculations of the campaign, accurately described by Hal Baumgarten.

"Now, let me tell you a little about the German manpower. According to French underground, they told Eisenhower at the end of April, beginning of May, that they had 250 elderly soldiers of the 716th Wehrmacht Division guarding that beach, and that they were static troops. They were put in to work for the Germans, from Poland and White Russia. And the French Maquis said, 'These guys, they've been impressed into the German army, they're gonna surrender rapidly, they have no case of fighting the Americans.'

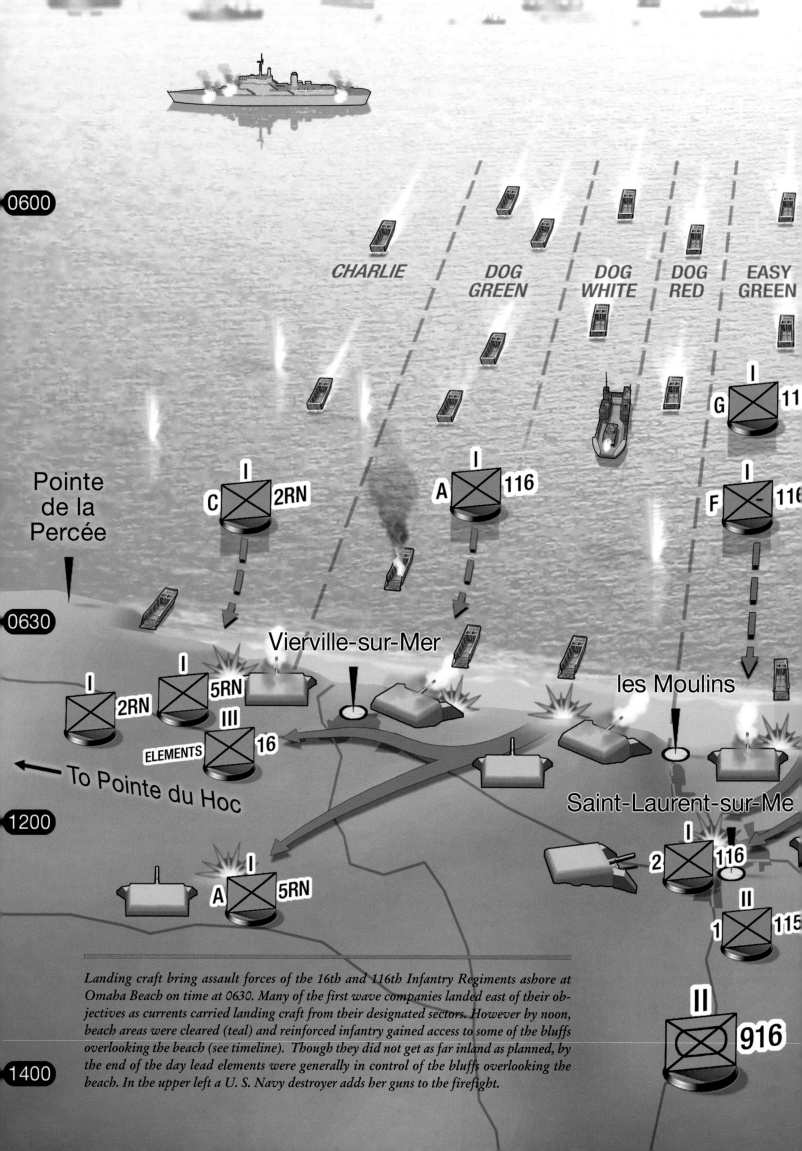

0600

CHARLIE

DOG
GREEN

DOG
WHITE

DOG
RED

EASY
GREEN

Pointe
de la
Percée

0630

Vierville-sur-Mer

les Moulins

G | 11

F | 116

C | I 2RN

A | I 116

I 2RN

I 5RN

III ELEMENTS 16

To Pointe du Hoc

1200

A | I 5RN

Saint-Laurent-sur-Me

2 | I 116

II 1 | 115

II 916

1400

Landing craft bring assault forces of the 16th and 116th Infantry Regiments ashore at Omaha Beach on time at 0630. Many of the first wave companies landed east of their objectives as currents carried landing craft from their designated sectors. However by noon, beach areas were cleared (teal) and reinforced infantry gained access to some of the bluffs overlooking the beach (see timeline). Though they did not get as far inland as planned, by the end of the day lead elements were generally in control of the bluffs overlooking the beach. In the upper left a U. S. Navy destroyer adds her guns to the firefight.

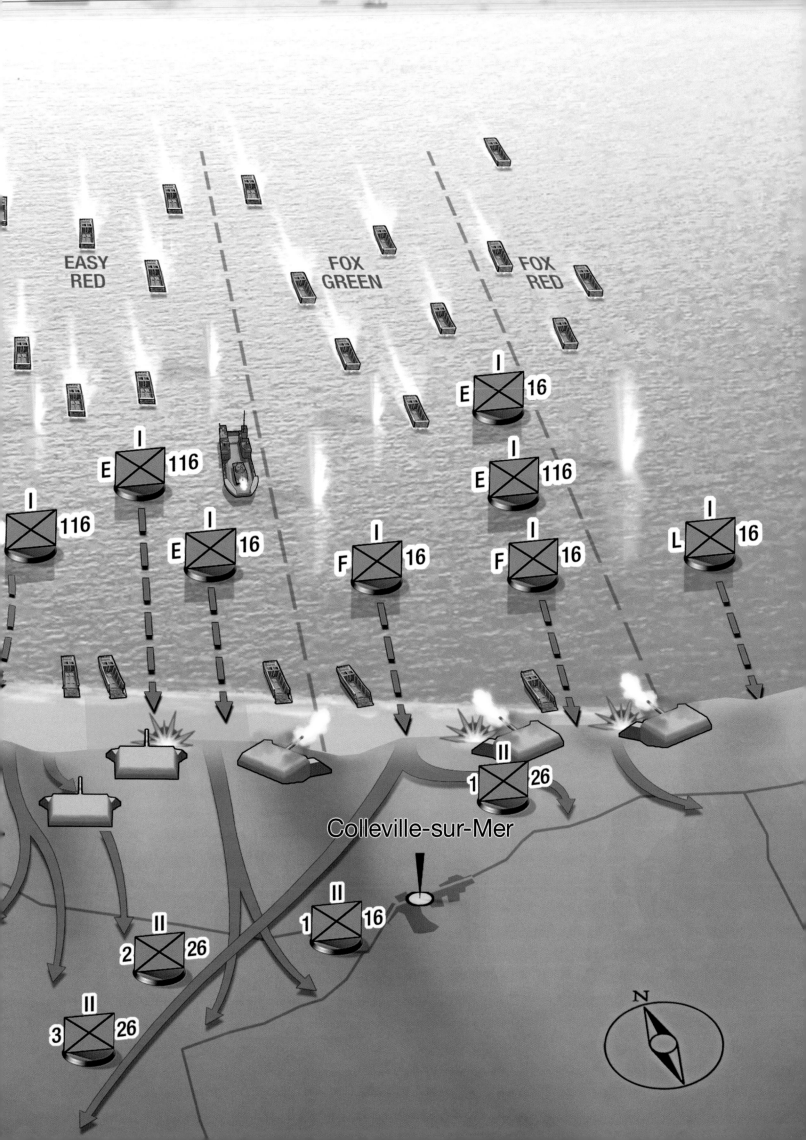

A dead American soldier lies on Omaha Beach prior to his body being picked up. Coincidentally, the two most common U. S. Army rifles of the war – the M1 Garand and M-1903 Springfield – lie together in the foreground.

"But unfortunately a German with a shotgun shot down both pigeons [carrying messages to England] in the early part of May, so Eisenhower was not privy to the information that they [had] moved in 250 young men of the 352nd Grenadier Division, which was Germany's best in France. They were young guys from Hanover, Germany, and their non-coms [had] fought on the Eastern Front against Russia. So they were hardened, battle hardened."

To Omaha Beach came boatloads of the men in companies A, E, F and G of the 116th, companies A, E, I and L of the 16th and 96 tanks of the 743rd in LCTs shoved to the beach. They were followed closely by army engineers and naval underwater demolition teams (UDT). To the right,

Company C of the 2nd Ranger Battalion landed near the foot of Pointe du Hoc. The German batteries which had opened on American naval vessels at 0535 now concentrated their fire on the beach invaders, with machine guns and mortars adding to the cacophony of weapons.

One of the LCVPs landing on Omaha Beach was PA33-4 with mechanic Tommy Harbour. PA33-4 carried men of Company A of the 116th. They were mostly from Bedford, Virginia. Company A landed on Dog Green near the Vierville draw, one of the most heavily defended sections of the beach.

"The picture [of] PA 33-4 is famous," says Harbour. "[It] shows us hittin' the beach. And the

American assault troops of the 16th Infantry Regiment, injured while storming Omaha Beach, wait at Chalk Cliffs, Colleville-sur-Mer for evacuation to a field hospital on D-Day.

first two soldiers that run out was shot. Shows them hittin' in the sand, face down. The next one that run out now, stood up on the ramp and looked down this-a way on the beach, turned and looked up this-a way and run off. You know, the Bedford Boys is 22 killed. I had them on my boat. That one that looked down the beach, looked into the camera, and on his helmet was [what] looked like a target. That was the Bedford Boys emblem.

"When they all got offa the boat, why here come Geronimo [another LCVP coxswain] in. He was an Indian. We all had a little Cherokee in us, I think. Anyhow, old Geronimo, his motor mac left the ramp down too quick, and he hooked it in the front of a cable on my ramp. I couldn't get it [the ramp] up. I was stalled, and the water was a comin' in. And Jones was a wantin' to get outta there, and I was wantin' to get out too. Next thing I knew, Geronimo pulled out, and the water was up to my waist. So there wasn't nothin' to do but start swimmin' out. So Jones and Shultz had done gone. I never did see them, I don't know where they went but they swum out and I swum out. Got out there, about, oh 40 or 50 yards, boat come along and picked me up, and they took me back to the *Bayfield*."

Over in the 1st Infantry Division sector, many men of the infantry companies were having the same problems. The machine gun fire was ricocheting off the metal drop down ramps of the

LCVPs. The men concluded they didn't want to be in the front when that ramp dropped down.

"I remembered, don't get in the front," says Albert Piper. "No way was I gonna go up the front. But I know that we were about 300 yards out to shore, and he said he was on a sandbar, and so they let us out. But you could hear that stuff hittin' out there before ya. I think somebody put me up on his shoulders and I went over the top. I'm sure Whittsen was the guy that pushed me.

"Well when I went down, I thought I was never comin' up. And he come right in after me 'cause I grabbed him by the back of his belt. He was about a foot taller than I was. And I cut everything loose, because I couldn't swim. And I had stuff that I'd carried since Africa. All that stuff I wanted to take home. Cameras and all. Cut 'em loose. The only thing I had was the radio batteries that I had to have, and the radio that I had to have when we landed. I had half of it, and like if you were with me, you had the other half.

"Now goin' in was rough. Wasn't too much firing because we were more off to the right. But when I got on the beach itself, we laid there for approximately four hours. Now, the reason for that is, there's a ridge line, you know. Now the machine guns were up on a ridge line. And if you got in where we were, we were off to the side, and most of the fire was on the left, so we could sweat it out for a while."

Vincent "Mike" McKinney was in the 16th Infantry Regiment, Company E landing in the first wave. A veteran of North Africa and Sicily, he made tech sergeant while his unit was in England.

"On our way to the beach my boat got hit twice. We landed. The ramp went down. The boat got almost full of water. It was still a little rough. When I got off the boat, I was up to my shoulders in water. Getting out of the boat I had to climb over several bodies that were just laying there, floating in the water.

"I was the first one on the beach [but] I wasn't the first one off the boat. The boat took a hit up in the front. And the others got shot; when the ramp went down they started through the water. The lieutenant made the shore all right. Other guys got hit going through the water. You couldn't run through the water. You had to struggle, you're holding your rifle up and trying to move your legs, and you have eighty pounds on your back, you're not moving very fast. As soon as the water gets a little lower you could put one foot after the other, and they were shooting.

"But when I ran across the beach, there was nobody in front of me. I didn't see a soul. I thought how eerie this was. Here I am in France, and the Germans are all over the place, there was supposed to be a whole lot of people there, and I don't see anybody. I could see little puffs coming out of the sand where they were shooting machine gun fire. They didn't have any big guns going off. It was mostly machine gun and rifle fire.

"It was a short beach, it wasn't too wide. Thirty, forty yards. It's not a Jones Beach [extensive and popular beach near New York City] or something, it was a narrow beach, from the time we hit the water line until we hit the start of the hill going up to the pillbox. I didn't want to run along the beach. I wanted to run right to where my pillbox was; I wasn't going anyplace else. Just straight."

Nearby, medic Charles Norman Shay went in with the 116th Regiment.

"As we approached the beach, of course, as you know, perhaps from history and from your research, the Germans had erected barriers well out beyond the low tide area, and we were not able to get very close to the beaches. In fact it's a few hundred meters to the beach and we were beyond that because we could not get up to the low tide area. We ran into the barriers, and once we ran into the barriers, the ramps were dropped and the order came to debark. Of course, by this time, all hell had broken loose because of small arm machine gun fire, mortars…artillery was flying continually from both sides…from the ships that were out at sea [that] were firing into the defenses of the Germans and Germans were firing back. And when the landing craft came into view, of course they opened fire on the landing craft.

"Once the ramps went down, many of the men that was…in my particular case, the men that was standing in the front end of the landing craft were immediately hit, wounded. We were loaded down with all sorts of gear, and when I left the landing craft myself I had to jump into the water. I landed in water up to my chest. Of course, my…all of my equipment that I was carrying, my boots, my clothing, became waterlogged, which made it additionally difficult to make any progress to the beach, but I eventually was able to get out of the high water. And I eventually made it to the first barriers that the Germans had erected that were out, that were not covered by water, and we used these barriers…in my particular case, anyway…used these barriers as protection for myself by going from one barrier to the next and trying to use them as a shield against the enemy small arms fire. And I was able to make it, like many other men, of course. I was not alone, of course, many of us made it by using this tactic to get to the beach.

"When we reached the beach, of course, we made it to the sand dunes that had bordered the beach. And this gave us much needed protection and once we reached this area, we were able to sit down and recover…regain our senses and to begin to think. I had been trained as a medic to treat the wounded, and I began to think that I had to continue on with my duties that I had trained for."

The 116th landed companies from the 1st, 2nd and 3rd Battalions in the first two assault waves. Hal Baumgarten was in Company B of the 1st Battalion. It landed on Dog Green sector, which was on the westernmost part of Omaha Beach, at 0700.

"Now the 1st Division was gonna land on the eastern part, which turned out to be the soft part. My other battalions, you know, the 2nd and 3rd Battalions, were gonna land in between, on Dog Red, Dog White…each had a dog insignia. Ours was Dog Green, the smallest of the beaches, most heavily defended.

"Company A and B landed right on target. The target was the white steeple of the church in Vierville-sur-Mer. But A Company had lost three boats to drowning. Company B lost two boats, one way to the east and one way to the west. The one way to the west went up the bluff and tried to free those Rangers at Pointe du Hoc. But my company, B, only landed with four boats. That's a total of 210 men coming in to face 450 on the bluff, in bunkers, with all that firepower."

As Baumgarten tells it, the manpower in Company B was soon reduced further. He describes in detail the first few moments as his LCA hit the beach at Dog Green.

"The first thing I saw a Company B boat on my left, port side, blew up, hit a mine. We were

A tank turret tops off a bunker on Omaha Beach near St.-Laurent-sur-Mer.

showered with wood, metal, and body parts, and blood, from on top. When our ramp went down [it was] the signal for every machine gun on that beach to open up on the exit to our ship. So Harold Donaldson, the lieutenant, was gunned down in the boat and several of the men around him. The fella in front of me, Clarence Riggs, was machine gunned on the ramp. I dove in [the water] behind him... [the] left side of my helmet was creased by a bullet.

"I was standing in neck-deep bloody water, with my rifle over my head. Now, I happened to be 5'10 on D-Day, and I weighed, with the equipment, well over 200 pounds. They put these combat jackets on these guys. I didn't wear it, 'cause my best buddy, who was the radio man in the boat, he said, 'Hal, don't wear that jacket, it's liable to drown you.' Now I listened to him, 'cause he was an old man; he was 25 years old and I was only a kid of 19. But anyway, these guys that wore these jackets, when they got into the water, pulled them down further. They were dark green canvas jackets, four pockets in the front, two in the back. They struggled to get their jackets off, and they couldn't. Some of them bobbed up and down; they got machine gunned in the water.

"So we hit the sand, we were running across sand at 300 yards out. I landed a little to the right of that one tank that was firing. But anyway, there were a group of us running across the beach with our rifles at port arms, which is the rifle across your chest.

"When we got to about 135 yards away from the seawall, a machine gun spray came from the trenches up on the bluff. And I heard a loud thud on my right front, and my rifle vibrated. I turned it over; there was a clean hole through its receiver, which is a little rectangular plate in front of the trigger guard. My seven bullets in the magazine section had stopped the German bullet. Another thud behind me to the left, and that guy was gone. I hit the sand behind the hedgehog, which is about 130 yards from the

Infantry soldiers at Omaha move along the shingle as they head toward a path through minefields that separates them from the beach exit.

seawall, and I observed to my right Private Robert Ditmar, Fairfield, Connecticut. I was yelling…

He tripped over the hedgehog, spun completely around, lying on his back, and yelling, 'I'm hit, I'm hit, Mom, Mother!' And then he was silent.

"I looked over to my left and Sergeant Clarence Robeson of Lynchburg, Virginia…I always mention their names and where they came from. I don't want people to forget about them. Clarence Robeson was staggering by me, without his helmet, gaping hole in the left side of his forehead, his blonde hair was streaked with blood. I was yelling, 'Get down!' And I guess he couldn't hear me anyway, the noise on that beach was horrendous. He staggered all the way behind me to the left, knelt down on the sand behind me, in about three inches of water at that time, 'cause the tide was coming in, and he started praying with his rosary beads. And the machine gun up on the bluff fired over my head, cut him in half.

"Now, there are only two of us alive from my boat team, Charles Connor and myself. We had 85 percent casualties, first 15 minutes. I was wounded five times; three times on June 6th, twice on June 7th. Now you might say to yourself, 'What kind of an idiot would keep fighting, being wounded?' Company L of the 115th was supposed to come in between 10:00 a.m. and 2:00 p.m. to reinforce us. So we were left with options: Stay there and die; give up the beach to the Germans; or fight wounded. We decided to fight wounded."

"Well, we landed," recalls Charles Shay, "We hit the beaches at 6:30 in the morning, and by the time we got to the beach, I don't know how much time had elapsed, but I can estimate maybe a half an hour, or maybe even a little bit more before we got to the shelter of the sand dunes and then I was able to regain my senses and continue on with that which I had been trained to do. And perhaps it was an hour by the time I was doing…already doing my duties, and I happened to glance back to the sea and I saw that there were many wounded men floundering in the rising tide that were not able to help themselves. They were doomed to drown if no help came to them, so I dropped what I was doing and I returned to the water to assist the wounded and to help…to drag them out of the water to the safety of the sand…above the high tide area."

The result of the misplaced landings and heavy enemy fire was that only one company, G of the 116th, had any unity and they were out of position. The others were scattered and intermingled. Company A of the 116th had extremely heavy losses and was out of action for the day. As Baumgarten described, Company B did not fare much better and no more landings were conducted directly onto Dog Green. Over on Easy Red, only a few units of the initial assault wave landed in the sector and they recovered reasonably well from the sporadic fire. But all of these men were out of position. Yet, the developing gap in the German defenses was advantageous to U. S. tanks gathering there on the beach.

Units of the second wave were getting stacked up quickly. The landing craft attempting to make shore, including the larger LCTs and LSTs beginning to make their way in, were hampered by the lack of success on the part of the engineering task force. They milled about in the surf. Men were crowding beach shelters and obstacles in the water. Destroyed radios and lack of communication in general made it extremely difficult for commanders to reorganize units and advance toward the critical beach road and draws.

The army engineers and navy demolition units that came in with the first wave suffered all of the problems encountered by the infantry soldiers landing on the beach; and, given the engineer and demolition units' missions, risked even more danger. Much of their equipment was destroyed

or lost on the way in. Explosive charges they carried were fired upon, either exploding and killing nearby personnel or being damaged and rendered useless for their intended purpose. Infantrymen seeking shelter and newly arriving boats got in the way of demolition efforts on the beach. The rising tide quickly obscured underwater obstacles. Only one of the six cleared lanes to the beach was marked. There was little in the way of implements left to mark it for incoming boat drivers. Working in full cooperation with the head of the army engineers, Colonel O'Neil, Lieutenant Commander Joseph H. Gibbons, USNR, commanding officer of U. S. Navy Combat Demolitions Units at Omaha, describes the difficult conditions under which the engineers and UDT sailors worked to clear the beach."

"After accomplishing our initial objective of sixteen, 50-yard gaps we were then to proceed to clear all enemy obstacles off the beaches. It was expected that all enemy gunfire would be neutralized by H-hour. The plan called for the Navy Combat Demolition Unit to land at H-hour plus three minutes. Unfortunately [enemy] gunfire was not neutralized and as we approached the beaches we were subjected to heavy enemy gunfire of 88-mm [artillery], 75s [-mm artillery], and rifle fire. In the engagement we suffered 41% casualties; 20% killed, 21% wounded. This excluded those who were wounded but were not evacuated from the beaches.

"The gunfire was intense, but we were successful in clearing initially six gaps [of] 50 yards each and three partially cleared gaps. By the end of D-Day we had been successful in clearing ten gaps completely. By D plus 2 [days], 85% of the enemy obstacles on the beaches had been cleared and by D plus 4 the beaches on Omaha were cleared of all enemy obstacles dangerous to invasion craft."

As bad as the situation was for the infantry, engineers and tanks in the first hours on the beach, it was worse for attached artillery. The use of DUKWs to ferry in artillery pieces was a complete disaster. Most of these were swamped in the significant swells in the bay that was only briefly and partially becalmed between storms. Many pieces were lost and the artillery was essentially a non-factor until they could land on larger craft. Tanks were the only firepower ashore for much of D-Day.

In a bomb crater U. S. soldiers hold captured Germans, some of whom wear civilian caps.

their LCI to the shore of Easy Red Beach. On board was one platoon of the 6th Naval Beach Battalion, commanded by Beachmaster Lieutenant Commander Joseph P. Vaghi. The Beach Battalion was responsible for directing traffic to and on the beach between the tide limits. They were responsible for shore-to-ship communication, providing landing assistance for incoming craft,

"I went in with the headquarters, my own outfit," remembers Albert Piper. "But that's what we were gonna do, was work with the artillery once they got in headquarters. Because, see your headquarters took care of all your fire, you know, the radio operators and that. Now the 7th Field Artillery, which had to land with the 16th [Infantry Regiment], they didn't get a gun ashore. Now I didn't know that for a while, until I actually got on it…they didn't get one on shore. They got stuck in the water or, you know… there's no way in God's world that you could set anything up on that beach."

Sixty-five minutes after the first soldiers hit the beach another group of navy men negotiated

rendering aid to the wounded, returning wounded (and anything else) to ships at sea and doing minor repairs to landing craft. To keep everything moving as efficiently as possible on this busy beach less than 10 kilometers in width – and doing it under fire, of course – the knowledge, skill and valor of the Beach Battalion was essential to success of the invasion.

"The beach was cluttered with thousands of beach obstacles placed there by the Germans to thwart an invasion attempt by the Allies," explains Vaghi. "A Navy Underwater Demolition Team had landed prior to our arrival and was successful in clearing away some of the obstructions, so as to permit movement into the beach by various landing crafts assigned to this and other beaches.

"My first awareness that what we were doing was for real was when an 88-mm shell hit our

LCI(L) and machine gun fire surrounded us. The Germans were in their pillboxes and bunkers high above the beach on the bluff and had an unobstructed view of what we were doing.

"The atmosphere was depressing. The top of the bluff behind the beach was barely visible; the sound of screeching 12- and 14-inch shells from the USS *Texas* and the USS *Arkansas* offshore were sounds never heard by us before; the stench of expended gunpowder filled the air and rocket launchers mounted on landing craft moved in close to the shore and were spewing forth hundreds of rounds at a time onto the German defenses. Purple smoke emanated from the base of the beach obstacles as the UDT prepared to detonate another explosive in the effort to clear a path through the obstacles to the dune line. This was the state of affairs as the platoon made its way to the dune line, oh so many yards away.

"Using the obstacles as shelter, we moved forward over the tidal flat under full exposure to machine gun fire as we finally reached the dune line. All C-8s [Vaghi's platoon] made the long trek including Commander Carusi. God was with us! Having reached the high water mark, we set about organizing ourselves and planning the next move. We were pinned down with little movement to the right or the left of our position and absolutely *no* movement forward. Because the UDT had opened gaps through the underwater obstacles into Easy Red, most of the personnel and vehicles came ashore on my beach with the result that we were very crowded and became 'sitting ducks' for the enemy fire.

"I believe the most dramatic event I experienced that morning was when an Army officer came to me and asked that I pass the word over my powered microphone that the soldiers were to 'move forward.' I gave the order after which an army

sergeant pushed a bangalore torpedo through the barbed wire at the top of the dune [and] exploded it, which then opened a gap in the mass of barbed wire. He then turned to his men and said 'Follow me.' The men rushed through the gap onto the flat plateau behind the dune line to the base of the bluff, a distance of some 50 yards or so through heavily mined areas where many lost their lives or were seriously wounded. The sergeant [who] said, 'Follow me' did not order his men forward, but actually went in front himself, which is the sign of a leader."

This sergeant had the right idea and commanders all along the beach were trying to convince their men to do the same thing. The only way they would survive and the operation would succeed was if they got off the beach. That was proving to be difficult. Sergeant Henry A. French landed with Company G of the 16th at 0700. He and his company commander, Captain Joseph P. Dawson, found themselves in position to get up the ridge.

"When we got up to this, I call it a levy, a berm, whatever, we were pinned down there so it was absolutely chaos. But anyway we were the first ones to get on top of the hill. And Captain Dawson said, 'When the wind blow, let's go!' Oh, he was excellent. He didn't say 'Okay, you men go here, go there and do this.' He said 'C'mon, let's go!' He was out front. One hundred percent.

"Dawson, he found the trails. You know, the Germans had their trails and he just helped me find one and there we went in with a couple machine guns and rifle [fire]. Colleville was our objective. But anyway, when we got to the top of the hill, I don't know how we got separated but myself and oh, I'd say fifteen to twenty more men, got separated from the company commander. And so we got into the woods up there and we got a little sniper fire but it was getting too late. So we just said well we'll find a place somewhere and we found a big ditch and we all got in it and hunkered down for the night."

The advance up the ridge by Company G, between St.-Laurent and Coleville draws, was paralleled by a Company E advance to their right. Together these independent actions began the movement up the cliffs and inland in the 16th Regiment sector because the draws were still heavily defended. They took the garrison, part of the German 916th Regiment, from the rear and forced them to surrender.

All across the front, soldiers, often just groups of beach survivors, banded together to try to get across the beach and up the ridge. Another major development occurred near Les Moulins, where a concerted effort was made to take the Vierville draw. Companies of the 116th Regiment and 5th Ranger Battalion were organized by Brigadier General Norman D. "Dutch" Cota, assistant division commander of the 29th Infantry Division, and other senior officers to move on either side of the village and up the ridge. These units struggling to move forward on Omaha Beach were facing the best of the German defenses on the Calvados coast. Hal Baumgarten describes the defenses he later researched but faced firsthand on D-Day.

"The pill boxes. They had tremendous firepower; they had a trench 30 feet above the seawall which had zigzag trenches and had a cocoon of underground tunnels to re-supply the people in it. They had three machine guns in there; they had riflemen…a good number of them…some with telescopic sights; and they could throw hand grenades on the beach below. So, that was part of their armament, plus there's a machine gun on their right flank, and the 75mm cannon which was only facing east, so it didn't bother us."

"Up on the bluff they had Tobruks [named after the Libyan stronghold in North Africa] which were [open] cement emplacements [from] which they fired their 105mm mortar shells down on the beach. Now, in the center of town [Les Moulins], they had a road going up into Vierville-sur-Mer. It meandered from left to right, 600 yards straight up. Well, this road was of great strategic value to the Allied command. The reason it wasn't open, General Rommel had two 8 ½ by 6 feet thick parallel cement walls [built]. And he had a machine gun guarding them, next to that 75mm cannon, and he had a tank trap in front of 'em and barbed wire and mines. Infantry is not stopped by cement walls, so we went up the bluff. But Colonel Ploger, who later became General Robert Ploger, blew the wall with 10 cases of TNT in front of the front wall, blew both walls at 5:00 p.m. One of my buddies, Charles Connor, who was in my boat team, went up the road at 5:00 p.m."

Destroyers like USS *Thompson*, on which Bud Taylor was leading a quad 40mm gun array, came in close, to about 200 yards off the beach, to clear out German strong points on the ridge, much in the way Taylor described this action earlier. This was extremely helpful to those soldiers making their way up the cliff including the Rangers at Pointe du Hoc. Four of the American "tin cans" and three from the Royal Navy, including *Thompson*, were commended by Admiral Hall, commander of Task Force O, for their close support direct fire continuing after the initial D-Day landings.

The Rangers were slowly making their way up the cliffs in front of Pointe du Hoc. They were delayed 40 minutes on the way in and the work of getting ropes and ladders heading up the cliff face was very slow. Confusion over what was happening there caused the next Ranger units in to move over to Dog Green Beach. Eventually, the Company C Rangers made the crest but the other Ranger companies and part of the 116th Regiment that were to wheel west through Pointe de la Percée were running far behind schedule. Company C found the casemate abandoned, but then discovered the 155mm guns in a camouflaged position further inland. These were abandoned also. However the 1st Battalion of the German 914th Regiment counterattacked and pinned down the Company C Rangers who were as yet unreinforced. They would be cut off and alone on the crest of Pointe du Hoc throughout the night.

Indeed, things were running behind schedule on both flanks of the attack. Though they were on the bluffs, the 16th Regiment and part of the 116th in the east were not close to the projected beachhead maintenance line beyond Colleville and St.-Laurent. On the right, the first soldiers of the 116th and Ranger Battalions, reinforced in the afternoon by the 115th Regiment, were just getting off the beach. But while the German commander at Pointe de la Percée observed through the haze and smoke of the morning that the beach was a mass of bodies and huddled men, the situation was changing. The combined force of all elements of the American attack was beginning to push against the frontline regiment of the 352nd Division. And while reinforcements were requested, the division had more urgent problems to the east where other Allied forces were landing in front of Caen.

The American high command was also beginning to feel a change in attitude after limited communica-

Fast moving landing craft carry Companies G and H, the second wave of the 16th Infantry Regiment's 2nd Battalion, past the heavy cruiser USS Augusta.

tion in the early morning portrayed disaster. A V Corps staff officer in a DUKW began criss-crossing the beach to give on-the-scene reports. By mid-morning he was able to report that the situation was improving as mixed units got off the beaches and advanced toward the draws and moved up the cliff face to the high ground.

"We were there for, I'd say, 3 ½, 4 hours before we moved," says Piper. "Because when you look up, you could see all the men up on that ridge, and they had no place to go. You could see 'em diggin' you know, but no place to dig. Well, I was gonna be smart, see. I saw 'em, and I figured, the hell with those, it's shorter over here. So I start to go over there, and a voice said, 'I wouldn't go there if I were you.' And I couldn't find him at first, 'cause he was over here. And I looked and it's a guy with no legs. But they had him [in a] tourniquet. And you know there's a time mark on tourniquets. And they tell you, certain minutes, loosen 'em, let 'em bleed a little bit, tighten 'em back. So I did that, and then I got in where I belonged.

"But it took us a long time to get up there. And when I got up there, man you had one hell of a time diggin' in, because everything was loaded. They had a trench up on top, the Germans did. We jumped in it, then we couldn't get out of it because of a sniper. Every time you stick your head up, *zing.*

"When we would get mines, you'd fish for them with your bayonets and stuff like that, cap 'em. Then they got smart and they put one under the other, so when you picked that one up, that blew up. They had Bouncin' Betties, then they had the 'de-nutter,' which was an English mine. It was like a little .22 pistol barrel, and when you stepped on it, step off of it, it would hit you in the nuts, but it wasn't accu-

rate, it would always hit you in the groin. Lot of fun."

Hal Baumgarten received a serious wound to his cheek and jaw in the morning, but as he stated he felt his best option of survival was to continue fighting and moving forward. Like many others, he was also suffering from mild shock and depression from what he saw around him.

"I saw all these buddies of mine dead, and I didn't know anything about plastic surgery. I thought, 'What are they gonna do with that face and a missing jaw and the teeth and gums on my tongue…my tongue was even cut.' I figured they're not gonna be able to put [my face back] together. So I joined eleven other guys about 1 o'clock. We went up the bluff. I called us the walking wounded, 'cause some of them were wounded worse than me. And we're goin' up the bluff, this 100-foot bluff. We went half-way up at least, to where those zigzag trenches were, which was 30 feet above the 25 foot [sea] wall.

"We turned right when we got up the bluff, and we went a little to the right of a hotel that's there, hotel-casino, and we went further in, and we came to a farmhouse with a stone wall. And the Germans were in there, about five of them. And they took us on, and they were firing at us. One of them made the mistake of puttin' his head above the wall, and I knocked him off, 'cause I was super expert [with a rifle]. So anyway, that little skirmish ended in about an hour with a hand grenade from us. And we moved on. We hit a machine gun nest with another five guys, and we fought with them and by the time we finished, there were seven of us left out of the twelve.

"Now we got up to the [ridge top] beach road that goes all the way down the beach to Pointe du Hoc. We got behind the bocage, or the hedgerow. We hadda crawl, 'cause we were under fire by shells. And while I was crawling, I felt something hit me in the left foot. It turned out later that it was a castrator mine. A castrator mine [or 'de-nutter'] is a mine that the Germans put in the ground, with three metal prongs sticking up. So when a guy steps on these prongs, and steps forward…they got like a pistol in the ground, shoots a bullet between your legs. So that's why they call it a castrator mine. But instead, this bullet went on my left foot, between the great toe and the third toe. Blew out, split the big toe in half; blew out my second metatarsal; compound fracture of the third metatarsal; and I later lost the second toe.

"So I got against the hedgerow, I took off my shoe…there was a bullet hole through my legging, in fact took the shoe off and emptied the blood out, like you would empty water from a vase. And I put on a beautiful bandage. I was always good in medicine. I put powder in, I put a nice pressure bandage on. There was a hole completely through the foot, I could look right through it. But anyway, shells started coming in right then. Ripped off the bandage, pulled the shoe up, laced it and jumped behind the hedgerow. We stayed there until about 12:30 in the morning, June 7th."

Meanwhile, back on the beach, medic Charles Shay was doing what he could amidst the carnage.

"I began to focus on treating the wounded… makeshift splints, tourniquets to stop serious bleeding, bandaging wounds, and in general trying to make the wounded comfortable. I knew that I had been trained to do this particular job, and that's what I was concentrating on. I was not concentrating on perhaps dying or losing my life. I didn't have time to think about this. I only concentrated on that which I had been trained to do.

"It was constant, small arm fire, mortar fire, and machine gun fire, and I don't know how I was never wounded, I don't know why…I had protection someplace.

"I stayed on the beach. As I told you before, I had become separated from my unit. I was operating independently, treating the wounded. And then there was much confusion and chaos, and the officers and the sergeants, the enlisted men that were able to make the beach, they began to organize the men to proceed inland and eventually, the beaches became much calmer because the men that proceeded inland had knocked out much of the opposition. It became a little bit freer to move up and down the beach, and that's just what I did. I moved up and down the beach looking for wounded people.

"I found a fellow medic [who] had been seriously wounded. I knew that he was dying because he had a very serious stomach wound. He was probably bleeding internally, which I could not help him with, and I gave him a shot of morphine. I bandaged his wounds as best I could, and well, we said goodbye to each other because I knew that he was dying and we would never see each other again. I laid a wreath on his grave up in Omaha Beach, up in the cemetery. He had been awarded the Silver Star posthumously for his actions."

The beach was still laced with artillery and small arms fire, but with the five draws in the process of being secured and the road through the St.-Laurent draw open, beach traffic began flowing in the afternoon as more and more follow-up units came ashore. This was accomplished with the continued success of the naval gunfire which was being directed by naval fire control parties when they were able to land. Under this fire protection army engineers were able to cut through the dunes and obstacles on the beach to

One of the five French-made 155mm guns used by the Germans at Pointe du Hoc peaks out from a camouflaged position in an orchard. All of the weapons were moved from the original battery overlooking the sea, at first confusing army Rangers who were assigned to silence them.

provide lanes for tanks and heavy weapons to move off the beach.

"So, finally we landed at Omaha Beach," recalls Jim Weller. "And it took us all day to get on the beach. And the reason why, there was all the hang up. And I take my hat off to anybody that carried a rifle in the infantry, they're the poor guys that had to secure the land to get the tanks on, and see, them poor guys, these young guys are getting slaughtered and paying the price. The machine guns was eating them up. Because the Germans had everything zeroed in.

"So, finally, like I say, we had about 300 some odd people in my battalion. We was just a battalion of 18 tanks and we were supporting a division. They used us any way they want. And what actually happened, we were supposed to land on Fox Green. So guess what? We landed on Fox Red. Everything that was planned didn't work."

Also arriving in the late afternoon with the 115th Infantry Regiment was Captain James M. Roberts, aide to Major General Gerow.

"We stepped off the ramps they lowered from each side of the landing craft and went down to our necks, and the waves were splashing around. Had to hop off the bottom a bit until I didn't have to hop anymore. Then I was totally soaked, including getting sand in my carbine, which I was equipped with as a company grade officer. But we got ashore. The beach was a terrible mess of people. Things had been going on since 06:30 in the morning. There were casualties all over the place. Anyway I got back laying against the

Soldiers of the 29th Infantry Division disembark from LCI (L) 412 on Omaha Beach during one of the post-assault waves. In the background anti-aircraft halftracks that could not negotiate the steep stone shingle have become submerged in the rising tide.

small hill leading up from the beach. I tried to fire the weapon, but it didn't [fire] because of sand and seawater. So I field-stripped it, then I didn't have anything to wipe it dry with. I pulled out the tail of my shirt to dry it and put it back together to keep firing.

"I was supposed to find a squad that we would put the general in when he came ashore. So I picked up another guy, and said we've got to get out of here. There was a little bit of a ravine coming down to the beach. So I was going around that end to go out to this ravine, and we were shot at by some concealed weapons on the other side. Obviously, the Germans were still there, so we flopped down and each of us fired a couple of rounds in that direction. That kind of quieted them. We kept on going up the hill. At that point, our frontline was about 300 yards ahead of us. I was supposed to wait until the general got ashore, so I went back and stood on the edge of the hill and looked over the English Channel. It was just unbelievable! Ships as far as you could see, ten miles one way, ten miles the other. It was quite a sight.

"On the way across [the Channel], I was chatting with another fellow who was my age, same rank, both captains…we were like two peas in a pod, really. On D-Day Plus 1 I had to go back to the beach, I don't recall what for. They had not policed up the bodies. I accomplished whatever mission it was, but then I ran across the corpse of this officer I was telling you about. He was lying down dead, a hole in the middle of his head. He's there, and I'm here, and I really got shaken up over that one. That was an instant I'll never forget."

Charles Norman Shay was administering to the wounded on the beach until some time in the afternoon.

"Troops that landed behind us, the 26th Infantry Regiment in the 1st Division landed behind me and these troops begin to move inland. I just followed some of these men that were moving inland, and I saw many dead American and German soldiers on the way in, and I spent the night in the field. I had to lay down because I was exhausted."

The 26th Infantry Regiment was to support the 18th in actions the following day. On the evening of D-Day, companies of the 16th and 18th Regiments were becoming bogged down in the area between St.-Laurent and Colleville. Those same American units pushed past the villages, neither was captured on D-Day. To the west, the 116th Infantry was settling down between Vierville, which had been captured at 1100, and St.-Laurent. The 115th Infantry had come in too far east and ended the day near St.-Laurent, some distance from its proposed objective, Longueville.

Things were winding down for the night when the V Corps commander arrived at Omaha Beach, according to Captain Roberts.

"He didn't get ashore until 9:00 o'clock that night. By that time, things were settling down somewhat. We had established, you couldn't call it a camp, but a place to put in his tent, a couple hundred yards from the edge of the hill. I had gotten someone to help me put up basically a pup tent for the general. He was not exactly thrilled with the quarters. I went back down the hill and set myself down in a ditch, and I thought to myself, if every day is like this one, I'm not going to survive this war."

He did survive, as did many others, but the toll for taking Omaha Beach was nearly 2,000 American casualties. In order that those who perished would not die in vain, much more progress would have to be made on June 7.

Across the Vire estuary on the Cotentin Peninsula the landing at Utah Beach started out much better for VII Corps than the nightmarish assault of Omaha Beach did for V Corps. Logical reasons for this were the more favorable terrain, the more effective beach bombing by the Ninth Air Force medium bombers and the fact that the airborne landings had diverted the attention of the peninsula's German defenders.

All of the units headed to Utah Beach in the first wave were from the 4th Infantry Division commanded by Major General Raymond O. "Tubby" Barton. One regiment of the 90th Infantry Division was held in reserve for a follow-up landing. The first assault units, as planned, would land on the beach in front of the village of la Grande Dune in a 2,220 yard front. The 8th Infantry Regiment and the 3rd Battalion of the 22nd Infantry Regiment made up this force. Since the month before D-Day had revealed enemy activity in the St. Marcouf Islands north of Utah Beach, detachments from the 4th and 24th Cavalry Squadrons were landed there at H minus 2 hours. They found the location heavily mined but abandoned, and the Americans held the islands through the day against German artillery shelling.

The naval gunfire preceding the invasion did not clear out all the enemy strong points, which were well concealed. Invasion warships and the close-in support vessels did enjoy relative safety, however, as the German batteries were mostly sited

As Operation Overlord *continued more German prisoners were gathered up across the Normandy landscape. A medic and a soldier holding an M3 "grease gun" are among those who observe the long line of POWs.*

to cover the beaches rather than the bay. The bay was more sheltered off Utah Beach, and the LCVPs approached the beach without incident. Although 15 minutes late because of the loss of their control boat, all but four of the 32 Duplex Drive tanks assigned to the first wave made it in under their own power.

A strong unanticipated current worked to the advantage of the first wave at Utah Beach. The landing took place 2,000 yards to the south of the planned beach areas and a few minutes late. Thus the assault force escaped the stronger defenses that covered the originally-planned landing area. As a result, the Utah Beach landings were accomplished with few U. S. casualties. Engineers and demolition units cleared the beach and landing approaches in one hour. By H plus 3 hours only sporadic gunfire harassed activities on the beach. Albert Skorupa came in with the 1st Engineer Special Brigade, Company C, of the 531st Engineer Shore Regiment (ESR). He remembers his first impressions of Utah Beach, being among the first of the Americans to land there.

"It looked like a nice sandy beach and it was good because we went in at low tide and you could see all the obstacles. It was great because if we went in there at high tide...they had a thing that would blow [up] the boat. We could see all that and it made it easier for us. And the Navy made a mistake, they dropped us about a quarter of a mile from where we were supposed to be dropped. It was better for us. The first guys that go in, they put a marker. A red marker for a red beach, a blue beach, and a yellow beach. That gave the guys coming after us [an idea of] where to go. Instead of all over the place they knew to go to the red beach and that's where you land, which was good.

"The Navy dropped us off in the water chest high. Then we got out of the water. We had

eighty pounds of C2 to blow up the wall. We went up over the wall because there's sand up against the wall. Then we blew up some obstacles on the beach. We caught a couple of prisoners right then and there and we turned them over to the prison stockade that was there. We wore our blue stripes across our helmet. We had orders not to take any orders from anybody unless they had a blue stripe, which was a pleasure and a half because you could tell people what to do."

David Troyer and his company mates from 3207th Quartermaster Company landed in an LCM at the same time as the 531st ESR to assist on the beach. Having witnessed so much of the loss of Quartermaster Corps equipment and men in *Exercise Tiger*, Troyer was very familiar with lessons learned from that tragedy.

"For D-Day some of the changes that were made...they never had a full company on a single ship. The 3207, for D-Day, was on two different ships. One of the things that happened for *Exercise Tiger*, when these ships were hit, it knocked the PA system out and they had no way of getting word down in the holds to evacuate. So for D-Day on my ship there were five ship runners. They were four officers and I was the only PFC. We had to learn the ship from one end to the other without going up on deck in case the ship was hit.

"We had a certain hold we was responsible to evacuate, and I just happened to have the hold that my platoon was in, part of the 4th Division infantry. We set up on deck outside the ship's captain's office. We seen everything...heard and seen everything from the very start. We heard the planes go over, the paratroopers go over at midnight. At 0300, we started going overboard to small landing craft and they circled out there until 0630, when we all started heading for the beach.

*LCVPs and other landing craft come ashore in
this aerial view of the assault landing at Utah
Beach on June 6, 1944.*

"I went in, going in the first wave, the 531st Engineers, beachhead engineers, and part of our company acted as MPs, directing heavy equipment. They had blowed a hole in the seawall, the main inland road on Utah Beach. That road today is named Daniel Road after one of my comrades. He was killed there and the road behind the seawall was named Oly Road, after one of the 531st Engineers. We got about halfway from the water's edge to the seawall and German 88's opened up on us and our lieutenant called us in, told us to make a run for the seawall. We was behind the seawall for a while until things quieted down just a little bit. We dug in behind the seawall, just got our fox holes dug…they had ordered us to move down the beach and inland. They had landed…the navy had landed us about 200 [2,000] yards from where we was supposed to land and we went down the beach.

"And leaving the area…I was one of the last ones, my section one of the last sections to leave the area…determined 88s opened up and just blistered the area we had vacated. I had went about 15 yards and got thrown on the ground, my legs spread wide apart. I took a piece of shrapnel, size of my double fist. I had it between my legs. An inch or two either way, it would have got me, but I felt the heat from it. I laid there long enough that that shrapnel cooled off and I carried that piece of shrapnel in my duffel bag for about a year before I threw it away."

The actual landing location did place all units out of position to reach their first inland objectives, so improvisation came into play at Utah Beach as it did at Omaha. But the light opposition to the landing allowed units to reorganize and move out together. The initiative was taken by assistant division commander Brigadier General Theodore Roosevelt Jr., who personally reconnoitered new routes to the causeways leading over the flooded back beach. For his June 6, 1944 efforts Roosevelt was awarded the Distinguished Service Cross (DSC), later upgraded to the Medal of Honor (MOH).

The 2nd and 3rd battalions of the 8th Infantry Regiment moved along roads on the left toward Pouppeville and Ste.-Marie-du-Mont. They were supported by tanks of the 70th Tank Battalion. The 1st Battalion was to advance in the center through Audouville la Hubert toward Ste.-Mère-Église. The other two battalions of the 22nd Regiment, landing at H plus 85 minutes, were to join the 3rd Battalion advancing north. The 12th Regiment coming in at H plus 4 hours was to advance in the center and seize the high ground west of the Merderet River. All units were to be on the lookout for their airborne comrades. On Utah Beach the armored units were able to advance inland over the causeways which the paratroopers had secured. One of these was the 65th Armored Field Artillery Battalion, the unit in which Pete Chavez drove an M-7 self-propelled howitzer.

"We landed in the first wave, you know, on Utah. It was right there at Ste.-Marie-du-Mont or somethin' like that. [They actually assembled a few miles north at La Houssaye]. We were tryin' to get to Carentan so we could join with the 101st you know. They jumped there and we were taking it by land and we were supposed to meet 'em there."

North of Ste.-Marie-du-Mont, batteries of the 191st Artillery Regiment of the 91st German Air Landing Division were sited inland of the flooded area. Earlier in the morning they tangled with the 101st. Later in the day they fought with the 3rd Battalion of the 8th Regiment as they advanced west. German soldier Joseph Horn was a 21-year-old telephone lineman who managed to elude capture for several

Jeeps and trucks head for shore at Utah Beach aboard a Landing Craft, Tank. The Jeeps are equipped for traveling partially submerged with a large pipe to the air intake and waterproofing of the gearbox.

days in the vicinity of Ste.-Marie-du-Mont. He remembers the activity that began after midnight on June 6 through the advance of the Americans from Utah Beach.

"On Monday evening, June the 5th, I remember I was allowed to eat from 10:00 o'clock until midnight. It was shortly after midnight that I heard the sound of very low-flying American airplanes, perhaps 200 meters high. I saw parachutes coming down. Some were white, some were blue, and some were camouflage. I was given orders to take a position and hold there. In the days before, I was laying wire for three hours walking in several directions.

"The area I was in was not under water, but most of the area around the town was a bit under water. Sometimes under the moonlight, I could see the American soldiers running, and once in awhile I could hear a clicking sound from time to time but I didn't know until much later what that was [he was hearing the U. S. paratroopers' cricket clickers].

"The American Navy ships were firing into positions all around us, and I remember my friend was in the top of a church tower that was hit. He was spotting for the artillery while the steeple was hit."

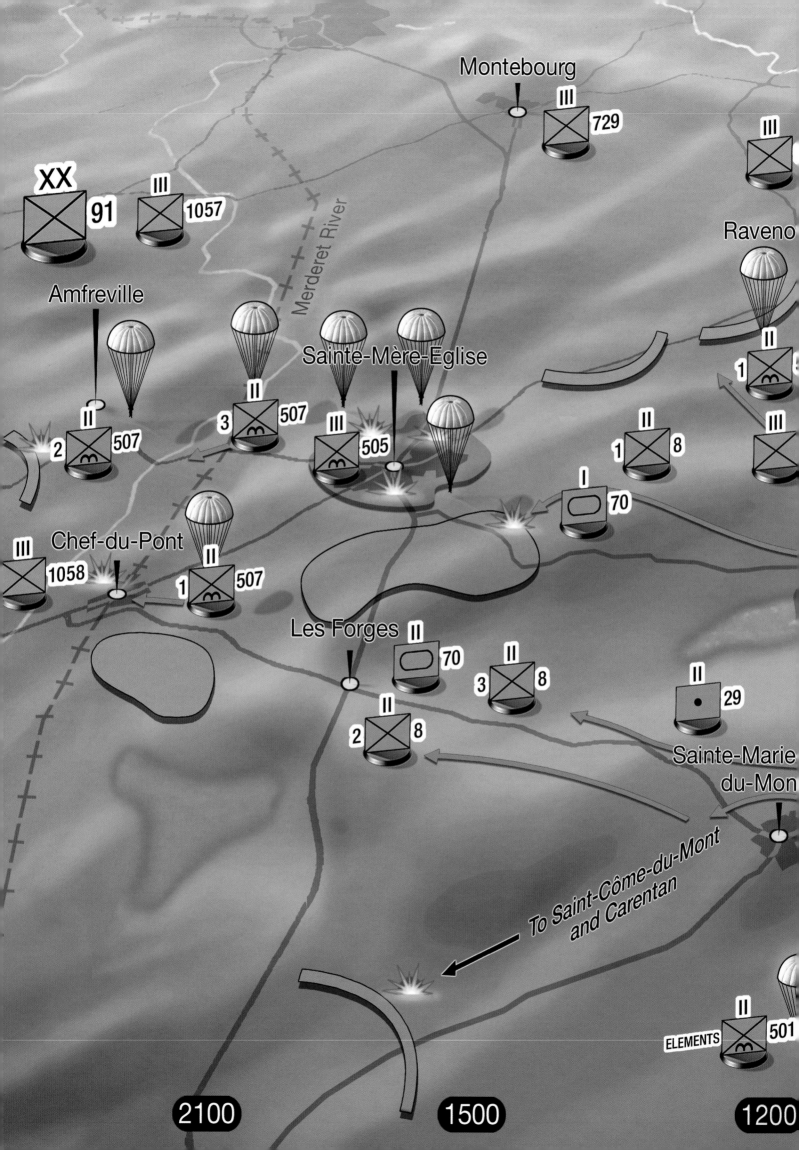

Montebourg

III 729

XX 91

III 1057

Merderet River

Amfreville

Raveno

Sainte-Mère-Eglise

II 2 507

3 507

III 505

II 1 8

I 70

Chef-du-Pont

III 1058

II 1 507

Les Forges

II 70

II 3 8

II 29

2 8

Sainte-Marie
du-Mon

To Saint-Côme-du-Mont
and Carentan

II
ELEMENTS 501

2100

1500

1200

uinéville

At Utah Beach three regiments of the 4th Infantry Division landed with much less resistance than their comrades at Omaha Beach. The timeline shows the rapid progress inland of the columns of infantry from the 8th, 12th and 22nd Regiments and their supporting units, despite having to negotiate flooded backwaters and minefields. However, scattered drops and skirmishes fought by men of the 101st and 82nd Airborne Divisions kept beachhead exits from being secured and several pockets of strong German resistance (gray shapes) prevented the linking of airborne and ground units.

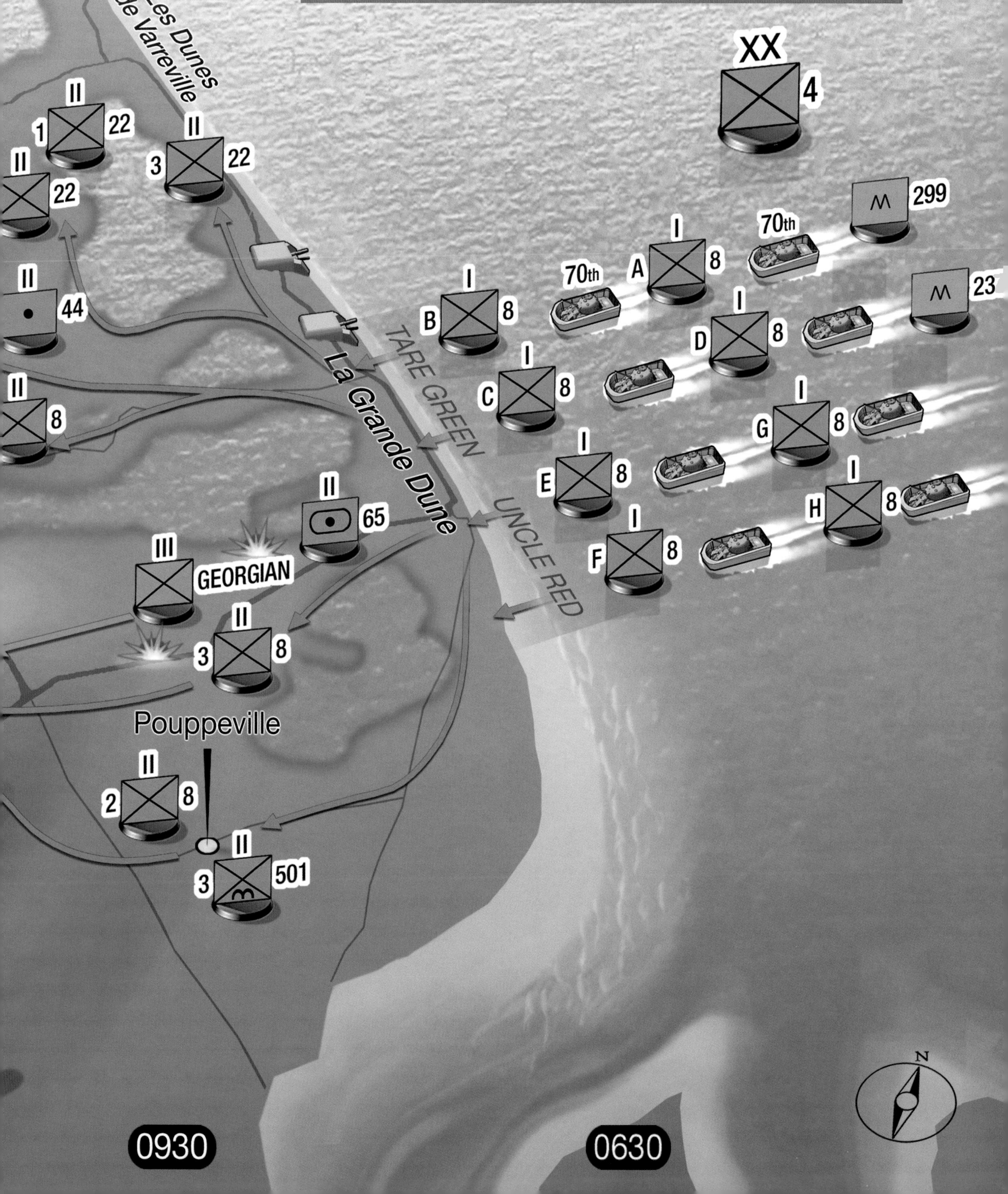

Fort de Saint-Marcouf

Les Dunes de Varreville

XX 4

1 II 22

3 II 22

II 22

299

70th

II 44

70th A I 8

B I 8

C I 8

D I 8

23

II 8

E I 8

G I 8

TARE GREEN

F I 8

H I 8

La Grande Dune

UNCLE RED

II 65

GEORGIAN

3 II 8

Pouppeville

2 II 8

3 II 501

N

0930

0630

Despite shelling from the 191st and other concealed German artillery units inland, the buildup on Utah Beach continued close to schedule. J. J. Witmeyer, a non-commissioned officer commanding a platoon in the 12th Regiment, landed at H plus 4 hours.

"When we made the invasion and I landed at Utah Beach on June 6th, the general in charge of the five American invasion troops which were the 82nd and 101st Airborne, the 4th Division...and then he had [additional] troops at sea that were in reserve...he was from New Orleans. Never ever acknowledged by the city. His name was

A group of medics wade ashore at Utah Beach from a Landing Ship, Mechanized (LCM). Confused by the sand bars and dodging fire from shore batteries, some landing craft dropped their loads far off shore.

'Lightning Joe' Collins, and he was VII Corps Commander.

"Well they put us off [the transport to the LCVP], about ten miles out...we came down rope netting. And I had a platoon of forty men, and I kid about it because that thing's made out...the landing craft there is made out of three-quarter inch plywood. But they painted 'em grey like that ... [to make it] look like steel to us. So anyway it was about ten miles out and they circle around until they do whatever formation they needed and then headed for the beach.

"Well it was very rough because the storm was on at the time, and the ship I

was on would be up and the landing craft would be down. Couple of my guys fell from the net. Sometime the net would be all the way down into the boat, and the next time the bottom of the net'd be 3 or 4 feet in the air. The landing craft would rock sideways, go up and down and not in sync with the ship, which is a bigger thing and it, too, is moving.

"There's a damned ramp, when you put it up it's about 7 foot high. You can't see out past it. Well, you couldn't make yourself heard because the flat bottom boat slappin' was like thunder, and motor's running in the back. You couldn't even hear people speak."

American reinforcements arrive at low tide on Utah Beach. Among the debris on the beach after the D-Day assault were German "Beetle" tanks that were packed with explosives. However none of the remote-controlled devices detonated.

The 12th Regiment landed and headed inland. Neither it nor the 22nd Regiment would reach their objectives because once they passed over the causeways, which the paratroopers had secured, they were bogged down by natural marshes. The 12th did make contact with the 502nd PIR holding the northern flank of the 101st at St.-Germaine-de-Varreville.

"I spent the night with a paratrooper, I think his name was Ferguson," says Witmeyer. "And sometime during the night we observed some movement out between the beach and us. Didn't have any real idea of where we were. We knew we were in

France, but we had missed the landing site by about a mile. And we didn't yell out because everybody started firing, but we kept a couple of bushes in our sights until daybreak. And we thought sure as hell somebody [was] crawling up on us. It was kind of spooky anyway."

Nineteen-year-old Michael Campisano from Massachusetts was with the 4th Engineer Battalion, Company B. They followed the 12th Regiment off the beach through the center of the area established by the 8th and 22nd Regiments' lead elements. But they were not involved in engineering operations initially.

"Well when we hit the beach basically we were all what we call combat infantrymen, we weren't engineers. We acted as though...just like the army infantry did. Moved up as quickly as possible and then we met our first resistance. And from that point on for the first week we were nothing but infantrymen.

"We landed about 3 to 4 miles off target, but...the Germans were completely surprised. And...I say that because six or eight hours after we pushed them back...we saw the road leading to Ste.-Mère-Église laden with thousands of bicycles. That was the way they came down from Cherbourg, which was approximately 18 to 20 miles away...to meet us."

Unlike many of the units on Omaha Beach, most of those that landed on Utah Beach retained unit cohesion. Campisano discusses the make-up and organization of his unit which included heavy weapons.

"We carried our own weapons, M1s. We had .30 cal. air-cooled and .30 cal. water-cooled machine guns, and some BARs...basically infantry-type weapons. We had the regular divisional setup

where we had...each lieutenant had a platoon and...staff sergeant, and each squad had a sergeant and a corporal. I was a corporal. Their leadership was the key to our whole setup because they told us what to do. We were small individual brigades, so to speak, led by one officer who was led by a captain above him. And they gave us direction right on the beach. As soon as we landed, they took over, told us what to do and we moved forward."

Fred Purdy came in on D-Day with the deployment of signal corps men who were to establish long range radio communications with SHAEF in England. But that didn't happen right away, as Purdy explains.

"We couldn't understand why we were going to be on the beach in Normandy because our equipment that we used could not go with us. We had to go, and the equipment to follow. We went across and then invaded... you know, we were like a little pebble of sand in the big sand pile. That's how small you feel in a big group. We went in the second [wave], I believe, at Utah Beach. And it was quite an experience, with all the equipment, and all the soldiers, and ones that didn't make it...and the Germans that didn't and all...but they got us off the beach immediately.

"The first waves of the combat engineers had cleared a path, maybe several paths, but behind the barrier of the beach it was flooded. But there were walkways out of mounds of dirt across the flooded area, and the combat engineers had already cleared up the mines and so on, and we walked between the white tapes, back to the parallel loop. And we spent the first night in the field off the beach at Utah Beach. No real instance of combat, but a lot of shell fire.

"At that time, we had no real assignment, except to stay alive. We saw the first day in Normandy...we run into a guy from the 82nd Airborne who had jumped the night before. He was telling us his experience and that he had been captured and the German had rubbed a submachine gun on his gums, trying to get him to respond, 'so he could shoot me.' And he said, 'Then our group retook me and some more prisoners.' I asked him what happened to that German that rubbed his gums and he said, 'I don't think you want to know.'"

Another unit that arrived on Utah Beach during the late afternoon was the task force of 82nd Airborne Division infantrymen and tanks under the command of Colonel Edson D. Raff. Concerned about rendezvousing with the 82nd paratroopers at Ste.-Mère-Église and also clearing meadows in the area for the evening landing of gliders carrying men of the 325th Regiment, Raff pushed his force behind the advance of the 8th Regiment's 3rd Battalion toward les Forges. But northeast of les Forges, the 91st German Air Landing Division had a large stronghold on high ground blocking the road to Ste.-Mère-Église. Raff pressed the attack but it failed, leaving the seaborne and airborne wings of the division separated. The gliders came in on schedule at 2100 and were mauled by German fire and many of the aircraft that did land broke up in the constricted bocage meadows.

Except for failing to establish communication with the 82nd and stopping short of their D-Day objectives when the terrain and German defensive maneuvers halted their progress, the 4th Infantry Division and attached units had a reasonably successful day. Total casualties for the seaborne units were 200, a tenth of those suffered at Omaha Beach.

THE BRITISH AND COMMONWEALTH BEACHES

The success of the operations carried out by the British 6th Airborne Division on the extreme left flank of the invasion area set the tone for how things would go for the landings and the inland penetration of the British forces on June 6. It would be in succeeding days that a breakdown would occur in the invasion's eastern sector.

The beaches, designated Gold, Juno and Sword, from west to east, were separated by the Calvados reefs. These reefs also required careful consideration of the tides. The Eastern Naval Task force moved into the area and the warships pounded the coastal batteries for two full hours. Airplanes had laid down a smoke screen on the eastern flank of the task force because Sword Beach was in range of powerful German guns at Le Havre. Three German torpedo boats did venture out under orders from Admiral Krancke into the eastern part of the bay and launched torpedoes among task force ships. A Norwegian destroyer was sunk in the raid.

The landing troops of the British Second Army were unaffected by this event and loaded into their landing craft to motor over to the beaches, subdivided into sections as at the American beaches from west to east; "Jig" and "King," three sections each; "Mike," two sections, "Nan," three sections; and three sections of "Queen" at Sword Beach. The Second Army also landed seven commando forces, of 500-600 men, British and some French, to fan out quickly and capture key points away from the beaches such as Port-en-Bessin.

At 0725 June 6, as scheduled, one hour later than the American landings because of the tides, the initial assault units of the Second Army made landfall on the three beaches simultaneously. On the right, the British 50th Division came ashore east of Arromanches on the beach called Gold. They were able to land without much trouble even though tidal conditions prevented the timely clearing of beach obstacles. The only ferocious resistance to the British landings came at la Hamel on the west edge of Gold Beach, where the German 916th Regiment, 1st Battalion defenses resisted stubbornly.

To the left of the 50th Division, the Canadian 3rd Division landed on the beach designated as Juno in front of Courseulles. They also had an opportunity for moving lead units off the beach quickly, but beach congestion was a problem at Juno as well. The easternmost beach was Sword, near the mouth of the Orne River. The British 3rd Division landed on Sword in front of Lion-sur-Mer and Ouistreham. Part of this division then turned east to cross the Orne and link with the 6th Airborne. Harry G. Jones was a lieutenant in the 2nd Battalion, King's Shropshire Light Infantry. He led his platoon ashore in that 3rd Division landing.

"As we got closer to the beach a landing craft carrying tanks, which was following close behind, received a direct hit from a German shell. The ship burst into flames and began to sink. There was nothing we could do to help the crew diving over the side of the blazing ship to escape the flames and exploding ammunition. Our landing craft ground to a halt on the sloping sandy beach, and I gave orders to my platoon to disembark. The beach by this time was covered with knocked out vehicles, personal equipment and some dead bodies. The time was ten minutes past 10:00 o'clock, the 6th of June 1944.

"We had been issued waterproof trousers which, at the time, we thought was a good idea, but when I leapt off the landing craft, being only five feet and a half tall, the tide swamped my trousers and I had one hell of a struggle to get to the waterline. I waddled on to the wet sands, and my first action on Fortress Europe was not to fight German soldiers but to tear off those blasted trousers!"

The lack of serious opposition on the beaches, except on the extreme right where the German 916th soldiers contested the advance throughout the day, allowed the British and Canadian soldiers to move toward the high ground, a ridge called Périers Ridge. It was the next objective for the advance units. The left of the 50th Division was facing the 441 Ost [East] Battalion, the weakest unit in the German line of defense in the area. The Ost Battalion dissolved leaving the road to Bayeux undefended; but in the smoke and confusion of the battle, the gap was not noticed immediately by British commanders.

"We reached the southern perimeter of Hermanville," says Jones, "and I turned into an orchard with my platoon where we hurriedly dug shallow slit trenches with our entrenching tools to prevent casualties from enemy shell-fire. On previous briefings, we had been informed that Sherman tanks of the Staffordshire Yeomanry would join us in this assembly area, and the plan was that we should ride on these tanks and attempt to capture Caen on D-Day.

"Unfortunately, the tanks had great difficulty getting off the very congested beaches, and some were knocked out by German 88mm anti-tank guns firing from a ridge about 800 yards to the south of us. This ridge became well known as Périers Ridge. Enemy small arms and machine-gun fire was also coming at us from

the direction of the ridge, but we still waited impatiently for the arrival of the Staffords' tanks."

Les Davis was a tank commander in the Staffordshire Yeomanry, C Squadron on D-Day. He was just as glad to get off the beach and toward the firing as Jones was to see these tanks come up.

"We actually got on to the beach about 9:00 o'clock, I should think. The leading infantry by that time were off the beach itself, and dug in on the far side of the coast road, in a ditch. Our original idea had been that we would get off the

British soldiers approach Sword Beach on a landing craft. The impact of so many Allied craft off Normandy and in the Channel impressed Group Captain P. W. Stansfield of the RAF 2nd Tactical Air Force Photographic Wing. "So great was the procession of ships and craft in convoys crossing the Channel as far as the eye could see, that it was unnecessary for me to fly a compass course. I merely flew in the general direction of the convoys."

boat, and form up in a field the other side of the coast road. But the squadron commander immediately sent me off up the road to find [out] about this gun they were complaining about on the Périers Ridge, so I chased off there.

"We didn't know at the time who the infantry were...even when we were carrying them on the backs of our tanks, I haven't got a clue as to which regiment they were. They didn't have any [cap] badges; they had steel helmets on, without badges. We fed them, sometimes, but there wasn't time to socialize and ask who they

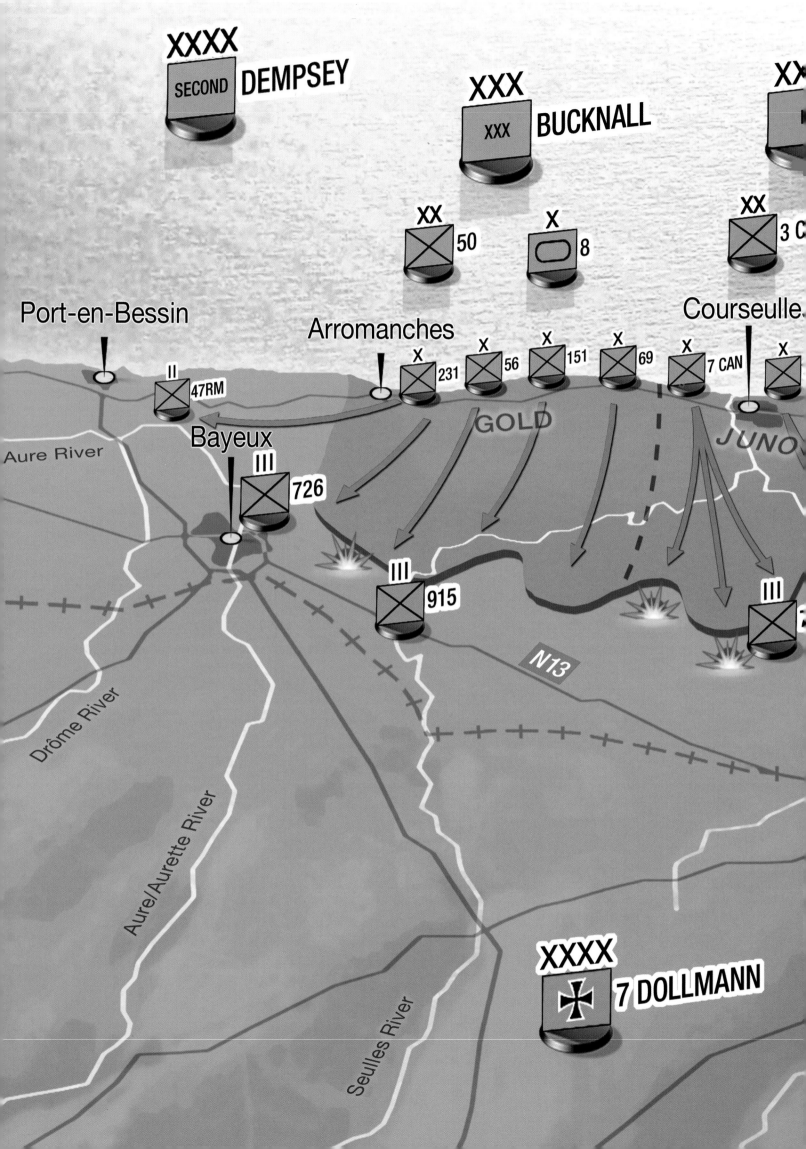

XXXX
SECOND DEMPSEY

XXX
XXX BUCKNALL

XX

XX
50

X
8

XX
3 C

Port-en-Bessin

Arromanches

Courseulle.

II
47RM

X
231

X
56

X
151

X
69

X
7 CAN

X

Bayeux

GOLD

JUNO

Aure River

III
726

III
915

III

III

N13

Drôme River

Aure/Aurette River

XXXX
7 DOLLMANN

Seulles River

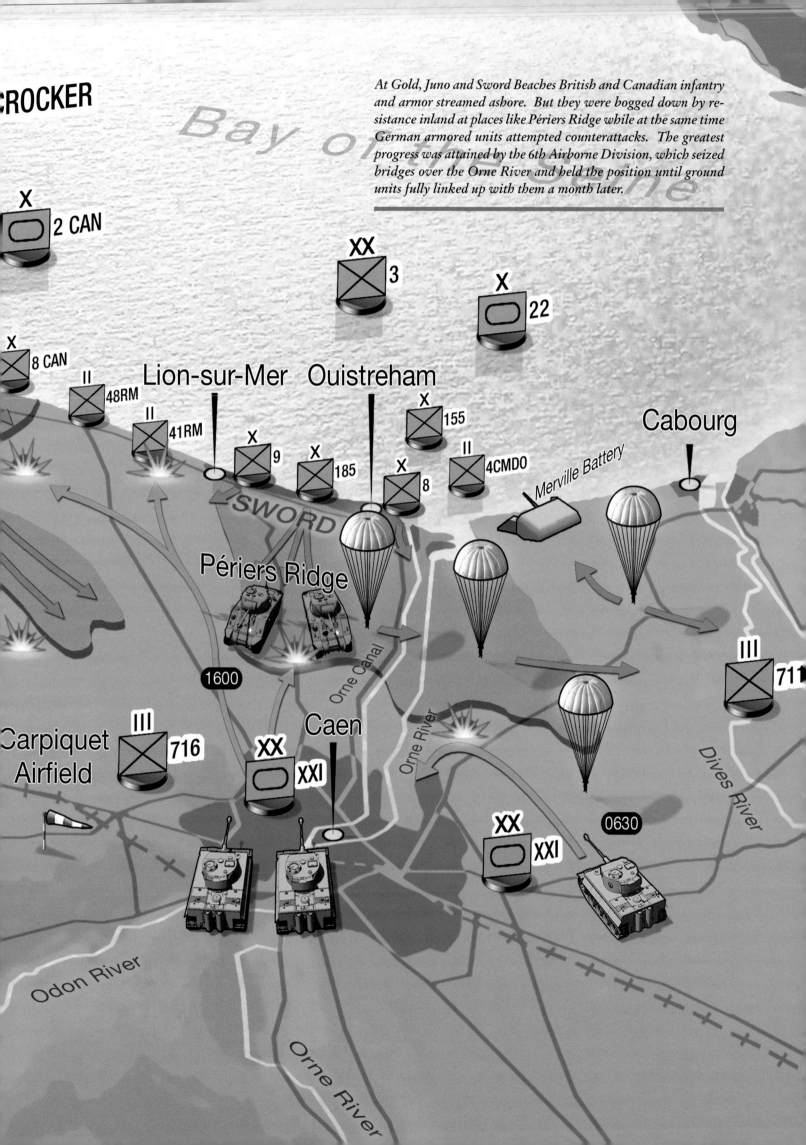

CROCKER

Bay of the Seine

At Gold, Juno and Sword Beaches British and Canadian infantry and armor streamed ashore. But they were bogged down by resistance inland at places like Périers Ridge while at the same time German armored units attempted counterattacks. The greatest progress was attained by the 6th Airborne Division, which seized bridges over the Orne River and held the position until ground units fully linked up with them a month later.

X 2 CAN

XX 3

X 22

X 8 CAN

II 48RM

Lion-sur-Mer

Ouistreham

II 41RM

X 9

X 185

X 155

Cabourg

X 8

II 4CMDO

Merville Battery

SWORD

Périers Ridge

Orne Canal

1600

III 711

Caen

Orne River

Dives River

Carpiquet Airfield

III 716

XX XXI

0630

XX XXI

were, what job they were on. At one time, we were supposed to be supporting the Highland Division, and I spoke to one of the soldiers, and said, 'Hullo, Jock', and he said, 'Who are you calling Jock, Brummie?' He was a Staffordshire bloke who'd ended up with the Scots…that happened a lot."

British soldiers storm ashore at Sword Beach on D-Day. A few infantrymen and paratroopers rendezvoused. R. G. Lloyd jumped with the 12th Regiment and landed among a small group in early morning hours. "We made our way in a small party across open country to our objective, where about 100 of our unit were already in position. Enemy opposition increased, and for a few hours we had a very hectic time. Shells passed overhead. This was HMS Warspite firing her big guns at targets well inland. We could hear the noise of the beach invasion. Daylight came. Yes! This was D-Day and I was in Normandy."

vicinity of the Vire River had them dispatched to that area in the morning. They had to return on foot if they couldn't commandeer bicycles or unreliable French trucks. The 915th Regiment returned just in time to plug the hole left by the pullout of the 441 Ost.

Some crack German soldiers, men in the 915th Regiment, were forced to counter march twenty miles after initial reports of paratroopers in the

The panzer division closest to the Allied beachhead was the 21st. Initially, the 21st was ordered to move to the Orne River to deal with the 6th Airborne paratroopers. However, after the sea

A Cromwell tank leads a column of the 22nd Armoured Brigade, 7th Armoured Division inland one day after their D-Day landing on Gold Beach.

invasion commenced they were rerouted to protect Caen. Moving up to the vicinity of Périers Ridge, they launched an attack against British tanks and infantry in the afternoon, but they were unsuccessful. Feeling unsure of their gains, however, British commanders halted short of two important objectives – Bayeux and Caen – on June 6. They felt better about tackling the subjugation of these cities in the morning. By that time, the new defensive line the Germans were struggling to create would be in place.

The moral conflict of war came quickly on D-Day to thousands of soldiers who had never fired a gun in anger. This anguish added to a myriad of other emotions the Allied ground troops were feeling on this pivotal day. A wonderful illustration of this comes from 18-year-old Canadian soldier Joe Womersley, who trained with the 1st Battalion of the Black Watch in Scotland. He was on a patrol on the front as Canadian forces advanced inland from Juno Beach on D-Day.

"I was then sent out to a regiment that was going to land in the invasion of Normandy, which I did. We had some trouble coming in. I lost my gun in deep water and picked another one up and used that. We fought quite a way up into the evening, and we ran into some stiff resistance.

"So my first personal experience was out behind German lines after crossing through a minefield, which every next step you're going to have your leg blown off. The night was cloudy, but every once in a while the moon would break through. Away we went, and we got maybe half a kilometer out and we got into the German lines. And the light...the moon came through the clouds, and I could see the silhouette out in front of me...a German soldier standing by a Tiger tank. My officer nodded at me. He just nodded. I'd been trained and knew what to do. I went around the back of this tank, and I had a knife and I jumped him from the back. I got the tip of my knife and I put it into his Adam's apple, not all the way. My officer came forward and...I was telling the guy to take it easy, he's not going to get killed.

"He started to struggle and I did it... so fast. I slit his throat. And he dropped down so fast. I was actually crying when I did this, because in my early days at school at the choir I used to listen to the Ten Commandments, and the one in there was, 'Thou shall not kill.' Anyway, I grabbed his coat, got his wallet, got everything. We headed back through this minefield to the headquarters where the company had their interpreters and their interrogators and stuff.

"I look at my hands and there's blood everywhere, down the tunic to the boots. I pulled this wallet out and his name was Günther Meyer, and he'd been at home on leave in Dresden. And this was about three weeks before D-Day. He had a picture of his wife and himself. His wife was holding... I would think a three-month-old baby, and a two or three-year-old boy on his knee. That particular occasion has been in my life forever."

THE END OF THE DAY

As darkness crept in on the late spring evening on the Normandy coast, the Allied commanders had to assess how the long and intense planning worked out on D-Day. The most serious problem as the day came to a close was the isolation of the 82nd Airborne Division in pockets along the Merderet River and the high casualties sustained in the division, especially among the glider troops. The paratroopers were in desperate battles around the bridges over the river and with Germans trying to retake Ste.-Mère-Église.

Tom Blakey finally found his way back to A Company and he and many others in the 505 PIR were in a battle to take and hold La Fière Bridge and the causeway leading to it west of Ste.-Mère-Église.

"If they [the Germans] could've got tanks across that bridge," says Blakey, "They could have interrupted the back of Utah Beach, that's why they wanted it so bad. If they could tear up the 4th Division...that would have been the end of Utah Beach."

Both 82nd Airborne Division commander Ridgway and assistant division commander Gavin were heavily involved in actions of their unit that day. Gavin was actually leading paratroopers in the intense actions at the bridges over the Merderet River. Dean McCandless was at the temporary command post of the 1st Battalion as the struggle along the Merderet continued throughout June 6.

"We took a lot of casualties. Keeler, my company commander, was POW. Kobos, my sergeant was also POW. Late in the day, our command post...we were getting mortar fire and artillery fire and we had runners coming and going back and forth to units. Only two officers left there, the adjutant and me, the communications officer. George Golden and I.

And we think they found out our damn compone [command post]…we better move this thing."

Wounded soldiers lie on the deck of a transport for their trip to hospitals in England. They were ferried from the beaches in small landing craft. As in other D-Day photos, unit patches were obscured by wartime censors.

Elsewhere, the Allied line was stabilizing, although few units had reached the hoped for end of the day objectives – the D-Day phase line, which was roughly along the Paris to Cherbourg highway through Caen, Bayeux, Carentan and Ste.-Mère-Église. The only large counterattack, by the 21st Panzer Division, was contained. But Caen and Bayeux, seemingly there for the taking, remained in German hands.

By the end of D-Day the Germans were digging in, bracing for further Allied advances, with most of their panzer divisions trying to sneak past Allied air cover. One desperate attempt to bomb Omaha Beach failed miserably as British and American ships used the four enemy Junkers bombers for target practice. Whether or not this June 6 invasion was *the* invasion or another was coming in the Somme River region, the LXXXIV Corps was going to need some help. And units were coming as fast as conditions on the ground would allow, from all over the OB West command. The invasion had begun; the shores of Normandy were breached, but France was not going to change hands without a great deal more fighting.

The Battle For La Fière Bridge

The situation inland from Utah Beach was one of the most challenging of all those faced by General Omar N. Bradley's U. S. First Army at the end of D-Day. Although one battalion of the 82nd Airborne had captured Ste.-Mère-Église, it and part of another battalion spent most of the day fighting off a German counterattack. The other scattered 82nd Airborne units failed to achieve their objectives; securing a bridgehead east and west of the Merderet River and north of the Douve, as well as linking with the flank of the 101st Airborne Division. Separated from the main force and west of the Merderet were part of the 2nd Battalion of the 507th PIR, isolated in a firefight at Amfreville, another group from the 507th nearby north of Gray Castle and much of the 508th PIR, clinging to a defensive position on Hill 30 north of the Douve.

Even though the German general in charge of one of the three divisions on the Cotentin Peninsula, Wilhelm Falley of the 91st Air Landing Division, was killed by American paratroopers D-Day morning as he returned from the scheduled war games in Rennes, his troops put up a continuous and spirited fight. At the center of this fight was La Fière Bridge over the Merderet. The bridge and another downstream at Pointe du Chef, both a few miles west of Ste.-Mère-Église, proved to be troublesome but necessary objectives. With intentionally flooded ground all around, these two bridges were the only exits from the Utah beachhead. As long as the Germans controlled them, the Americans were bottled up. At the close of D-Day neither bridge was secured. Lieutenant Dean McCandless found himself in the middle of the back and forth action there on June 6.

"[Lt. Col. Edward C.] Krause's battalion took Ste.-Mère-Église and we took the bridge. They knocked out a tank the minute they came in. Take out a tank, Germans come to try to get it, and they'd kill 'em. We took a lot of casualties. Late in the day, we were getting mortar fire and artillery fire. Here comes a GI walking up with an M1 thrown over his shoulder and we tell him to get down, he's gonna get his butt shot off. That was General Gavin. He said, 'You're doing fine. You achieved your objective, you're holding 'em just fine.' But we didn't have anywhere to go anyway. So we just dug in and stayed. Days later we could get there and get organized and ready to fight and then we had radios and equipment with us but those first two days we only took what we could carry by hand."

Paratrooper Tom Blakey was positioned with his company, Company A of the 505th PIR, in the vicinity of La Fière Bridge.

"A Company [1st Battalion, 505th PIR] was the lead team to get to the bridge. Most of them landed right where they should have been and they were almost on top of the bridge. Most of the A Company was there in force. They [men from the 507th] stayed with us, we wouldn't let them go any place. We needed men too badly."

La Fière Bridge was taken in the morning, but almost immediately lost to a German counterattack. The 1057th and 1058th Air Landing Regiments were squeezing in on the 82nd Airborne's positions from three sides.

In this photograph an 81mm mortar team of the 325th Glider Infantry stands by to add to the pre-attack bombardment for the June 9 assault on La Fière bridge and causeway.

"[The situation at the bridge...] chaotic will explain it, absolutely chaotic. That's one of the problems with the bridge, nobody knows exactly what happened, nobody knows exactly how many people were there. There was enough to do what we had to do, but that was all. There was a lot of killing going on in that area. We killed a lot of Germans, we killed those two tanks that they sent at us...the other one backed off and we never saw him again. That's what they wanted that bridge for because that bridge was the only bridge in the area that would hold tanks.

"Some of the fellows and me almost ran out of ammunition and one of the fellows came up with a Jeep load of ammunition for us. There was people out lookin' for gliders...taking what we could have used out of it. They got a Jeep from General Gavin...he and [General] Ridgway was a couple of miles apart. Ridgway was in Ste.-Mère-Église and Gavin was at the La Fière Bridge."

Assistant division commander Gavin was busy trying to supply enough men to hold one or both of these two Merderet crossings. But he lacked the manpower to hold the bridgehead. Meanwhile, Lieutenant Colonel Charles J. Timmes' 2nd Battalion of 507th PIR was holding an orchard halfway between La Fière Bridge and Amfreville after being repulsed from that town shortly after their landing. In a three company attempt to retake the bridge at noon a company under Captain F. V. Schwarzwalder rushed the bridge and causeway, then continued on to reinforce Timmes. But they could not secure their position all the way back to the bridge and became cut off as well. Lieutenant John Marr was in this group.

"We spent D-Day night and D plus 1 [day and] night in a perimeter defense, backed up against the water in what is now Timmes' Orchard, which is very near Amfreville and that was a place that was called the Gray Castle. It was an old French castle, and that happened to be the 91st German Division command post. We patrolled out...and of course we got repulsed by automatic weapons fire and some mortar fire on D plus 1. And D plus 2, Timmes sent me on a patrol at about 8:00 in the morning to go to the Gray Castle behind some tall trees and so on. We didn't really know what was over there, so we wanted to see what it was that we were getting the fire from.

"I was unsuccessful in my patrol and we threw up white phosphorus grenades to make a smoke screen. Went back and I reported to Timmes that nobody was going to go into that castle today through the fire that they were doing as we approached through the wooded area. And so then he said, 'Well, why don't you go across to the northeast and see what you see...if you can locate any friendly troops over there.' He wanted me to take a patrol and I requested that he just let me take my runner because we'd [be] more likely to make it across than [if] we had a bunch of soldiers. And he said, 'Okay, do it your way.'

"And so I took Carter, my runner, and we went out to the north. There was a road running out to the north of the Timmes' Orchard, to the water's edge. And we found out there was a [submerged] cobblestone road headed toward the railroad section house, which was on the far side of the water, about 1,200 yards away. So we just started following that road out there, broad daylight, and the Germans never took notice of us at all, never fired on us the entire trip. The head of the family that occupied the section house offered to take us up the river in his boat, which he guided with a long pole. He poled us up the river to the far side and to the treed area where the 325th Glider Infantry had landed and assembled on D plus 1.

"One of the battalion commanders of the regiment put us in a Jeep and headed up the road to deliver us to the division command post so that we could tell our story. And on the way to the division command post, we met [General] Ridgway coming our direction in his Jeep and I briefed General Ridgway as to what we were doing over there. We had no communication with the division during those three days that we were in there in Timmes' Orchard area. We had no radios, we had no wire, no way to really communicate with him, and we were trying to hold on to what ground we had in the area that we were assigned to establish an airhead line. The division didn't know where we were either.

"So Ridgway told the battalion commander to take us on to the division command post, which he did. And we briefed the division staff and they told us to go and take a rest. So we went out into the woods and took a much needed nap. And along toward evening one of the 82nd headquarters people came and got us

This photograph of the Merderet River from La Fière Bridge was taken by the U. S. Army's former chief historian, General S. L. A. Marshall. The idyllic scene Marshall captured looking north toward Neuville-au-Plain belies the bloody battle which had taken place on and around the bridge just a few weeks earlier.

out of the woods and said, 'Okay we got a plan, and we need your help.'"

The plan was for Marr to lead the 1st Battalion of the 325th Glider Infantry down the railroad and across the swamp on the sunken road he had discovered.

"Somewhere around... probably 9:30 or 10:00 by the time it was dark enough, the battalion and their vehicles went down the road, crossed over the railroad, went into Timmes' Orchard and the battalion commander met with Timmes and made a battle plan to attack the Germans from the rear, on the western approach of the causeway."

The glider battalion commander wanted a paratrooper who knew the area to accompany each of his companies. Marr went out with C Company to attack the churchyard overlooking the causeway. The Germans at the west end put up white sheets and began surrender talks while they maneuvered their weapons for enfilading fire. The glider troops were caught out in the open in fields.

"The enfilading fire took its toll," says Marr. "People were out in an oats field, and beyond in another field as well, adjacent field, to the right flank of our attack. And so there was a tremendous exchange of fire in there, and as daylight broke, the attack failed, but not before a soldier named DeGlopper, Charles DeGlopper, had gone on a rampage with his Browning Automatic Rifle. And he took out a lot of the defenders, and kept going until they finally killed him. He was the only guy to win the Congressional Medal of Honor in the Normandy operation with the 82nd Division.

"Now then, what happened next was, that having seen nobody out in this oats field...and the oats were about 3 feet high and getting ready for harvest...and I looked up toward the churchyard, and against the berm were two soldiers from C Company, and they were the wiremen who were laying the field wire along with the company as it advanced. So, I called over to where they were, and I said, 'Okay, we need to, we need to get us a withdrawal thing here.' I couldn't see any Germans. I couldn't see any glider people. So I decided that what we had to do was to crawl through that oats field, back toward the way we came. We'd be guided by the wire that they had laid up during the darkness hours. And they had an EE-8 radio telephone, and we were able to get communication back to the Timmes' Orchard.

"And so we started crawling, a little at a time, about three body-lengths, so that we would not be making big waves in the oats field to attract the Germans. So we did that all the way down this field, which was about 300 yards long, and then we started up a slope on the other side, and came back to the juncture of the hedgerow where we took an alternate course earlier in the night.

"What I did not know at that particular time was that the division had already, they had a backup plan to attack the Germans on the west side of the causeway, if the night attack had failed. The attack started at 10:00 [a.m. on June 9] but it was preceded by artillery fire from the 82nd Division Artillery and the 90th Division Artillery, and they fired many concentrations on the churchyard area where the German main defense was.

"The situation was desperate, and the division had to take action, and their action was to mount an attack across the causeway, and that attack was led by the [325th] gliders and a composite company of the 507 was placed in readiness at that point by General Gavin, who was on the eastern approach to the bridge on the causeway. And he had placed this composite company in readiness under Captain Bob Rae to attack forward...he was to go and push through to the other side. The battle [for La Fière Bridge] was, as S. L. A. Marshall said, 'was the fiercest battle in the European war.'"

Spurned on by the 82nd Airborne Division leadership and backed up by Rae's company from the 507th, elements of three companies of the 325th Glider Infantry crossed La Fière Bridge and established a bridgehead on the west side despite intense fire from German infantry, artillery and tanks. They even endured some friendly fire when American cannons fired into their positions in the village of le Motey. But they secured their position and, as enemy fire began to wilt, linked with Timmes and the 327th to the north and Captain Charles G. Shettle's outpost of 508th PIR men on Hill 30 to the south. The last of the important D-Day bridgehead missions of the airborne troops was finally accomplished, paving the way for the infantry to move into the far reaches of the Cotentin Peninsula.

Sam M. Gibbons was a Florida native who served for four years in the 101st Airborne Division and served his native state in the U. S. Congress for 34 years.

Jim Weller, in a photograph from 1943. He first enlisted in the Marines in 1938 but lied about his age and his mother had him brought back home. In 1942, when he was old enough, he volunteered for the army.

Garth Webb (center) and members of the 14th Royal Canadian Artillery pictured here on D-Day. Webb, of Midland, Ontario, Canada was a junior officer who landed at Juno Beach in command of a troop of M-7 mechanized guns.

Albert Piper is seen here in Vermont in 1939 during the early part of his army career. Piper penned song parodies to amuse his army buddies.

Brooklyn native Vincent "Mike" McKinney joined the peacetime army in 1940 and reported to Governor's Island, home of the 16th Infantry Regiment. He served in the Mediterranean before the 1st Infantry Division was assigned to *Operation Overlord*.

William Funkhouser was born in Ohio but grew up in the Shenandoah Valley of Virginia. He was assigned to the Big Red One (1st Infantry Division) and landed at Omaha Beach in the first wave on D-Day.

Ernst Floeter, seen here in 1944, volunteered for the regular German Army to avoid being drafted into the Schutzstaffel (SS) and began his service in the German Labor Force building the Autobahn.

CHAPTER 3

FIGHTING IN THE HEDGEROWS
BUILDING THE BRIDGEHEAD

n order to achieve *Operation Overlord*'s main objective – creating a secure Allied lodgment in France – things would have to continue to unfold in favor of the Allies. This included weather. By June 7, the window of favorable weather was still open, but changes were developing. This would affect the reinforcement of the ground units on the beaches and, significantly, the number of covering sorties flown by the Allied tactical air forces. Having been ordered to Normandy, German armor reinforcements were able to travel with greater speed when not harassed by enemy aircraft.

Since the Allies did not achieve their D-Day objectives, what were they doing about it on D plus 1? The V Corps, recovering from the hard fighting at Omaha Beach, had to deal with exhaustion and confusion among the assault regiments. On June 7, the majority of new objectives were assigned to later arriving battalions of the 115th, 175th, 18th and 26th Infantry Regiments. More critical was the lack of supplies – less than 5 percent of projected supplies arrived at Omaha Beach on D-Day – especially ammunition and beach obstacle clearance equipment, and there was a lack of vehicle parks off the beach to organize armor and mobility assets.

General Dwight D. Eisenhower, Lt. Gen. Omar N. Bradley, and Major General Joseph Lawton Collins meet at the Château de Francquetot, northwest of Carentan. In this region Lawton's VII Corps, along with the airborne divisions, fought hard to take Cherbourg and secure the Cotentin Peninsula.

Without solutions to these logistical problems, combat success would be extremely difficult.

But the combat troops forged ahead and on the right flank of the corps, the 18th and 26th Regiments crossed the Aure River and pressed the remaining elements of the German 352nd Division, reinforced with the 30th Mobile (bicycle) Regiment, into a decreasing amount of real estate in the Drôme River valley. At the same time, elements of the British 50th Division were closing in on the east. The British had already marched into Bayeux before noon on June 7 while the 47th Royal Marine Commando fought throughout the day and into June 8 to take Port-en-Bessin. The British and Canadian soldiers also cut the main road between Bayeux and Caen. Yet they could not complete the encirclement of Caen nor could they penetrate defenses north of the city. Colonel Goth observed the predicament of his German 916th Grenadiers in the middle of the 325th Division sector.

"By the evening of June the 6th the enemy had managed to open up breaches and reached the westernmost point of Vierville and the outskirts of St.-Laurent and Colleville. [On] June 7 the regiment stuck to its positions. We were threatened on two fronts; to the east, around Bayeux, by the British and to the west by the Americans. I was given permission to fall back southwards two or three kilometers during the night, a move that we were to repeat several times over the next six weeks."

U. S. 1st Infantry Division forces failed to break the German hold on the Drôme Valley through

June 8 and in hard fighting the Germans were able to extricate the trapped 726th Regiment. While this was counter to Hitler's direct orders not to yield any territory, the LXXXIV Corps commander, General Erich Marcks, concurred with the division commander that it would be better to save the soldiers to fight another day. That would become a familiar pattern in LXXXIV Corps tactics. By D plus 3 the Americans had made a junction with the British 50th Division west of Bayeux, but the area around Formigny was far from secure. Fields surrounded by hedgerows appeared as soon as the attacking forces arrived on the high ground and the terrain was a hindrance to continued progress.

General Leo Freiherr Geyr von Schweppenburg commanded the Panzers in the west until defeatist tactics angered Hitler.

On the western flank, the V Corps' forward progress was only a few miles from the beach. They were far from a juncture with the VII Corps, but a re-energized 116th Regiment, supported by tanks, pushed toward Pointe du Hoc and relief of the Rangers, whose numbers were dwindling. Naval gunfire kept the German 914th Regiment at bay in that area, but German artillery was slowing down the American column approaching from the east. At the same time, the 115th Regiment was opening up some space on the high ground to the south-

General Friedrich Dollmann and his Seventh Army were charged with containing the Allied breakout.

General Erich Marcks, commanded the LXXXIV Corps whose troops were on the front line in Normandy.

west, assisted by the 175th and artillery units that landed on D plus 1.

The VII Corps had not reached its D-Day objectives on the Cotentin Peninsula either. While progress on the afternoon of D-Day had been made clearing out beach resistance to the north of Utah Beach, it was not without cost. This progress was halted when the 22nd Regiment advance reached Battery Marcouf (Crisbecq) and Azeville, about a third of the way to Cherbourg. But they had the greatest advance of any of the VII Corps units in the first two days.

At the end of D-Day only a small patrol of the 82nd Airborne Division had reached the line of ground troops – the 8th Infantry Regiment line southeast of Ste.-Mère-Église. Plans were made for an attack on the morning of D plus 1. However, at the same time the Germans were renewing an attack of their own by the 1058th Regiment on Ste.-Mère-Église that was stalled on D-Day. Reinforced, the German attack proceeded east while the 8th Regiment and an armored and infantry task force moved north into the town. The VII Corps force split and enveloped the Germans between Ste.-Mère-Église and Neuville. When the 1058th came across the largest massed group of American armor to that point, about sixty tanks, they were intimidated into a retreat. The German commander then decided to form a de-

A damaged Sherman tank belonging to A Company of the 741st Tank Battalion is towed by an armored recovery vehicle through the streets of Colleville-sur-Mer on June 7.

fense line between Ste.-Mère-Église and Cherbourg to blunt any further American advance.

By this time, the rest of the 325th Glider Infantry arrived with little incident at their designated landing area near les Forges. Part of this force joined a battalion of the 505th PIR north of Ste.-Mère-Église, but the bulk of the 82nd was still stalled in its efforts to command the Merderet River crossings. The four-day battle continuing at la Fière Bridge and elsewhere along the river was delaying any movement directly to the west of Utah Beach.

On the southern flank of the VII Corps, the 101st paratroopers were still holding their positions along the Douve River, but were unable to make any progress due to isolation and lack of ammunition. They did, however, succeed in capturing nearly all of a battalion of the 6th Parachute Regiment who were advancing in an open field between the 501st and the 505th PIR. General Taylor organized a task force with tanks that made a modest advance toward St.-Côme-du-Mont, but that was the furthest southern penetration of the division on June 7.

Throughout this early fighting the naval guns in the Bay of the Seine were the best artillery support for U. S. First Army. Naval fire control parties ashore were adept at finding targets of opportunity and radioing coordinates to the war ships. The ships also launched spotter planes to find targets.

There were thousands of rounds expended in this support through June 11. One bombing mission by the battleship USS *Arkansas* knocked out a railroad bridge, a stretch of track, and the train that was occupying it.

While the naval artillery was devastating to targets inland as far as 15-20 miles, the sorties made by the Ninth Air Force and RAF Second Tactical Air Force were instrumental in preventing the much needed German reinforcements from moving to the Normandy fighting. Fritz Baresel was part of the reconnaissance force in the Panzer Lehr Division, one of the first panzer units called in to reinforce the coastal units. He talks about the difficulty of dealing with the Allied air attacks.

"The air superiority of the U. S. Air Force during and after the invasion was impressive and the hedges in Normandy didn't help to hide [us]. We were several times the recipients of carpet or saturation bombings...very scary, noisy and wondering what to do about it. Most bombing and strafing however was from P-38s, we called them 'Jabos' [Jagdbombers]. It forced us to move mainly at night."

The French Resistance also played a part in slowing down the German relief columns. There was little the Germans could do about these spontaneous sabotage incidents. Once the invasion began it was too late to track down and arrest FFI members. German air interdiction was also extremely limited. With only 815 aircraft in France and the Low Countries in June 1944, the Luftwaffe could do little to oppose the Allies in the air. Most sorties went after shipping in the Channel.

An American convoy rolls through the devastated city of Isigny on June 19. Although the city was not heavily contested when Americans first entered on June 8-9, naval bombardment had taken its toll on the Norman town.

ADVANCES EAST AND WEST

On the extreme eastern flank of the invasion, in the area held by the British 3rd Division and 6th Airborne, the 21st Panzer Division had some company. Having given up on the offensive to keep the British and American forces from linking up, the panzer division was pulled back into a defensive line north of Caen. Field Marshal Rundstedt then ordered the 12th SS Panzer Division and Panzer Lehr, then arriving in the area, to join the Seventh Army. He put Geyr von Schweppenburg in command of this reinforced armor group. The German leadership then sought to plug the gaps in the shredded 325th Division. A plan to drive a wedge through the British and Commonwealth forces and retake Courseulles was abandoned after too much time elapsed in creating a plan of action. German leaders then looked to stem the British breakthrough, perhaps even to retake Bayeux.

Meanwhile, Rommel, who had returned to France to direct the efforts of the Seventh Army, was concerned about the threat to Cherbourg. In order to prevent the Americans from completing their march across the base of the Cotentin Peninsula, he called up the 77th Division and 17th SS Panzer Grenadier Division from Brittany. A rumored American airborne landing at Coutances, some distance south of the peninsula base, fueled the decision. Rommel reasoned that the Allies were throwing everything into the Normandy invasion, so Brittany could be stripped of key units for the moment. Despite what was occurring in Normandy, Hitler and the OKW still believed a second invasion was coming.

With George S. Patton still in England, and the Allies keeping up an effective ruse that his massive army was assembling on the Channel coast, the German high command still believed an invasion was coming to the Kanalküste. Interestingly, two sets of American orders came into Rommel's hands during the first few days of the invasion that outlined American objectives including Cherbourg and St.-Lô. This information contained no orders for the British divisions, however, so this chance intelligence wasn't conclusive enough to change German strategy. To the most astute observers like General Dollmann and Field Marshal Rundstedt, it could have shown no second invasion was coming. Rommel was more concerned about local problems. A visual inspection by a top officer revealed no American airborne activity at Coutances, so Rommel diverted the II Parachute Corps to St.-Lô, which he most likely would have done even without knowing American intentions.

General Eisenhower, on June 7, toured the landing areas with Admiral Ramsey aboard HMS *Apollo*. Ike was concerned about the lack of progress in joining the two American corps of the First Army and expressed this to his top commanders. General Bradley ordered the 29th Infantry Division to move quickly on this linkup mission. The most pressing need in supplying the ground troops was ammunition. The supply effort was still running behind schedule; unloading on the beach was a slow process and the Mulberries, though started, would not be finished until June 16. Former New York railroad barges were pressed into service, hauling tons of ammunition across the Channel towed by LCIs. They came under the fire of a small but concerted Luftwaffe attack, but delivered the ammunition to Omaha Beach on time.

Since there was still a threat from the Luftwaffe, however weak the effort was, anti-aircraft guns were an important part of the equipment being brought ashore. And with the guns came one of the more interesting groups of specialty troops. Barrage balloons were part of the static defense in England. And with the invasion came a portable version of that defense. Bomb-equipped barrage balloons were floated above anti-aircraft and other guns for protection and in the First Army they were operated by the African-American barrage balloon battalions. William Dabney, from Virginia, followed his brothers into the army as a volunteer. After basic training he and many other black recruits were trained at Camp Tyson, Tennessee specifically in handling the barrage balloons. Trained in England in combat procedures as well, he landed on Omaha Beach on D-Day.

"Well, when we first hit the beach we was being aware of the mines and every-thing. There was still guns going off on the ships out in the English Channel and they was shootin' from the hills so the first thing we did was take cover. I lost my balloon. I carried a balloon with me on the beach, it was attached to me, with a bomb on it and of course it got shot out from under me.

"I was a crew chief. Two guys went in with me…they was right behind me when we went in. We didn't have a certain place to set the balloons up, but we had to wait to get some more equipment in. And our job, as we hit the beach, was to guard those 90mm anti-aircraft guns. My site was right under a camouflaged 90mm…my foxhole…and we would send those balloons up at night when our aircraft stopped patrolling in the daytime. We would

German armored infantry vehicles, camouflaged to escape air interdiction, gather in a Normandy village for a counterattack on Allied forces in June 1944. At right is an SdKfz 251 halftrack which served a variety of transportation and weapons carrier functions.

have our radios, we would know exactly when to send our balloons up when they stopped patrolling during the day."

In pursuit of the SHAEF order to close the gap between the two American corps, 29th Infantry Division leaders ordered forward the fresh 175th Regiment on D plus 1. They were to rapidly advance toward Isigny and cross the Vire River to meet with the 101st Airborne, which was ordered to the same location. On the flanks of the 175th, the other two 29th Infantry Division regiments were ordered to clean out remaining pockets of resistance.

On the night of June 7, the 175th Regiment started out for Isigny, preceded by tanks of the

Sergeant Curtis Cullen of the 102nd Cavalry Reconnaissance Battalion developed these steel cutting teeth to deal with the size and depth of Normandy hedgerows. Shown here welded to the front of an M5A1 Stuart light tank, they were made from German beach obstacles. They aided movement of armored vehicles through the hedgerow country and prevented their undercarriages from being exposed to fire while attempting to mount the natural obstacles.

747th Tank Battalion. In about 24 hours the town was taken and the German 352nd Division was forced to fall back to protect its left flank. To the 175th's right, the 116th Regiment and the remainder of the 2nd and 5th Ranger Battalions broke through and relieved the besieged Rangers at Pointe du Hoc. They then continued west to clear out remaining pockets of resistance along the coast. This was necessary because in independent actions small groups and individual German soldiers were still shelling and firing on Omaha Beach. The 115th advanced to the Aure River, securing the entire high ground between the river and the beach.

In order to effect the junction of the corps, the 101st Airborne, including the 327th Glider Infantry that arrived by sea, needed to take Carentan on the way. Rommel considered Carentan a key strategic city and ordered reinforcements from the 17th SS Panzer Grenadier Division and II Parachute Corps there. The 101st advanced south from the positions held north of the Douve with tanks and the 65th Armored Field Artillery. Standing in their way was St.-Côme-du-Mont defended by the 1058th Regiment. The glider infantry got bogged down in the hedgerows east of the town while the 65th fired 1,500 high explosive rounds into the town. Pete Chavez, M-7 driver in the 65th Armored Field Artillery, describes maneuvering his armored vehicle through hedgerow country.

"Oh, that was murder. But we'd get behind 'em…the Germans were on the other side. That was as good cover for us as it was for them, but I guess they had the advantage over us. And finally, we had some tanks, you know, that somebody rigged a kind of a fork in front of 'em, and we could push them hedgerows, make a path or somethin' through there, you know. I don't know who they belonged to, most of them. The ones that had them forks. Somebody else furnished them, you know. [Like maybe the] armored division that was there."

The constant pressure from several sides caused St.-Côme-du-Mont to fall on June 8, but Major F. A. F. von der Heydte managed to extricate most of his force and regroup them for the defense of Carentan. The American units proceeded south in a broad front, the 327th on the east. The 502nd PIR attempted to enter Carentan over the causeway but the going was tough. The 3rd Battalion commander, Lieutenant Colonel Robert G. Cole, led an inspired charge across the last causeway bridge where enemy strong points were grouped around a farm house. But this attack bogged down as did the advance on the east

by the 327th. The paratroopers settled into a kind of siege of Carentan and warded off several German counterattacks. Artillery, including naval guns, hammered the city. In Carentan, Heydte's men were running short of ammunition. With Americans at every turn, the first German air resupply mission of the Normandy campaign was carried out on the night of June 11-12.

While this was going on, part of the 327th crossed the Douve east of Carentan and on June 10 affected a rendezvous with a recon company from the 175th Regiment. This was the first meeting between the two American corps. Impatient for progress, First Army brought in more units and placed the mission under Brigadier General Anthony McAuliffe. To the east, V Corps units guarded the eastern flank of the operation. Just after midnight on June 12 the attack was renewed. A battalion of the 502nd moved in from the southwest about 0200, and the glider infantrymen entered from the other direction about the same time. They found few Germans to take prisoner. Major Heydte had accomplished another evacuation the evening before and created a new defense line southwest of the city.

The Americans discovered this as General Taylor ordered the 101st to probe to the southwest. They were to meet a portion of the 82nd Airborne, which was finally in control of the Merderet River and moving south and west from the river. Paratroopers like Tom Blakey were glad to be finished with the difficult battles to secure the Merderet River crossings and were ready to move on to the next challenge.

"Most of us went back to Ste.-Mère-Église and got into a battalion formation. We went south and then across the peninsula. We crossed from Ste.-Mère-Église to a little town called Saint-

Sauveur-le-Vicomte. There was a lot of fighting going on between those two places, between Ste.-Mère-Église and Saint-Sauveur-le-Vicomte...it wasn't a picnic. Of course there was bridges to take there also. [The problem of hedgerows]...that developed immediately. [Fighting in the hedgerows] wasn't easy by a long shot...they were very easy to defend but they were hard to take.

"We had a couple of country boys, farm boys, and the good thing about them is they knew a little bit about cows. We'd go to a hedgerow and look out into the field and if the cows were laying down, chewing their cud and peaceful, the chances are there are no Germans around. If the cows are up moving around and mooing, chances are somebody was there. If they were up moving around with huge udder bags full of milk it was because they hurt. When a cow gets her bag full and nobody milks it they hurt.

"So they ought to be milked and we milked them, and drank a lot of warm milk. A couple of us could milk but everybody can't help...just pulling on one of those teats doesn't get milk you have to know how to do it. Milking a cow is similar to riding a bicycle, you learn it and you never forget it."

The 101st was not making forward progress southwest of Carentan. On the morning of June 13, the 17th SS Panzer Grenadier Division counterattacked from Heydte's line and drove the paratroopers back nearly into Carentan. It took the help of an armored task force (that had been formed the day before to move southeast of Carentan) to stabilize the situation.

A 155mm howitzer of the 345th Field Artillery Battalion is shown participating in the bombardment that preceded taking the La Fière causeway on June 9.

Omaha Beach, called St.-Laurent-sur-Mer Port once it was secured, became the major entry point for equipment, supplies and newly arriving Allied units. A number of LSTs are parked at low tide while a few LCTs have come in further and wait the high tide to exit. In the foreground vehicles stack up on the beach while out on the water are anchored the transport and supply ships which crossed the Channel.

East of Carentan, soldiers of both U. S. corps were engaged in fighting for control of the Vire River and its crossings. The junction of the two corps existed, but it was not very strong or deep. Another entire corps, the XIX, was arriving to reinforce this area. Far to the east, the British and Canadians were facing a strong defense north and west of Caen, so progress in that area slowed to a crawl. But in the center, the American V Corps was on the verge of making significant progress heading south into the stretch of Normandy terrain called the Forêt de Cerisy.

On the beaches, the buildup of men was taking place while the initial invaders were advancing inland. More than 100,000 GIs were put ashore in the first three days. On the fourth day, Buster Simmons landed with the 105th Medical Detachment, a unit of the 120th Infantry Regiment attached to the 30th Infantry Division. He remembers the time waiting off Omaha Beach to land.

"On the morning of the 7th I was off the coast of France, sitting on this boat waiting my turn and that took a while. Time ran together out there...day was night and night was day. We were just there watching a few German airplane pilots...if they got off the ground and into the air they were dead, because our guys got them. They'd make a dive bomb rush at us and we felt sure that he had our nose marked on the end of that bomb...it came down and spread out, hitting on each side of the boat. We got through that mess, finally got out of there and went to the coast of France to a little place called Isigny."

The Bay of the Seine and the Channel on the French side were continuously patrolled by the smaller naval warships of the task forces – destroyers, destroyer escorts, PT boats and British patrol craft – on the alert for enemy surface ships, U-boats and aircraft. Anti-aircraft guns, fighter patrols and the barrage balloon battalions were at work to insure nothing disturbed the debarkation of the troops or the unloading of vehicles and supplies. A problem was that the LSTs took 10-12 hours to unload on the beach. By June 16, Mulberry "A" was operational at Omaha Beach, and the LST unloading time was whittled down to a 64 minute average. In the first two days, eleven LSTs were unloaded at the artificial port.

It was crucial that the buildup of soldiers, equipment and supplies keep pace with the advances made by the forces already ashore because more of those 58 German divisions in France were beginning to make their way to the front. Despite the constant threat of air attack, and the destruction of bridges and rail lines leading to Normandy, the panzer divisions and other German reinforcements made it to Normandy. The armored counterattacks that had weighed heavily in *Operation Overlord* planning from the beginning were becoming a real threat because the Germans simply refused to give up France without a fight.

THE CAUMONT GAP

In order to expand out of the beachhead area and keep a flank aligned with the advances being made around the city of Caen by the British and Canadians, U. S. First Army had new orders for V Corps. In conjunction with the newly-arrived 2nd Infantry Division, the 1st and 29th Infantry Divisions would head due south toward the Forêt de Cerisy. This heavily wooded high ground was a longtime objective in *Overlord* plans because it was perceived to be a location from which the enemy could launch a counterattack. The 2nd Infantry Division moved in between the two

D-Day divisions and the operation was launched from the Aure River vicinity on June 9. The advance was to be conducted by two of the three regiments in each division with supporting units. Always conscious of the possibility of a German counterattack slipping past the front line toward the beach area, First Army ordered the third regiment in each division kept in reserve.

The 1st Infantry Division regiments were able to reach their phase lines (a level of operational objectives) with little resistance by nightfall. The 29th, with an echeloned advance tying into the 1st's right flank on the Vire River had, except for one battalion, little trouble reaching its objectives on the north bank of the Elle River. The flanks of the German line were giving way. However in the cen-

ter, the 2nd Infantry Division, missing much of its heavy equipment which was waiting to be unloaded, had a rough time beginning its advance. What was left of the German 352nd Division was fighting to hold Trévières. However, by the next morning, Trévières was empty as the 352nd had pulled back to a new line south of the Elle River. This put them conveniently to the west of the 29th Infantry Division and therefore a major skirmish along their line did not develop in the next few days of the American advance. The 1st Infantry Division arrived astride the St.-Lô/Bayeux highway and the 2nd Infantry Division was south and west of the Forêt de Cerisy by end of day, June 10.

A British Sherman Firefly tank, a variation of the M-4, travels on a dirt road in Normandy. Despite having three armored divisions available, General Montgomery was unable to advance his forces far inland in the first weeks after D-Day.

German leaders, including Rommel and Dollmann, were concerned because the 352nd withdrawal, cou-

pled with Panzer Lehr's engagement with the British 7th Armoured Division southeast of Bayeux, opened a hole in the German defense line some ten miles wide south of the St.-Lô/Bayeux highway and Forêt de Cerisy. This was why the 2nd Infantry Division – able to rapidly move south with the German evacuation of Trévières – only found stragglers when they passed through the wooded highlands. With alarming situations developing south of Cherbourg, around Carentan and in the Vire and Taute river basins there was little to be done to rectify this situation. But the German leaders agreed someone must occupy the gap and so Rommel granted his subordinate commanders permission to send the 3rd Parachute Division and the 17th SS Panzer Grenadier Division to this "Caumont Gap." The 3rd Parachute was still arriving from Brittany. And while the 17th SS had units southwest of Carentan, much of the division's armor was still making a slow trip to the front. As a result, only the reconnaissance battalion of the division was able to arrive in this area north of Caumont by June 9. Other German units from Brittany, including the 353rd Division, were also ordered north. At the same time, a counterattack in the British sector was

These Panther tanks of the Panzer Lehr Division are preparing to counterattack the British landing beaches on June 6. They did not enter the fight that day but in the next several weeks they were at the heart of German resistance to the British Second Army.

planned on the evening of June 10 with parts of the 12th SS and 21st Panzer Divisions to relieve some pressure on the Caen defense line; but this was cancelled when the British stepped up their effort against Panzer Lehr and the 12th Panzer Division. The organizer of this operation, General Geyr von Schweppenburg, was critically injured and most of his staff killed when Allied fighter-bombers struck his headquarters that same day. Though control was passed to Seventh Army, German armored operations suffered from the results of this attack.

When the 1st Infantry Division probed south toward Balleroy on June 10 and took prisoners from the German reconnaissance unit, it was perceived by Allied intelligence officers that perhaps they had come across the leading edge of the massed armor counterattack that planners had predicted would come by D plus 3. This caused much consternation in what to do, so the advance stopped for two days while intelligence was sorted out and units were refitted. By June 12 the three division front was ready to move and the 1st Infantry Division was given the most ambitious assignment, to push directly south and drive a wedge through this suspected gap in the German line.

Panzer Lehr had bested the British 7th Armoured Division in a battle at Tilly-sur-Seulles on June 10 and 11. It was hoped the U. S. 1st Infantry Division could clear a path for the British 7th Armoured to move around Panzer Lehr and south of Caen. However, the 1st Infantry Division advance was also ordered to proceed with a dose of caution. Once reaching each phase line, the regiments would have to receive headquarters approval to go further. The other two divisions on the right would advance in an echelon back to the Vire. It was hoped the entire operation would also force the Germans to take some of their attention away from the VII Corps advance on Cherbourg.

The 1st Infantry Division advance moved rapidly and patrols were probing the village of Caumont by nightfall. Here momentum changed rapidly. Elements of the 2nd Panzer Division were arriving on the field and contested the 1st Division gains. Originally moving forward to conform to the "Big Red One's" flank, the British 7th Armoured Division became isolated when their countrymen in the 50th Infantry Division did not close up. The British 7th was challenged by armor of the arriving 2nd Panzers and had to pull

This German Panzer IV Ausf G was among the most prevalent tanks in the Wehrmacht armored forces available to General Geyr von Schweppenburg to oppose the Allied advance.

back to a river line defense northeast of Caumont. Its flank exposed, the American 1st Infantry Division had to dig in around Caumont. The best opportunity for a Normandy breakout up to that time, during the second week of June, was shut down.

In the center and left, the slightly more modest objectives of the U. S. 2nd and 29th Infantry Divisions were not being met. As regiments of the 2nd advanced down the St.-Lô/Bayeux highway they were challenged by the crack infantrymen of the 3rd Parachute Division. A rise called Hill 192, despite being pounded by artillery and fighter-bombers, continued to hold up the 2nd Infantry Division regiments. To the right of the 2nd Infantry Division, the 29th Infantry Division regiments ran into the fire of the German line along the Elle River north of St.-Lô. General Bradley decided to call off these attacks on June 13. More divisions were arriving and making their way to the front and he wanted the XIX Corps to take up the western part of the line where the V Corps held only a weak connection with the 101st Airborne in the area of the Vire-Taure Canal. One of the new units, the 30th Infantry Division, took over part of the responsibility from the 29th

on the left flank. The first regiment of the 30th to see combat was the 120th Infantry Regiment.

Second Lieutenant Frank Towers was a "ninety-day wonder" from Vermont. After serving 14 months as an instructor at Camp Wheeler, Georgia, he was assigned to the 120th Infantry Regiment. The regiment arrived in England in February, 1944 and came ashore in France on D plus 5. Towers talks about the differences he and his comrades found between their training and fighting the German army in France.

Burned and damaged houses in Caumont. The German defenses here were razor thin when the 1st Infantry Division probed the area in mid-June but the opportunity for an Allied breakthrough was not exploited.

"Actually on the 15th of June we had our first contact with the enemy and we were in combat for 185 days thereafter. The early days of combat we found to be severely different from the training we got when we were in England. A bullet would go overhead or strike someone and it was a live bullet...we had been training with blank bullets...and we realized if a bullet struck a man, he was dead or seriously wounded and it was kind of a traumatic shock to us.

"Another one of the things we encountered was the hedgerows at Normandy. We heard about hedgerows but we had no idea what they were, really. We had seen some in England, they are very small and low, perhaps one foot high, but hedgerows in Normandy were 6 to 10 feet high and 10 to 12 feet thick at the base. We were prepared for tank warfare, or at least support...the tanks would go merrily rolling along across the fields. This was not so because the hedgerows were small fields of about 100 feet by 100 feet...or 100 feet by 200 feet, that was a big field. Our fighting in Normandy was from hedgerow to hedgerow, 100 yards at a time and it was very slow. We got way behind our schedule, the anticipated schedule they [U. S. commanders] had made.

"We got down to the area of St.-Lô and the 29th Division was attempting to get in and capture St.-Lô which was a critical communication center for railroads. The 29th Division had tried for several days to get into St.-Lô, and had failed because the Germans had control of the high ground which was surrounding St.-Lô. It was our mission to clear out the high ground to the west of St.-Lô and after a few days we did that."

The action Towers described was on the western flank of the line running from northwest to southeast parallel to the German line. After the

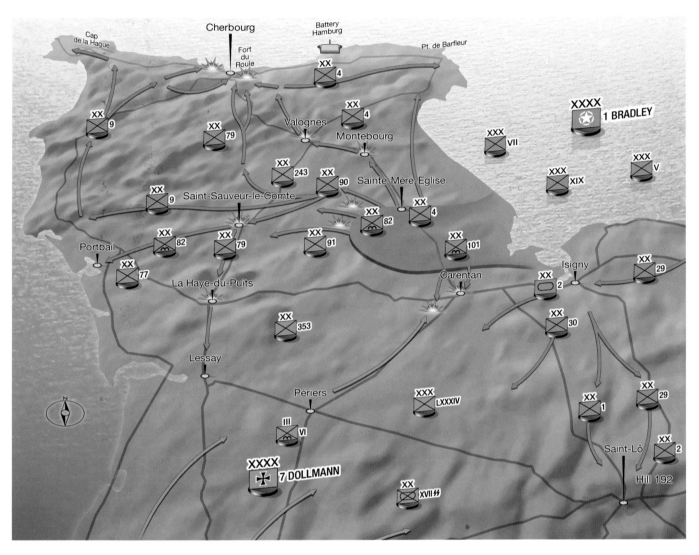

attack by the 120th Regiment on June 15, the regiments of the 29th and 2nd Infantry Divisions began a three-day attack across the hedgerows and hills surrounding St.-Lô. The 1st Infantry Division held firm at the salient in Caumont. Even though they were short of forces nearly everywhere, the Germans used terrain and determination to battle the American regiments all along the line. The only significant accomplishment by

The U. S. Army VII Corps was responsible for taking Cherbourg and cleaning out the Cotentin Peninsula with the assistance of the 82nd and 101st Airborne Divisions. Field Marshal Erwin Rommel could not bring units from Brittany and elsewhere fast enough to stem the tide in the many battles fought on the peninsula. Hitler and Rundstedt were still unwilling to empty the Pas de Calais area of troops, believing a second invasion could still come there. Meanwhile the U. S. V Corps and the newly-arrived XIX Corps became bogged down by German defenders in the area around St.-Lô.

the V Corps in the three days of battle was the taking of Hill 192 by the 38th Regiment. Like the Army of the Potomac in front of Richmond in 1862, the First Army could see the steeples of St.-Lô five miles away, but couldn't get to them. The action in this sector would settle into a defensive stalemate through the end of the month while things heated up on the Cotentin Peninsula.

TAKING CHERBOURG

The VII Corps' main task after establishing the Utah beachhead was to cut off the Cotentin Peninsula in order to isolate and then capture the port of Cherbourg. The desperate fighting along the Merderet River was indicative of much of the rest of the fighting on the peninsula, punctuated by periods of rapid advance. While the 4th Infantry Division, accompanied by the 505th PIR, moved north, with the first objective a series of artillery emplacements between the Merderet River and the coast, another force that included the 325th Glider Infantry and 507th PIR headed west to seal off the peninsula.

Soldiers of the 82nd Airborne Division take cover in a ditch outside Saint-Sauveur-le-Vicomte on June 16. After five days of fighting against stiff but decreasing opposition from the German 91st Air Landing Division, the paratroopers reached the line of the Douve River, the last water obstacle before the west coast of the Cotentin Peninsula, by noon.

First up for the 4th Infantry Division were the artillery strongholds at Azeville and Crisbecq that had turned away the division on D-Day, followed by another line of artillery and infantry east and west of Montebourg and extending to Quinéville on the bay. Here the German units that had unsuccessfully attempted to counterattack at Ste.-Mère-Église dug in around standing artillery forts. Shutting down the big guns in this region was urgent because they could still lob shells into Utah Beach. Beginning on the June 8 and continuing for eleven days the 8th, 12th and 22nd Infantry Regiments fought determined resistance.

Between the Merderet and the Douve River, as paratrooper Blakey of the 505th PIR indicated,

In Saint-Sauveur-le-Vicomte, a paratrooper carrying the tripod for a .30-caliber light machine gun sprints across a street. A disabled American 57mm anti-tank gun sits in the foreground.

the going was slow and bloody. The hedgerows made convenient and formidable natural earthworks. The 82nd Airborne Division paratroopers were joined by 90th Infantry Division soldiers, recently arrived. The 90th was going to be the first American division in *Operation Overlord* to have a command overhaul because of incompetence.

The attack of two regiments of the 90th (the unit's 359th Regiment was in the 4th Infantry Division group to the north) began on June 10 and got off to a very bad start. The 357th Regiment ran into a sturdy defense put up by the German 1057th Regiment just west of the Merderet. On the left, the 358th Regiment was struggling as well. While the 82nd Airborne Division units were progressing to secure the southern flank along the Douve,

the 90th struggled to advance – even when their third regiment was brought in from the north.

Small things were indicative of the 90th Infantry Division's lack of proper execution in what its men were trained for. Some of these were noted by Al Webber, the replacement infantryman who had distinguished himself as a marksman in training. His is a vivid recollection of his first days on the Cotentin Peninsula, and how he and a few others moved around, trying to take their place in the 90th Infantry Division's advance across the peninsula.

"Aboard ship coming over I was promoted. I was made a 'salty' corporal and I was assigned to direct finger exercises and other more martial exercises on deck to a squad of men. This squad, we sort of stayed together and a lieutenant would occasionally visit. I was a 'salty' corporal on shore and I kept my eye on a handful of teenagers.

"We landed in Normandy on Sunday [June 11]. We could hear the sounds of war...it seemed all around us. You'd hear *rat-a-tat-tat,* sounding very close at hand and then you'd hear a sort of answering. There was no front line. So we just walked...we were told to stay on the road, don't go off. The Germans very kindly had driven that home with little signs that had a skull and cross-bones with 'Achtung! Minen'...mines along the edges. We finally got through the swampy area out into the notorious hedgerow country and we were told to pull off into a field and settle down with our K rations up against the hedgerow and get a meal...and if we could, get some sleep.

"Monday and Tuesday it was move here and then there and we just stopped at the front...our front which was the 90th Division, 358th Infantry. It moved forward a little and then we'd stop and they were too busy fighting to accept replacements at the time. It was very, very busy and the 90th took an awful beating. Unfortunately they had rather poor officers. I didn't know this at the time. I found out by reading about it they were not tactically and strategically [effective]...probably everything should have gone more smoothly than it did and the replacements should have gotten into the division more quickly.

"We didn't stop on into Tuesday. We walked past a field and there was a field hospital but we walked right past that. I remember the men talking about medics and they said when you get hit you'll be coming back to it. So I said 'Fine, take good care of it.' So we moved inch by inch and moved very close to the action but not in it. Tuesday night we ate early. We were de-trucked and were very close to a little town called Pont

l'Abbé and this was the division that the regiment was having a tough time taking.

"So, I led my squad...it was dark by this time...along a sidewalk and just again following the rear end of the last man in somebody else's squad...and suddenly all hell broke. This tremendous explosion about 15 feet up. The Jerries, I guess, had a lot of ammunition stored there... Everybody got flattened out. Nobody was hurt. And then, they must have been the 90th people said, 'Come on, come on, come on in here.'

"My squad and I think two other squads went into this building...I didn't know what it was...the basement and they said get some sleep so we bedded down and got some sleep. I woke up in the morning and something was crawling over me on top of me. I looked and it was a rabbit. God knows if they were pets of someone but there were about fifteen rabbits hopping around and snuggling up to the men because I think they were frightened. We had a 60[mm] mortar set up right outside us and they started getting active. And the Germans got into it and what I learned later on, the sound of the 88's...*zzzzinggg...wham!* And they were a very flat trajectory and we were low. They were hitting the upstairs of the building we were in pretty heavily but we were not in the line of fire.

"We were gathered together I think by a replacement officer who made himself known...very young. I don't think he was a day over twenty. And he told us we were in C Company, 358th Regiment of the 90th Division. He said it was Texas and Oklahoma National Guard, which didn't mean a hell of a lot to us...we were all New Englanders.

"We were told to be...'lock and load, lock and load'...be ready and do what you're told. 'Everybody follow me on the double,' and we ran out of our building which was now getting hit hard and over to another building where we spread ourselves along a wall. And we lay there, wondering what would happen next. The Jerries started looking...they were looking for us with mortars and you would hear *boom, boom,* and you'd cringe and *boom*...and it's gone. And they'd come back...same thing... and they did this for three hours and they never hit the building."

By June 13, VII Corps had had enough, the 90th Infantry Division commander and the unit's regimental commanders were replaced and the 9th Infantry Division was brought in to take over the lead. On June 14, a push past Pont l'Abbé was begun by the

505th PIR (relieving the 507th), 325th Glider Infantry and the 358th Regiment from the 90th. On June 15, as the assault moved slowly against the prepared defense, the paratroopers found a hole on the south and pushed into and beyond Saint-Sauveur-le-Vicomte.

"We're advancing, you know," says Dean McCandless, communications officer in the 505th PIR, "And we're goin' across there...there were paratroopers...troopers runnin' across the bridge with everybody shootin' at 'em like nothing was happening. But we were aggressive solders. I remember some of the ground troops were annoyed with us because we would charge ahead and outrun 'em. [And they'd say] 'You're gonna

A patrol in the streets of Saint-Sauveur-le-Vicomte on June 19. The Germans were already withdrawing from the city that day while Rommel tried to form a rear guard west of the Douve. He wanted to delay the American push westward long enough to get the 77th Division moved south to Haye du Puits in order to fight another day.

get out and get cut off, you're gonna get cut off.' And we said, 'Oh, come on, man. We start off cut off.' But it was our thing…if we could find a soft spot we'd rush through and get around behind 'em. And so we got across to Saint-Sauveur-le-Vicomte with ease, really. And then we fought a little ways up."

The 90th Infantry Division was still fighting with some sluggishness and was left behind to guard the right flank while the 9th Infantry Division moved west through light opposition and took Barneville-sur-Mer. Along with the 82nd Airborne, the 90th was soon reassigned to the new VIII Corps, which was charged with protecting the gained territory on

the Cotentin Peninsula while the VII Corps invested Cherbourg.

Trapped inside the encroaching VII Corps advance in the central Cotentin Peninsula was the German 1057th Regiment of the 91st Air Landing Division including telephone wireman Ernst Floeter.

"The Americans were sitting practically all over the place, and our division commander was killed the first day. And I had the impression it was complete chaos on both sides. So on the eighth we came to a place there where, like farm, we bunked in a storm building and somebody got hold of a message that the

---

Aerial view of Lockheed P-38Fs of the 38th Fighter Squadron. The fighter-bomber's twin fuselages allowed for extra gasoline storage for extended range. Failure to check Allied air supremacy cut off supplies and reinforcements and doomed Hitler's order to hold the Cotentin to the last man.

Americans are attacking next morning so we had to dig our first foxholes. And then the next morning I got ordered to frisk four or five Allied prisoners. I don't know whether they were Canadian or American, but they were all afraid and shaking. I felt sorry for these guys. I wish I could have spoken to them, then I could give a little more encouragement, but I hope they made it through.

"While doing this we had incoming fire from the American mortars, so we rush to our foxhole and to cover and then suddenly, in the background, the Germans are retreating. So somebody called out, 'Get out of here.' So I ran about 20 minutes, it was completely chaotic. After a while I looked around me, there were only strange people. And the rifle they gave me didn't work, for heaven's sake. So I had some hand grenades, that was about all that I had. Then I found a Luger pistol on a German soldier and I had this, at least something to defend myself. But I never shot anyone. And then, by good luck, I found my unit.

"And from then on, we retreated, stopped, dug our foxhole. Then we got mortar fire from morning until night. On the 11th I got wounded, I got a big piece of shrapnel in my back, but it was just a superficial [wound]. On the 13th of June we had to retreat at night. The Americans were shooting at us with strafers [fighter aircraft] and I got a piece of shrapnel right on my throat, and as I came to my senses I was all alone, and suddenly somebody grabbed me by my collar. And he turned me around and ran right into my unit. There was nobody around but my guardian angel. It's true [chuckle]. And somewhere around there on the 18th of June, we were a group of about 60 men and officers, all like a combination of all German outfits…infantry, artillery…just a group of stragglers."

On June 14, while the assignments were being shuffled within the units moving between the Merderet and the Douve rivers, Al Webber and his replacement squad was absorbed into a group sent to guard the flank of the advance where a bridge over the Merderet had been blown after the GIs crossed it.

"A man with a strong Texas accent said, 'My name's Pettigrew and I'm the platoon sergeant now. So what we're going to do is send a squad out. You guys are going to dig in our side of the bridge and keep your eyes open and if anything moves shoot it.' It was rather quiet. It seemed to me we were going away from the action. We walked out on a causeway again…it was the Merderet…and we started to dig into the iron-like clay. I was paired off with a fat fella named Tad, a Missourian. So we both dug away and then, nothing. All the action, the noise was back somewhere off to our right.

"Then suddenly out of the blue, *ratta-tat-tat*, just like the movies, down between us. Nobody got hit by the first [volley], somebody got hit by the second and the corporal, he got up on his knees with field glasses looking down this causeway…I guess it was a wooded area. And that must have disturbed the Jerries because they sent over the one that hit me. I suddenly felt wham, a tremendous blow on the side of my head. No pain, it just felt as if somebody took a sledge hammer wrapped it in a pillow and whacked me in the head. And a head wound you bleed, oh boy do you bleed. Here I am with gushing blood, and I said, 'Tad, see if my ear is still there, will you?' He said, 'Christ you'd better start praying, half your head is gone.' I said, 'Can you help me? Can you do any first aid? I'm not good at it.' And he tried to put a bandage on the half of my head that was still there. The lieutenant came over and he gave me a shot of morphine, but through all this I felt no pain whatsoever but it was strangely dream-like.

"A couple of the boys, must have been four of them, carried me out to, I think the same dark dungeon [where we met Pettigrew earlier]. I had some coffee there and one of [the medics] said, 'How old are you, son?' I said, "Nineteen, sir. Today's my birthday.' He didn't know whether to laugh or cry. He shook his head. I just lay there. Some other guys were coming in and I couldn't see if they were my buddies or not. A litter on a Jeep, back to the field hospital, and slap some more morphine into me. That evening I was on an LCT on my way back to England."

THE DEFENSE WEARS DOWN

Despite the criticisms of the effectiveness of the Atlantic Wall, the German defenses in Normandy were often very sophisticated and complete, on and off the beach. It was the garrisoning of these defenses that was the issue as June wore on. One of the last strong points before the outer defenses of Cherbourg was Valognes. It was on the direct road, N-13, from Paris; the highway that ran through such highly contested places as Montbourg, Ste.-Mère-Église and Carentan. At Valognes the VII Corp would be facing the fresh German 77th Division from Brittany rather than the war-weary 91st Air Landing and 6th Parachute divisions.

But even these fresh soldiers needed food, ammunition and fuel. General Dollmann put in a new request for air support, transportation and even reinforcements from the Fifteenth Army. He would receive none of these. Field Marshals Rommel and Rundstedt echoed in communication with the OKW the need for more support to face the very real Allied threat in Normandy. Instead, OB West received a visitor, Adolf Hitler, who came to Soissons, northeast of Paris, to meet with the West's senior commanders on June 17.

Rommel and Rundstedt wanted a shift in strategy in the West that would enable them to move units easily, giving up some territory while strengthening other areas. Hitler's answer was to insist that they not yield any ground and to issue commands to every unit to hold until the last man. However, Hitler did agree to rearrange things in other theaters so four new panzer divisions would be coming to France. With these, he urged the commanders to launch the ultimate counterattack that would set the Allies on their ear.

Though Rommel wanted the 77th Infantry Division withdrawn from the peninsula rather than be trapped in what he considered by now the inevitable fall of Cherbourg, Hitler denied his request; but confusion in orders allowed some of the 77th to escape down the west side coastal road while part of the division was caught. The 77th was not in Valognes, however, when General Barton's 4th Infantry Division probed the city on June 20. Only rubble remained there from previous bombings.

Cornered in the tightening hold the Americans had on the peninsula was Ernst Floeter. After days of moving away from the VII Corps ad-

---

Top: A Luftwaffe crew loads a torpedo and prepares to launch a Heinkel He 115. The HE 115 was the largest and most powerful twin-float seaplane in World War II and besides serving as a torpedo bomber it was used for mine laying and reconnaissance. Bottom: African American soldiers man a 155mm howitzer in Normandy. Although the black units were segregated, they performed most of the functions of other ground combat troops. They have been following the advance of the infantry and are establishing a new position on June 28.

vance, he and others in the 1057th were cornered in a field.

"We were all around St.-Sauveur, in that vicinity there, south of Cherbourg. Because the Americans, they cut already across the peninsula and we were inside the periphery. We were caught in a trap. So on the 18th our commander gave us the order to cover. As you know, the Normandy [region] is all criss-crossed with hedgerows. So I lay down there about noon and then in the evening somebody got me and said, 'The Americans are here.' So they surrounded us, and they shot over at us, they hollered at us. They could have killed us very easily, but they didn't do it.

"And so after a while, one of our lieutenants called out, 'Stand up and shoot.' Instead, somebody took out his towel and started to wave that white towel and out of the corner came the first GI. So I got up and my first impression, my first thought was, heaven thanks, no more rifle to build [clean, assemble]. So at least the first part of my wish came true that I became prisoner. So we were sitting in the long line there, and the officers, they kept to themselves. My impressions from the Americans who could not have been any better, they were fantastic. First they took care of our wounded, and then they took care of us, and then after a while somebody came and went through my pockets, and I had a little good-luck piece and he threw it on the ground and said something in French. He said, 'Vous-parlez Français?' 'Oui, monsieur.' So I asked him in French if he would be so kind and give it back to me the souvenir. He picked it up and put it in my pocket.

"So, after a while we had to turn around and walked about a half a mile into a ditch. There we stood with our hands on our heads, and by some stupid movement, my glasses slipped down and just could hold them with my teeth and I thought, 'Well, if I let my glasses go then they are gone…if I put glasses on by myself, I'm gone.' And a GI came back and put them on my nose. So another nice episode from the friendly soldiers. And then next day, we ended up on Omaha Beach. We came over the dunes. I saw down there the beehive of the landing point, and I thought, 'Any German that can think of victory is an idiot.' It was amazing."

General Collins was ready to order the VII Corps to attack Cherbourg's *Landfront* fortified line. He even had a captured copy of German LXXXIV Corps orders which gave a good idea of the plan for defending Cherbourg. A three-division front was formed with the 9th on the left, the 4th on the right and the latest addition to the American force on the peninsula, the 79th Infantry Division, in the center. J. J. Witmeyer received a battlefield commission from sergeant to lieutenant and was ready to lead his platoon as part of the attack.

"I was in the 79th Division. We took the 90th Division's place in the center of the line. On the 19th we started with heavy storms. On the 22nd we were on the outer defenses on the *Landfront* side of Cherbourg."

Those heavy storms were part of increasingly bad weather that developed during the Cotentin operation. It gave some credence to the reason the Third Air Fleet of the Luftwaffe gave as to

"Whale" pontoon runway sections of Mulberry "A" at St.-Laurent-sur-Mer are seen twisted and rendered useless by the storm of June 18-19. In the background stands one of the tall "Lobnitz" pierheads that anchors the seaward end of the runways. The destruction of the artificial pier forced a return to beaching LSTs for supply until other port facilities were secured elsewhere in Normandy.

why they couldn't put planes in the air. A greater reason was lack of landing fields. Some days American tactical air operations also had to be scrubbed. This was an unfortunate but also unavoidable part of the campaign, and it was not unexpected. However, on June 19, the day Collins three-division assault began, a real weather disaster struck.

The first big storm came out of the north to wreak havoc on Allied sea and port operations. Ironically, June 19 was also the day the Luftwaffe launched one of its largest bombing attacks, 113 sorties. Their effect was minimal compared to the damage done by the storm which did not end until June 22. More than 800 British and American naval craft were damaged or destroyed. The Omaha Mulberry was a complete loss and was not rebuilt. The British Mulberry was damaged. Supply operations at Omaha and Utah Beaches were suspended through the storm, with just a trickle of ammunition coming ashore. Even after the storm ended, Omaha Beach, the Allies principal "port" in June, and the sea lane in front of it were so covered in debris they needed a major clearing before normal unloading operations could resume. The situation increased the sense of urgency for taking the port at Cherbourg.

THE FALL OF CHERBOURG

General Collins was satisfied when the storm began to dissipate on June 21 and the three divisions had closed in around Cherbourg; the 9th Infantry Division worked through heavy fighting on the west side of the city and was poised at the inner defenses, the 79th Infantry Division fought up the N-13 highway from the south and the 4th Infantry Division bypassed a few coastal batteries to arrive on the east side. Collins issued a surrender demand that evening, in several languages to reflect the diverse nationality of the approximately 20,000 Axis soldiers in the city. General Karl-Wilhelm von Schlieben, who was commander of the German 709th Division and was in charge of the Cherbourg defense, allowed the ultimatum time to expire without comment. He did appeal directly to Hitler for reinforcements, pointing out the severe deficiencies of his situation. And although reinforcement by a parachute regiment from Brittany was considered, there were no planes available to drop them in the city and the harbor was closed.

On June 22 Allied medium and fighter-bombers launched an air attack on Cherbourg that was designed to demoralize the troops more than to destroy the city. There was a lot of fighter strafing involved. Fighter and dive bomber assistance continued as two U. S. infantry divisions arrived a mile from the city and began the assault on the inner defenses. The 4th Infantry Division was held back to guard the east flank. On June 25 the navy was called in to engage the naval guns of Cherbourg and the nearby coast. USS *Nevada* arrived from England with a task force of cruisers and destroyers to engage the Cherbourg guns while USS *Texas*, USS *Arkansas* and other Allied ships worked on Battery Hamburg to the east. Woodrow Derby was on *Nevada*.

"We went into Cherbourg harbor to knock out all the German guns there. The Germans had 15-inch guns and they really shot at us, the *Texas* and the *Arkansas* were the other old battleships that were there. We didn't get hit with a shell there but the *Texas*, I believe, was hit with one shell from those guns. We knocked them all out, and our troops went in there to unload all their supplies and everything."

The unloading would come much later. But the afternoon-long bombardment of these targets, directed by air and land spotters, had a positive effect on the ground campaign advance into the city. *Texas* did take a hit from Battery Hamburg that killed one man and damaged the superstructure and some of the supporting ships were damaged by the shore batteries. *Nevada* just had a near miss. The naval bombardment allowed the VII Corps soldiers to storm into the city on June 25. Building-to-building fighting took place over the next few days in the first battle of *Operation*

Fort du Roule was the principal land-facing fort the Germans used in defense of the city of Cherbourg. The multi-level fort was taken by members of the 314th Infantry Regiment of the 79th spurred on by acts of individual bravery and leadership.

Overlord in a large urban area. J. J. Witmeyer led his forty-man platoon into the city.

"When you go through a town, the people on the right side of the road are responsible for you on the left because if somebody's in the building, he can't fire at you. He gotta lean out the building…he doesn't do that…so the guy on this side looks this way and this way. And one of the first houses in the city of Cherbourg, I dashed in the house. As soon as I got inside there's two Germans sitting there on the floor, with their legs straight out, the rifles laying in their laps. I killed them the second time [because] they were both dead already. Somebody had dragged them in there, but you don't have time to analyze.

"I carried a .45 [cal.] Thompson [submachine gun] and you fired at peo-

ple…you had an M1 rifle, you fired at people and they fall down and we'd take credit for that. When you have to fire at somebody, three feet, two feet, a big difference between shooting somebody up close…when you see his ring, or his eyes or whatever. And unfortunately I had to do some of that."

Civilians mostly stayed hidden during the action, but Witmeyer had one encounter on the approach.

"I had one lady on the way to Cherbourg, she ran out screaming at me and pounding on my chest, because we were the first American troops she had seen. Moving up on the pillbox, and she grabbed me by the arm and pulled me inside and there was a kid about three years old…was dead

HMS Glasgow *(foreground) and USS* Quincy *fire on the Cherbourg seaside defenses from outside the harbor on June 25. They were part of an eighteen ship naval gunfire mission sent in support of advancing American land forces.*

on the bed, big artillery shell. What I'm trying to say is she hated America…she hated the war, you know. And in effect she was holding me responsible. I had nothing to do with the artillery round."

The key fort controlling the city defenses on the south was Fort du Roule. The top priority for the 79th Infantry Division was capturing this powerful bastion which had a large field of fire in front of it, impeding any advance into Cherbourg. Howard Proud was in charge of a wire team assigned to establish communication between various headquarters of the 79th. He recalls some of the dangers involved with establishing the telephone lines.

"There were many artillery shells and the German artillery was fierce. It was not like ours. Ours was a boom. Theirs was a crack. Whenever you went out with that wire you were in danger yourself of being shelled because it was a very active area. And you learned to preserve yourself. If you had a telephone wire and it had a short in it, you could communicate through the [other] wire and the ground [acting as electrical ground], and sometimes that worked."

The assault on Fort du Roule began on the morning of June 25, just hours before the naval bombardment began. The mission was assigned to the 2nd and 3rd Battalions of the 314th Infantry Regiment, while the 313th advanced into the flats southeast of the city. Initial "softening up" of the fort by P-47 fighter-bombers had little effect. Machine gun nests protected the fort and had to be taken by infantrymen who applied large doses of cunning and guts to the task. After a day-long fight the fort fell.

"Two of my guys got the Congressional Medal of Honor for combat there at Fort du Role," re-

calls Witmeyer proudly. "I have the French Legion of Honor, that's France's highest decoration.

"We took two more pillboxes, including the very last one on the beach. And then we were shelled by our destroyers, because people were having trouble taking the beaches in their sectors and they were calling for assistance. And I wasn't in the pillbox but five, ten minutes when it was shelled. Come to find out the navy was shelling it. And it's a frightening thing. I wasn't panicky, but you get a lot of rattle, a lot of vibration, you get a lot of dust flies. Pretty long story how we got out of that. I had some pretty good soldiers."

The fall of Fort du Roule started a capitulation of the port. Surrenders began on June 26 when Schlieben was surrounded in his underground bunker. Propaganda broadcasts all over the city brought out white flags from the garrison on June 27. By June 28 occupation forces entered the city. The harbor, destroyed as a last resort by Hitler's orders, was a complete mess with exploded facilities, sunken ships and other damage. Navy engineers assessed what could be done to rebuild it, but it would not be a rapid recovery. Although the first Allied ships were able to dock at Cherbourg by the end of July, the port was only restored to limited regular use by mid-August 1944 and by then it was too far from the Allied front lines.

American forces were sent to Cape Barfleur on the eastern tip of the Cotentin Peninsula, and Cape de la Hague, on the western tip where a garrison had to be subdued. Battery Hamburg and other strong points were taken under control. With the fighting ending in the Contentin Peninsula, attention focused on the line drawn in the sand across the base of the Normandy hedgerow country and what the Allies needed to do to cross it.

Top Left: A GI stares at a dead "last stand" German sniper in Cherbourg on June 27. *Top Right:* German defenders of Cherbourg, including Adm. Walter Hennecke (right) and Gen. Karl von Schlieben (hidden from view) surrender in front of an underground bunker on June 26. *Bottom:* An American patrol files between damaged buildings on a narrow Cherbourg street.

After the German withdrawal from Valognes an American Jeep and truck wind through debris in the destroyed city. The center of this key town was destroyed by Allied bombing and shelling as the VII Corps neared Cherbourg on June 24.

American Medical Teams In Normandy

During the cross-Channel invasion there were casualties, as in any other conflict. Those not killed instantly or captured fell into a number of categories of wounded, and medical treatment appropriate to the wounds was given by various types of medical providers. The most basic level of care was given by the individual soldier themselves, or their buddies or commanders, from basic first-aid and medicines the men carried. During the D-Day campaign, many of the sol-

Left: This watercolor captures the wonder and weariness of a typical American infantry medic in Normandy. ***Bottom:*** *Medics of the 4th Infantry Division administer to soldiers of the 8th Infantry Regiment on Utah Beach.*

diers on both sides were new to combat and the effect of weapons and shrapnel on the human body. Even if physically able to treat themselves, shock often incapacitated them. They relied on army medics or navy corpsmen to take care of them. Medic Charles Norman Shay shares his recollections of what happened the day after his harrowing experiences on D-Day.

"The next day, I continued on, and I eventually found my medical detachment that had already established a medical aid station, and I reported in.

Then I was eventually reunited with the F Company, what was left of F Company.

"We had a few days because we had to recuperate. [We] lost 40 or 50% of the strength of our platoons. They had to have replacements, and it was two or three days before we were able to…continue to move on. By that time, the backup troops that had landed after us had already continued on, had secured the beach…had secured the village that we were assigned to occupy, and that was where I found my medical detachment. I was assigned as a medical aide there. Once we had received replacements…infantry men as replacements…and were reorganized, we were moved by truck into our next position."

James Baker was from Harlem. He enlisted in the army in 1942 after having begun his college education. He liked medicine but did not have enough credits at the time to qualify for the army to send him to medical school. Of the choices of service branches offered to him, he chose to be a field medic. From the time he entered the southern states by train on a government voucher through his training in Abilene, Texas he endured constant episodes of discrimination as an African American. This even extended to the base in Texas where he learned to be a medic. In early 1944 he sailed on the *Queen Mary* to Scotland, then was sent to England with his unit, the 494th Port Battalion, in preparation to land on D plus 1.

"I was aboard the ship with other guys. I had gone down one level below the deck. And all of a sudden there was a *boom!* It was an explosion…we had hit an acoustic mine and the ladder that we used to go down from the deck level

A French woman looks on dejectedly as American medical personnel examine the legs of her young daughter at a field hospital on the Cotentin Peninsula.

down to the next level fell. We were down there in the dark. We didn't know what was happening, if we were sinking or what. And somebody got the ladder, put it back up and we came running out of there like rats out of a hole. Trying to get up on deck to find out what's going on.

"They started calling for medics. Now on board the ship, we were the medics for the 494th Port Battalion and we were all black. And most of the rest of the ship were white. But people started hollering for medics and they didn't care the color of your skin at that time. They just needed people…people down on the bottom level…where the trucks and tanks and things were. And some fellas had fallen down and we had to get those big flood lights to shine down there so guys could go down and bring up the wounded so that we could try to patch them up.

"And the very first guy that I was assigned to work with happened to be a white guy whose head had been decapitated…and…I used to not wear my dog tags like a lot of guys. But I didn't have this guy's dog tags and I didn't know who he was. Well here comes another fellow, he happened to be a sergeant, carrying the head of a soldier. And he was looking for a body and I was looking for a head. And at that point I started reaching in my pocket and pulled my dog tag out and started wearing it because that was the first warning. I was gonna wear my dog tags from then on."

Baker ended up landing in the Dog Red sector of Omaha Beach in a landing craft accompanying the bodies of some of the casualties from the mine explosion on his ship.

"I landed on Normandy beach carrying one end of a guy who had been killed. 'What are we to do with these bodies?' They said, 'Put them on the beach and another outfit will come along and pick them up.' And people hollering 'medic, medic,' all over the place and we were running from one person to another. And I remember there was an officer who had been shot in the knee and he was squirting blood. You know, you learn that if you can stop the bleeding, often you can save a life…whenever somebody got his guts shot up, or his head half off, you know you can't do anything for him so you just give him some morphine and let him die in peace.

"And I was working on this officer who was just squirting blood and he [chuckle], he said to me, 'I'd rather die than to have a nigger put his hands on me. Just leave me alone.'

"I said, 'Sir, one of us got a problem and it's not me.' And he wasn't in a position to do very much 'cause he was hurting. And the blood was squirting and I'm trying to stop the blood and he's sayin' leave him alone 'cause he'd rather die than have a black man touch him. And I was almost to the point to want to follow his orders [laugh]…there were so many other people hollering medic. And you just run from one guy to the other 'til you can try to get some control…as much as possible. And that happened for a few days while we were still pinned down. The Germans were still up on the hill firing down. They had land mines and machine guns and barbed wire and that kind of stuff to deter our advancement. But we finally pushed them back and we were there for a few days… moved up ourselves up to a little town called Vierville-sur-mer to a building and set up a clinic."

Beyond the front line care of the medics were the field hospitals at the battalion and regimental level. Both the Allies and the Germans were really on interior lines of supply in Normandy; that is they could both trace a direct route back to their home base. For the British and Americans, it was back across the Channel to England.

For the Germans, it was traveling the roads and railroads – which their dual enemies of the French Resistance and the Allied air forces made increasingly difficult – back to Germany. Therefore both sides quickly evacuated those who were not seriously wounded to standing hospitals in their home countries.

For those who were too seriously wounded to be sent to England or were on death's doorstep, the aid stations were the next step, followed by the field hospital. Surgical technician Eddie Sutton served in a First Army emergency surgical unit for those most seriously wounded on the battlefield.

"I made the invasion, D-Day, at Omaha Beach. The propeller sheared on our boat and we sit there waiting for somebody to pull us around. And a PT boat said they would come by and get us if we could catch the rope...or the tow. And we caught it and they pulled us to, I guess, the side of the front. We got off that boat that

night in an orchard, and we camped there for a few days. Our team wasn't together. See, we was in separate boats to get there, and we assembled after we got there.

"We had teams that did this on the field. And that included an anesthetist, two surgeons, and two enlisted men, and a nurse...a female nurse if we wasn't in danger of being shot. We were with the front line troops...behind them, not up at the front...but it could be any infantry, artillery, anti-aircraft, or those type of outfits. They strapped patients on Jeeps then and would transport them like that if they didn't have ambulances available.

"We didn't have a hospital. We had portable units, and we would set up in a building, just a surgical thing, but we would be between a field hospital and the front line somewhere. Six trucks, and our surgical unit was set up on a 6x6 truck, see...it had autoclave [a high-pressure steam sterilization machine]. Any type of a thing

Army surgeons and nurses perform an operation in a tent field hospital.

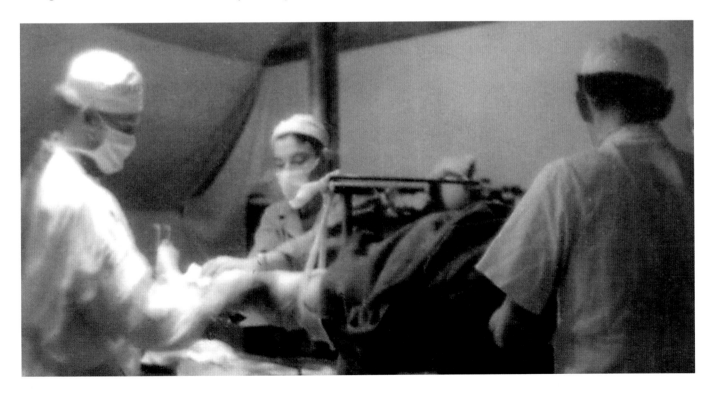

that you'd have in surgery at that time, we had it there. For sterilization, we had a very good sterilization program. We had alcohol in five-gallon containers, and we would sterilize our instruments with alcohol, and a lot of times, we could autoclave and that would sterilize your towels and sheets and what have you. If we couldn't get supplies, we had to do laundry. When the supplies came, we got sufficient supplies for a time.

"Most of the patients that we got never lived. We did surgery on them...hips blown off, legs, arms, bones, really, really damaged people. Severely damaged, but if they were able to be transported to a field hospital, we didn't do surgery.

"One guy, for instance, was from Tennessee and my major was from Tennessee and the guy said, 'Doc, I don't really care, but I've got two children and I'd like to go back to Tennessee and see them.' And that major stayed with that guy until he died,

about 30 hours. Things like that, you know, and it was touching, really touching. Yeah, if you wasn't careful, you'd get...it would get personal."

The U. S. Army Nurse Corps was very much in evidence in *Operation Overlord* and this included staffing field hospitals with female nurses. Muriel Kappler was a young Minnesotan who was interested in nursing and after graduating from a nursing school she and two friends felt the patriotic calling of joining the war effort. The three were assigned to different nursing units. Muriel went to Normandy. She remembers the trip across the Channel and landing at Utah Beach.

"Well, I'll tell you, I was very young and we really, I don't think any of us had any fear. And we, I know that night we slept where the nurses were, down the hatch, and there were just ships around us. All I remember was the planes above and the shooting and our getting off the ship and hav-

The 42nd Medical Battalion field hospital, where Muriel Kapler was a nurse, at its temporary location at Holy Mother Church outside of Ste.-Mère-Église.

ing to go down this rope ladder. And we were told to spread [out] as soon as possible, so that we were ten groups. And of course we had our back packs and gas masks, because they didn't know if gas would be used, or what. We just had our regular combat jackets [and a helmet] and of course we were in fatigues, that's what we wore all the time, you know, even in our tents when we were working. We never saw a white uniform, or anything like that.

"[We were the] 42nd Field Hospital [attached to the] First Army. We had three platoons, and we were completely separate except for administration. And then each platoon had six nurses, and we had three doctors and an administration officer and that was it. We had a chief nurse. And a dentist, but he went from place to place. We had many corpsmen and drivers, you know, ambulance drivers and supply people. A pharmacist who was, you know, a lay person.

"And I don't know if somebody came and…I know I have no idea how far we walked. It could have been half a mile, it could have been a mile. And we got to…it was the 82nd Airborne that had hit the beach there, [actually the 4th Infantry Division] I think, and so there were just bodies lying all over, and all we could do was help the medics who were already there. And they weren't from our unit, they were medics that had gone in with the airborne.

"[Triage] was all you could do, 'cause our equipment…we got separated from our men. They got off at Omaha Beach. It was a mix-up, and a lot of our equipment was lost. So I don't know when we finally…third or fourth day that we finally set up our first unit. I think it was St.-Marie-du-Mont.

"Well, we had the, you know, the men, had to set up the tents, of course. And there was a surgical

tent, and a shock tent, which I worked in. X-ray tent. And then one for the administration. They had the pharmacy. And then, in the middle of those four tents was the Red Cross. And then outside of it was where the men slept and we had our tent where the six nurses slept, and…so that was it [chuckle].

"We got them in, five, ten minutes off the line. That's where our mortality rate, they said, would be 95%, and it was only 5%. And we got all the cases that couldn't be taken, you know, back, 'cause all the others were shipped right back to England. And then we would…our unit…we moved with the lines, we could always hear our own gunfire. I worked in the shock tent and you poured in plasma, and blood, and got their blood pressure up to 100, and then they went into surgery. It was a surgical tent and the post-operative tent. [The shock tent doctor would diagnose] and decide when they should go in, into surgery.

"I think it was in our first place that we got a message from the Germans that we should move, because they were going to bomb it. And we got it at night, so we moved at 10:00 at night, 'cause we were near an ammunition dump. And they did bomb, and we did move. But at that time, they would stop, you know, shooting when they went over the Red Cross. But of course that didn't keep up very long either.

"The Germans that had been wounded, you know, they got exactly the same care as our men. But our men did not want us talking to them at all. They'd say, 'If you have a minute to talk, you talk to us.'"

These are just a few of the other heroes of the D-Day invasion and battle for France; the ones that save life instead of taking it away.

CHAPTER 4

BREAKOUT FROM NORMANDY
PLANS AND COUNTER PLANS

General Bernard Montgomery, assessing the situation in his 21st Army Group, was dissatisfied with the slow progress being made by British and Commonwealth forces in moving south and southeast of Caen. The Germans continued to check progress into the city on the north and west. True, because of its proximity to the Seine River and direct route to Paris, the British sector of the Allied Normandy front did receive the most attention from German resources; but other than some inconclusive drives southeast of Bayeux, no territory of consequence had been gained since D-Day.

On June 21, 1944, Montgomery notified units in the British sector that a push would be made southeast from Tilly-sur-Seulles with the venerable British VIII Corps in the lead. In his explanation of the drive, Montgomery indicated that it was important to do this to take pressure off the subjugation of Cherbourg. By all appearances, the American VII Corps was doing just fine on the Cotentin Peninsula without this maneuver, but for the British to break out of the German defenses in Normandy, it was necessary. However, the need to get the British VIII Corps positioned caused a delay in the start of the offensive.

This photograph captures a V-1 rocket in flight over London. "Buzz bomb" attacks began with ten V-1s launched on the night of June 12-13 and by the end of June 1944, about 1000 had reached the city, terrorizing civilian populations and damaging military assets in England.

On the other side of the line that ran from Caen and Tilly-sur-Seulles to Balleroy and the Elle River, the Germans were making plans as well. The promised six fresh German divisions were on their way and Hitler's counteroffensive to smash the Allied line was being worked out tactically. Geyr von Schweppenburg returned at the end of June and again was given command of Panzer Group West, to operate from the Drôme to the Orne rivers. Upon arrival of the fresh divisions – the 9th SS and 10th SS Panzer Divisions coming from the Eastern Front; the 2nd SS that had been only partially engaged; the 1st SS Panzer Division from Norway; and two infantry divisions from the south of France to take the place of Panzer Lehr and 21st Panzer Divisions – the plan was to launch a counterattack toward Bayeux to split the British XXX Corps and the American V Corps.

Transportation problems continued to weigh down German plans. So did a lack of artillery ammunition and the offensive was delayed. By the time things were ready, the British VIII Corps began its push southeast on June 25. The Allied offensive only gained about five miles against the German response with the Panzer Lehr Division in the lead. Once again, the need to plug holes in the line took German attention away from any offensive. Panzer Lehr had been fighting non-stop for three weeks and it was about spent.

"We saw some heavy fighting near St.-Lô, Bayeux, Argentan and Caen," says Fritz Baresel. "We hardly could move during daytime.

The Allied air force was everywhere. The reason for a reconnaissance force was to establish exact front lines and report to headquarters. We were not supposed to engage in battle, but to establish exact enemy positions you had to be close to the action. Unbeknownst to me, I was very close to my brother Hans with his U-boat in St.-Nazaire.

"One day we rolled on a side road at 90 degrees to a main road when we noticed a large tank column. As we got closer we realized they were English tanks and we beat a hasty retreat. Some of us turned around, but one particular vehicle tried to escape just by backing up...but they crashed through a hedge and didn't see the ground below. The vehicle turned over completely in the air and landed in the upright position, but the commander of this vehicle was dead under the tracks. Most likely he didn't even have time to jump to safety."

While Panzer Lehr Division and other engaged units waited for relief formations to arrive, the Allies continued to spoil the German plan. General Leonard T. Gerow, U. S. V Corps commander, moved the 3rd Armored Division on June 29 forward to drive back an enemy salient near the Vire. The Germans reacted, but the American armor then settled down into the line the next day. The six-division German offensive was watered down to two, and an ULTRA intercept read by Allied code-breakers allowed U. S. and British tactical air strikes to shut

The German Army continued to resist the Allied push out of the hedgerow lodgment area. Here two Mark V "Panther" tanks have been knocked out by American tank destroyers, a task always accomplished with great difficulty because they could not penetrate the front armor of the Mark V. Eisenhower asked Washington for better ordnance that would do the job.

A smiling Erwin Rommel is greeted by Adolf Hitler during one of their meetings in 1944. Rommel's sincere attempts to stave off the Allied advance through France were thwarted by decisions made by the Führer and the OKW. Rommel soon became doubtful of victory and sympathized with those plotting Hitler's elimination.

down the assault. In the meantime, Cherbourg fell, and an offensive Hitler considered in the west coastal region to drive north into the Cotentin Peninsula was also abandoned. Rundstedt wanted to concentrate the resources he now had into making a strong containment line across the Allied line of penetration inland from the invasion beaches.

Meanwhile, the Germans were not just losing soldiers, they were losing leaders. General Friedrich Dollmann died of a heart attack on June 28. Whether it was induced by the Führer's unreasonable expectations or the prospect of soon becoming a POW like Cherbourg's failed defender, General Karl-Wilhelm von Schlieben,

is unknown. On July 1, Rommel and Rundstedt attended a private meeting at Berchtesgaden with Hitler, and Field Marshal Wilhelm Keitel and General Alfred Jodl of OKW. The Fifteenth Army was still needed where it was, Hitler told the two western forces leaders, but some units would soon be dispatched to Normandy from the Kanalküste and elsewhere. The Führer was also willing to back off from launching any large counterattack in the West, but repeated the need to hold all territory to the last man. He believed the Allies could be worn down by attrition and new developments.

Among these new developments making Hitler optimistic were the V-1 flying bombs – which had begun striking London on June 12 – missile technology, and jet aircraft. Unspecified guerilla war tactics were also mentioned for use in the West. All of this was not significantly different from what previously had been announced and failed to fit the stark reality of the worsening situation. Rommel and Rundstedt returned to France without accomplishing anything except to deepen the lack of confidence they shared in Germany's Supreme Commander of the Armed Forces.

In this illustration American fighters down a German V-1 buzz bomb over England. Besides shooting down the rockets, a procedure called "tipping" was used in which the planes touched a wing against the V-1 wing to force it off course. Records show that 660 rockets were destroyed in the air.

When Rommel and Rundstedt, upon their return, made arrangements to withdraw German forces to a slightly compressed line – they did so *before* notifying OKW, which subsequently denied permission – the repercussions were swift. Rundstedt was presented the coveted Oak Leaves to his Knight's Cross by Hitler's adjutant, but the award was accompanied by a personal note from the Führer relieving Rundstedt of command. General Geyr von Schweppenburg was also sacked. Field Marshal Günther von Kluge replaced Rundstedt in command of OB West, but the mistrust of the leaders in the West would have ominous implications in the near future.

With Cherbourg captured, three of General Omar Bradley's American corps were freed to move to the west of Carentan to establish a breakout line. The VIII Corps led, moving south along the west peninsula road. It encountered resistance from the German II Parachute Corps. The 79th Infantry Division was in the VIII Corps van, and J. J. Witmeyer remembers an incident that stayed with him over the years.

"I'll tell you [about] the vengeful feeling. On about the 3rd of July outside of Haye-du-Puits…that was one of the sites expected to be used for the breakthrough 'cause there were crossroads and not much road junction. And a machine gun was tearing me up pretty good. I lost about fourteen men there. So I had two tanks attack and it looked like a field in front of me but it was a marsh. [The] machine gun was firing and I took…Martin Windhaus…my platoon sergeant, a little Italian fellow…he didn't weigh a hundred pounds…and my interpreter [DeSoto] and crawled behind a rock wall about not quite two foot high. And some of the Germans, maybe the French people also, used that for a latrine. And I didn't know that and I crawled through that, so I was unhappy about that point anyway. And the company commander was back at the road, maybe three-quarters of a city block, and he started yelling, 'Witmeyer, where you going?' So I yelled back to him, 'I'm trying to see where this machine gun's firing from.' And so he shout out, 'Get back in here.'

"And I told these guys, I said I'm not going back through that crap, I said I'm gonna go over this wall. And I jumped up on the wall…I don't remember whether I counted three or whatever I did…but I jumped on the wall and I took this Fiorello by the hand and I pulled him up on the wall and I had Windhaus and DeSoto. I don't know what they did, they were watching me and they stood up I guess. And the machine gun sprayed around, and it killed this boy through. Shot Windhaus in the head and DeSoto in the chest. And when I jumped down from the wall I had this young Italian guy and he died laying across my legs. I was sittin' on the ground and I said to myself, 'Damn, somebody ought to say something, you know.' A Catholic boy and I couldn't

As the 79th Infantry Division marched south after Cherbourg they ran into a large firefight at la Haye-du-Puits. Private Glen E. Robinson was "on point" for his platoon in the 314th on July 6 when small arms fire sprayed the road. "'Hit it!' I shouted. Sergeant [Edward P.] Keffer crawled forward to see if he could determine from where the heavy volume of fire was coming. There was a metallic pinging sound and he pitched forward beside me. 'You hit?' I asked, afraid there would be no reply. Slowly he lifted his head. A small stream of blood ran down the side of his face. The bullet had entered the front of his helmet, grazed his head and had exited at the back of the helmet. 'Man, that was close,' he sighed. The medics ran forward and quickly wrapped a bandage around his head, then helped him back to the aid station."

think of a fitting prayer. The only prayer I knew was the Lord's Prayer, and I said that over him and laid him on the z I called over 'Martin.' I says, 'Martin how you doin'?' He said, 'They shot off the whole top of my head.' I said, 'Can you get to this wall where I am?' And he said yes. And I said, 'I'll tell you what, I want you to get on your knees and I'm going to pull you over on my side.'

"And he did that and I pulled him over. You're not supposed to use your own first aid packet, but I took mine and I put on top his head…a compress about two and a half inches by four, and about an inch thick with gauze. And I pushed it down in his head wound, and then I tied it, because they got about two feet of gauze on each end. Made a big bow on the top, and of course it was extremely saturated with blood. And I remember as clear as looking at you, I said, 'Martin, you look just like my old grandma.' Had this big bow on top his head.

"Well he passed away. And then I hollered for DeSoto because he got hit in the chest. I did the same thing with him. When he got over the wall, I pulled him over and he survived that, and I was the only one out of the four of us that didn't get hit. I took care of all my guys. And my sergeant by the name of Phil Lepley…this was years later…he said, 'You know what you did?' He said, 'You took everybody's rifle that was around you and fired 'til it was empty.' I said I don't remember that…I just blacked out I think. And after that I never stopped killing Germans with revenge, and that's a fact. That's when I changed from a pretty smart soldier…foot soldier…to a combat soldier, to a killer. I'm not proud of that, I'm just telling you the way it is."

The German soldiers were showing resolve and resilience despite the difficulties of their position and friction among their leadership. This made the fighting hard and frustrating for the attackers and sometimes American soldiers were known to self-inflict wounds and show other signs of battlefield stress. Both sides also used psychological warfare techniques to break the stalemated situation. As the hard fighting continued, Bradley revised his plans and a smaller but still seemingly adequate line from Lesay to St.-Lô was proposed from which to launch the Third Army breakout. To that end, deception plans continued in England in which Patton was replaced in command of the fictitious First Army Group with Lieutenant General Leslie J. McNair. All other deception related to a Kanalküste attack, including setting a date – August 14 – was stepped up.

A U. S. airfield under construction, similar to the one built for the 366th Fighter Group. "That was the LeBrec family château," says Flight Control Officer Robert Balkom. "They just gave us an apple orchard. The engineers came in and tore the orchard down and put the runway in. This looks like an ordinary runway, but it was dirt with mesh over it, the same wire mesh used to reinforce concrete."

SETTING UP FOR THE BREAKOUT

On July 3, Bradley ordered the advance toward St.-Lô resumed. It was not easy for the ground units of the five American divisions on the line there. St.-Lô was an important communication center for roads and railroads passing through it toward the coast and could not simply be bypassed in the hilly bocage. Air strikes were called in but did not help much. Despite the fact that the airfield at Carpiquet had not been taken – the Canadians tried and failed on July 1 – the IX TAC was able to operate a third of the squadrons from Normandy via temporary airfields created by air force engineers.

General Dwight D. Eisenhower and Lieutenant General Omar Bradley listen to Major General Pete Quesada, commander of the IX Tactical Air Command, talk about the heavy bomber attack that preceded Operation Cobra.

Lieutenant Robert Balkom was a Flight Control Officer and commanded the detachment at one of these cobbled together landing fields in Normandy.

"I was with the 366th Fighter Group of the Ninth Air Force, which was flying P-47s. We did not have the luxury of a control tower, it was a one ton GI truck. We fortunately had an enlisted man who was a carpenter, and he built the plywood body. The [control tower] turret is from a B-26...a gun turret. We had to monitor four radio channels at all times. An enlisted man sat at a desk with antiquated telephones. We had another enlisted man at the end of the runway in a trailer with a pyrotechnic [flare] pistol, which he would fire if the pilots tried to come in with their wheels up.

"The P-47 was the heaviest single engine plane in World War II...seven tons. Here they were dive bombing with a 500-pound bomb underneath each wing. The front lines were at St.-Lô, just fifty miles away, up until the 25th of July. The fellows would take off with a bomb under each wing to bomb the Jerries and sometimes the bombs dropped and sometimes they wouldn't, because the dirt and the dust from the airfield got into the bombs' release [mechanism]. So they'd come back over the field you'd see them with a bomb still under the wing. We'd call the pilots and tell them to fly over the Channel and dive, and try to get rid of that thing.

"Sometimes it worked but sometimes it didn't. When they came in and landed, the bomb would always drop off. We had an engineer detachment on duty all the time sitting in front of this control truck. They'd be watching and watching for the bomb to drop and as soon as it did they'd go buzzing out in a Jeep and then the sergeant would come back to our vehicle and say, 'Well Lieutenant, two more revolutions and that one would have gone off.'"

Buster Simmons' 105th Medical Detachment was with the 30th Infantry Division in front of St.-Lô. He observed the way the renewed attempt to take the city started off slowly then gained momentum in the beginning of July.

"All we were doing was just probing the enemy and they were probing us, to see [what] our strengths and weaknesses were. Until we got enough land that we could put equipment on to start moving, that's where we started. July 7, 1944, that was the first day we really moved forward to the attack mode, we'd been static up to that point. St.-Lô was terrible, but we weren't the primary liberators of St-Lô, the 29th Division was. It was tough; there was not a single building in that town that wasn't destroyed or damaged to the point that it had to be razed."

July 4 turned out to be a memorable Independence Day for the Americans on the ground in France. General Eisenhower flew across the Channel in a P-51 Mustang piloted by the commander of the IX Tactical Air Command, Major General Elwood R. "Pete" Quesada, then Ike later drove his own Jeep behind German lines accompanied by only an aide and an orderly. Fortunately for the Allies, Ike's party found its way back to an American command post unscathed. At noon Bradley had the 1,100 American artillery pieces on the line fire a one shot salute – into the German lines.

But St.-Lô continued to hold out for another two weeks and culminated in house-to-house fighting that resulted in 11,000 casualties for the First Army. General Bradley planned a new offensive to get his army out of Normandy but it would not launch until the last week of July. Even though the main effort of landings in the six weeks since D-Day – bringing nearly a million Allied personnel into Normandy – was

Soldiers of the 30th Infantry Division, supported by a Sherman of the 743rd Tank Battalion, move through St.-Fromond on July 8. The division passed though this destroyed village on the way to their staging position for Operation Cobra.

providing combat troops, the support troops had important jobs to do also, and many were moved to France expeditiously through the buzzing port that was Omaha Beach. Sam Hobson became a battalion clerk in the 118th Regiment.

American infantrymen dash across a hedgerow-bordered lane near St.-Lô. The damaged vehicles in the road include a knocked-out Panther tank in the foreground.

thing and they were not sent back to the front lines. We were scattered over France. My company was separate, most of the rest of them, I had their paperwork in my hands."

"Within 24 hours [of D-Day] there's Germans and Americans back in the hospital, and we had to guard the German prisoners. Had to get these men, who were coming through to be replacements, trained and ready to be shipped to the front lines. The 2nd Battalion in August of '44 went over…we went to Omaha Beach. We stayed there on the beach a few days and from there we went to a little coastal town in France. We did training of some MPs to get these boys who just came out of the hospital adjusted to firing on the range. Some of them needed some help mentally and physically. They were not forced to do any-

Joe Sorrentino arrived in France assigned to salvage operations in the Quartermaster Corps.

"I know we landed in Normandy on [June] 12th. We landed in Utah Beach. Now of course, the fightin' was all finished there, but we stayed overnight. We hadda walk, when we got off…I

Top: Soldiers of the 29th Infantry Division move through St.-Lô. The division bore the brunt of the four-division attack to command the high ground and road hub along the Vire River. Bottom: An American truck burns after being struck by German artillery near St.-Lô on July 20. Even though the city fell a few days earlier, shelling and small fire fights continued.

don't know how many miles. We walked right through Ste.-Mère-Église. The parachutes were still hangin' from trees and everything like that. We can't take 'em down anyway. So next day, we got our trucks again and they brought us to Omaha Beach. Well the thing is we hadda cross a bridge in the town of Carentan and it was still under fire. We hadda cross one truck at a time. But nothing landed, so we were pretty safe. So we went to Omaha Beach. We really weren't on …I never did see the beach.

"We lived in the, what they called the hedgerow country. You probably heard about the hedgerows. And they were built up, they claimed…they were there for maybe hundreds and hundreds and hundreds of years. And the roots…roots got so thick that the tanks couldn't go through 'em. So after that was all over, they hadda prepare for a breakout. And one night I was on guard duty. So when I went back to my pup tent…that's where we lived, in pup tents…somebody woke me up, said, 'Hey Joe. You gotta come and see this.' I heard airplanes, and the sky, full of airplanes. Yeah, all day long. They kept bombin' around St.-Lô, and they start droppin' bombs, and the ground was vibrating. We were quite a ways from St.-Lô, but we still felt that ground shaking, it felt like a earthquake.

"We went through town [St.-Lô], it was nothing but rubble. But the area, the fields, we hadda pick up junk, but we didn't find nothin' that we hadda repair or anything, was mostly empty shell cases and stuff like that. Rifle belts, they looked like Mexican war, you know…they

Looking north along one of the main arteries running through St.-Lô shows a community in utter devastation – a real and symbolic reminder of the destruction rent by aerial bombing and unrelenting artillery shelling that was characteristic of the fight for Normandy.

Wehrmacht soldiers work on mechanized Nebelwerfer (rocket launchers) in the Caen area. The two rear vehicles are Wurfgranate 41s and the rocket launcher in the distance is probably a Wurfkörper M F1 50, built on the popular SdKfz 251 halftrack.

were layin' all around the place. We didn't [touch them]...that was the ordnance job."

Douglas Jenney from Maine was a wireman assigned to the 30th Infantry Division and landed with the division on Omaha Beach within the first few days after D-Day.

"Our job was laying wire for communications. I was with the 30th Signal Company in construction and we laid wire. When we were in England, we waterproofed our truck so we could drive off in the water. When we went in on the Omaha beachhead I was driving a 2 ½ ton truck. I drove off into water up to my waist when we drove to the beachhead.

"We didn't lay any [wire] right off quick. We were in the hedgerow country and we only had to lay short wires to the rest of the division. It seems that we were there for a month before they got in enough supplies and we had the

breakthrough at St.-Lô. We kept on the move all the time. They'd pull us back when we finished one place, and they gave us a rest for a week or so, then they'd move us ahead to wherever we was needed, especially the hot spots."

In front of the left flank of the Allied line stood the city of Caen, second largest in Normandy. Caen was a dichotomy of French culture. Its medieval beginnings were displayed in the historic center city, a citadel-like area protecting monasteries and other religious buildings. It was also a major transportation and manufacturing center with huge limestone quarries, steel mills, docks and railways. Finally, it was a center of Nazi military governance.

General Montgomery, after spending weeks trying to slink around the perimeter of Caen without success, decided the only option left to him was to take the city head on. As a preliminary

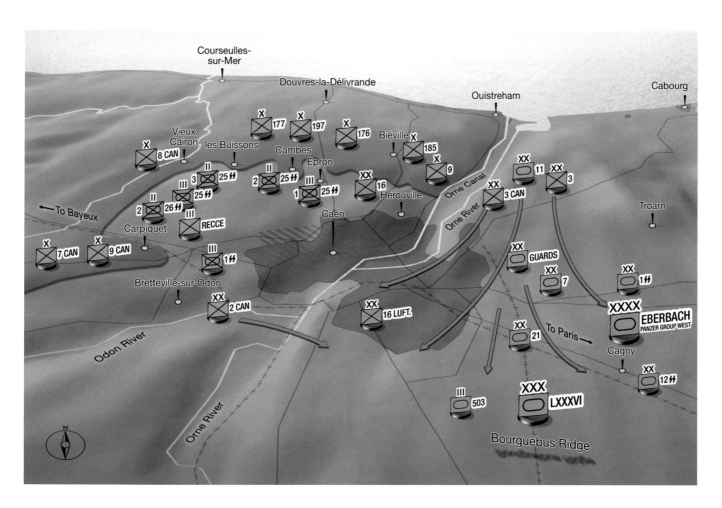

objective, Montgomery wanted the aerodrome at Carpiquet, a little southwest of Caen. He assigned the Canadian 3rd Division to the task on July 4. In the early morning hours an artillery barrage from 760 guns, including those on British warships in the bay, started the attack off in a big way. However, despite continued artillery support and fighter-bomber sorties throughout the day, the Canadians could not wrest the airport completely from the defenders, the 12th SS Panzer Division. Like all Waffen-SS units, the 12th was made up of loyal Nazis, in this case, young men from the Hitler Youth. In these days of disagreement among senior army officials, the

Operation Charnwood (upper left in map) succeeded rapidly in part because much of the German armor was pulled from Caen to escape bombardment. The rest of the forces in the city were overrun in the attack. After a brief respite, the Second Army readied for a push to consolidate and expand the ground held east and southeast of Caen. Operation Goodwood was designed to bring the Allied east flank out of the Normandy bocage but German defenders stalled the advance.

Führer gave much autonomy to the Waffen-SS commanders. The 12th soldiers were dug in among the hangers and refused to be dislodged from their mostly mortar and anti-tank gun defense. The airport remained in German hands in a virtually unusable state.

By this time new panzer units were arriving from the east. Every type of German tank in use in the West – Panzer IV, Panzer V (Panther) and even the monstrous Panzer VI (Tiger) – were included in the panzer and panzergrenadier divisions in and around Caen. Keeping Caen in German hands and the Allies on the west bank of the Orne River was such an important objective that virtually no German unit was held back except those that were too battle weary (such as the much-used Panzer Lehr Division that was moved away from the Caen front in the beginning of July). Unfortunately for the Wehrmacht, British intelligence knew almost as much about German troop dispositions as they did.

On July 8 Montgomery began *Operation Charnwood* by ordering Lieutenant General Miles Dempsey's Second Army into an orchestrated offensive against Caen from the north. The attack was preceded by 470 strategic bombers that laid down an explosive carpet 4,000 yards wide by 1,500 yards deep across the northern part of Caen. Monty convinced SHAEF to use the strategic bombers in *Charnwood*, and support it with tactical and

fighter bombers throughout the day. But other than permanently knocking out a few enemy tanks, the effect of the air attacks was merely to fill the city streets with rubble and kill 400 of the French residents remaining in the city. The Allied airmen were not intentionally careless, but carpet bombing techniques in support of ground attacks had not yet been sufficiently perfected – something the Americans would regretfully discover in a few weeks.

The principal challenge for the three divisions attacking Caen was that German troops were holding villages on the outskirts of the city and the stone houses, hedgerows and fences gave them natural defensive positions that were hard to penetrate. Tanks and other armored vehicles could not clear out these strong points without the help of the

Left: HMS Rodney *adds her weight of shells to the naval pounding in support of the British and Commonwealth landings on D-Day. She also led the naval barrage for* Operation Charnwood. *Right: A B-25 Mitchell Mk II of the Dutch Squadron, RAF flies over the Colombelles steel works, in the industrial section southeast of Caen. The resilient German lookout post held out until* Goodwood *on July 18-19.*

infantry units, and Britain – now five years into World War II – was running critically short of infantrymen and experiencing a decline in the number of infantry regiments that could be mustered. The "softening up" of the German defense line by air attack was only partially helpful as the area carpet bombed was thinly held and German troops and even panzers could hide from air attack. But the artillery bombardment from land and sea – the battleship HMS *Rodney*, for example, was firing nine 16-inch guns – aided the advance

throughout the day through sheer "shell shock" of the enemy.

Field Marshal Rommel directed the units to be involved in the fight that he and his men knew was coming. There was a strong desire to protect the panzer divisions and so both veteran and green infantrymen were in the front line to carry the brunt of the attack. The desperation of the German troops fighting in France was exemplified by the 16th Luftwaffe Field Division which was made up of

A British soldier offers a helping hand to an elderly woman after Caen's liberation, July 8-10. Much of the city was leveled during bombardment, leaving large numbers of the population homeless.

Winston Churchill inspects the ruins of Caen shortly after its liberation by British and Canadian forces. He is accompanied by Second (British) Army Commander General Miles Dempsey (center) and General Bernard Montgomery, commanding general of the 21st Army Group, both with their backs to the camera.

airmen and ground crews converted to fight as infantry. The Germans did make use of multi-tube rocket launchers and Commonwealth forces estimated that most of their casualties in June and July were from mortars and the Nebel-werfer multiple rocket launchers.

The three-division attack began at 0420, July 8 with the British 3rd Infantry Division and its armored support moving southeast to Lébisey Woods and Herouville, places from which they had been driven away on D-Day. At the same time, the British 59th (Staffordshire) Division moved down along the main road from the north, encountering stiffer resistance. Later in the day part of the 3rd Division came west to help them. About three hours after the jump off the 3rd Canadian Infantry Division and supporting units started their on-time advance on the villages northwest of Caen. At the village of Buron the fighting was hard and the Canadians fought off panzer counterattacks throughout the day. Elsewhere they made better progress including overrunning the aerodrome that had eluded them on July 4.

John R. Roberts was X Company Sergeant Major in the 2nd Battalion of the King's Shropshire Light Infantry (KSLI). The unit was in the 185th Infantry Brigade, 3rd Infantry Division. It saw a lot of action in the battles around Caen.

"Our company was to attack the ground to the west of Lébisey, and round to Caen. This battle took place over one day, and the very outskirts of Caen were reached, by which time the German, who had evacuated his troops as soon as the air-raid had started, he had this habit of pushing his troops back, so it was a fairly bitter struggle.

"I hadn't lost many men in that operation...I think I had one missing in the attack on Caen itself. I'd had one man near my rear HQ as we moved up from Lébisey. He was hit on the side of the head, and there was a hole through which one could see his brain. We looked after him. Later, I asked the MO [Medical Officer] about this man and he said 'Oh yes, he'd be perfectly all right.' He said they'd put a plate on him, grafted it over. I'd been very concerned for him. He was a corporal, a very good man."

German forces began to withdraw from Caen and the strong points on three sides of the city throughout the night. The British advance continued into Caen on July 9 and the city was considered liberated that evening, although snipers and other German rear guard troops had to be cleared out of Caen during the next 24 hours. The bridges south of the city were destroyed, so British and Canadian tanks did not pursue the withdrawing panzers and German infantry.

In the coming days, another offensive would not only be costly in men and materials, it would cost 21st Army Group commander Montgomery a loss of stature and trust. The battle for Caen was not yet over because the southern edge of the city, where the industry and rail facilities were situated, remained in German hands as did much of the land beyond the Orne River to the east and south, blocking the way to Paris. Therefore almost immediately after *Operation Charnwood*, Montgomery began plans for *Operation Goodwood*. It became one of the most controversial chapters in the Normandy campaign.

British troops cleared out pockets of resistance west of Caen on July 10 but the British leadership knew their next major thrust would be

Canadian M-4 tanks race down a rural road to position for an advance through the industrial suburbs of Faubourg de Vaucelles and Colombelles east and southeast of Caen across the Orne River.

where the main German forces were – to the southeast. Perhaps in an effort to secure another strategic aerial bombardment, Montgomery intimated that he was going for the gold – a push to Falaise, an important crossroads town beyond which the hedgerows and hills opened to relatively easy terrain in the direction of the Seine. General Eisenhower was very much for this idea that he felt was overdue and offered the air support if Montgomery could get the drive going during good weather.

On the other side of the Orne River, the Germans were following orders from Hitler to dig in to a good defensive line to stem any further Allied progress until reinforcements arrived. The Germans found good defensive positions in the villages north of a defensible ridge, Bourguébus Ridge, known to the British soldiers as "Buggerbus" Ridge. German artillery was stacked on the northern edge of the ridge and panzer reinforcements were assembled behind it for counterattacks. Everything in the arsenal was brought out, including 88mm flak guns, mobile heavy guns, giant Tiger II (King Tiger) heavy tanks and later the imposing Jagdpanzer IV tank destroyers. Two corps, I SS Panzer Corps and LXXXVI Corps, under the direction of Panzer Group West, received fresh infantry reinforcements as well.

Preliminary actions by Commonwealth forces took place from July 11 onward. One of these was a raid to deny the Germans their "eyes," two tall chimneys at the Colombelles steel mill. The 2nd Battalion of the KSLI was part of the attempt to destroy these key enemy observation posts.

A German 11.1-inch K-5 railway cannon fires its quarter-ton projectile. Eight of the guns, built by Krupp, arrived in the 1940 invasion of France. The 725th Railway Artillery participated in the German defense during Operation Goodwood.

"We did an attack on a place called Colombelles, the factory district on the east side of Caen," says Roberts. "There were no other serious casualties in the Colombelles operation, but it was a pretty hectic place, with shelling and mortaring."

Corporal Robert "Bob" Littlar was in Roberts' X Company during this raid that began at 0100 on July 11.

"In Normandy, the action I remember most for close engagement amongst buildings was when we were fighting our way into Colombelles, the industrial district, with a lot of railway sidings and warehouses. We were the lead company, the leading section had just got the other side of an alleyway, but then Jerry opened up so my section got into a building, which I got the lads to loophole. Jerry was no more than 30 yards away with MG 42s [machine guns], sited at low level with camouflage nets over the approaches. We were pretty much pinned down.

"My platoon sergeant decided that the only way we were going to make any headway was with a mortar, so he broke through until he found one of our 2-inch mortar crews and brought them back to our building. They managed to shoot the Jerry machine gunners out, but it was all a bit hairy."

The raid was called off when Tiger tanks overwhelmed the British armor accompanying the raid. Elsewhere, bridges held since D-Day by the 6th Airborne (who were not part of *Operation Goodwood*) were crossed for part of the three-corps assault to gain their starting positions. Other temporary "Bailey" bridges were laid across the Orne. What the Germans could not see from their observation posts in the high stacks of Colombelles or discern from intelligence was the extent of the pre-attack bombardment.

British infantrymen pose aboard Sherman tanks in the Operation Goodwood assembly area east of the Orne River and canal on July 18. The tank on the extreme right is equipped with a crab flail for clearing mines.

The *Goodwood* air support was greater than for *Charnwood*, hit more targets and took on several stages of strategic and tactical sorties during the early hours of the attack on July 18. The date was supposed to coincide with the commencement of U. S. First Army's *Operation Cobra*, but that was pushed back two days, and then to July 24, because of difficulties in taking St.-Lô and poor weather for air operations in that region. Added to the air strikes by more than 2,700 planes (the tactical operations were guided by RAF spotters riding in tanks on the front line) were rolling artillery barrages designed to creep ahead of the ground advance. For some German targets the British warships were in shelling range.

All of this bombing was designed to have a psychological as well as a destructive effect on the German defenders. And for many that was effective. The infantry rounded up prisoners who were temporarily deaf, mad or both in some of the villages first encountered. But not all villages were hit by the air attack and not all the defenders were stunned. As the three fronts advanced – the II Canadian Corps on the right pointing toward Vaucelles and the industrial area along the river, the British I Corps on the left and the British VIII Corps in the center heading in the direction of Bourguébus Ridge – they came under artillery and tank fire from villages and the ridge further south.

"For *Operation Goodwood* we were actually on the tanks, Staffs [Staffordshire] Yeomanry" says John Roberts. "It's no fun being on them when 17-pounder guns are going off, I can tell you. I've got some of the results, with this tinnitus.

"With X Company we captured a place called Troarn, to guard the left flank, while three armored divisions were pushed through to take the ridge. It was a dreadful day in some ways, because the weather turned sour in the afternoon, and it rained heavily. We lost some people from the battalion that day, I think three company commanders and sergeant-majors. Only Major Thorneycroft and myself were left that day."

The fighting on the right of the British line where the KSLI was located continued in villages and orchards west of Troarn. It was most important for the German LXXXVI Corps to retain Troarn and so the city itself held out for a time although the 185th and other British infantry brigades worked through territory on a line running to the southwest. In the center the fight was led by the armored divisions of the VIII Corps and there were many classic tank battles between the Orne River and Bourguébus Ridge as groups of panzers went on their own offensives. Lieutenant Lionel Knight was a troop leader in C Squadron of the Staffordshire Yeomanry. His tanks were right in the middle of this fight that went on from morning to late evening in the center of the British advance.

"I think we had another tank regiment in front of us which I believe was the Fife and Forfar [2nd Fife and Forfar Yeomanry]. It was going to be a bit of a charge. They laid down an artillery barrage in front of us, well, allegedly in front of us...it was landing all around us in actual fact...but they lifted eventually and moved on. A bit frightening, that.

"The Fife and Forfar went on first. And they got an awful hammering. I don't know how many tanks they lost. When we went through where they were there were tanks all over the place, some down in bomb craters, some on fire. We passed through them and our objective was a railway line, presumably the one that went into Caen.

"When I got there I heard a bang and came to a grinding halt. It was the first time I had a hit on my tank. A lot of smoke started coming in behind the turret so we all had to jump out. And of course our infantry wasn't up with us then. So it was a bit worrying but we did get out.

"The firing at us stopped. I thought we might as well get back into the tank again because it hadn't caught fire. The smoke we saw was from the tank's fire extinguisher vapor. The shot had gone right through behind the tank's turret and knocked off the top of the fire extinguishers as it had gone through.

"So we got back into the tank. We hadn't been there more than a couple of minutes and we got another bang. We'd been hit again. So we all jumped out again. This time the shot had hit the idler wheel. This is a wheel no more than about nine inches in diameter which is underneath the turret to carry the track. Of course, it had taken all the whiz out of it. Purely luck, it would have taken our legs off if it had gone through. So we were lucky. Twice."

The tanks had to pass over a steep railroad embankment on the route south. Then they were hit by anti-tank fire from villages that had escaped total destruction in the bombardment. A village called Cagny was at the center of the push being carried out against strong resistance by the Guards, 7th and 11th Armoured Divisions of the VIII Corps. Jack Armitage's battalion of the 51st British (Highland) Infantry Division relieved another unit in Cagny after the principal battle passed through the hamlet. He found himself in a situation that ultimately had him asking the question all soldiers in combat ask themselves.

"Well, there was a very intimate moment happened in Normandy. Now, I've told this and some people don't believe [me] and some do. But we were at a village called Cagny...we re-

A scene of destruction in the village of Cagny on July 19. Early the day before Lancaster and Halifax bombers dropped tons of high explosive bombs on Cagny. Later it was in the middle of heavy fighting.

lieved [another unit of] the 51st Highland Division in the morning and it was a perfect time to leave, because there was a ground fog. The unfortunate thing [was] that halfway through the changeover the fog lifted and Germans were sitting on the hill, looking right down on the plain. They shelled us unmercifully.

"Anyway, we eventually got an RAP [assembly point] established, not far from the village, just where the wall to the village started and there was trees there so we could move and couldn't be seen. And right opposite 30 yards away from us on the corner of the field was a German 88-millimeter abandoned, with a whole pile of ammunition. There was four [British] tankers, the guys with the black berets...tank

crews...loading ammunition into this truck. I guess they'd gotten an 88 [millimeter] of their own and were going to give the Germans some of their own back.

"So I thought, oh, I'll go and help them. And a voice said, 'Don't go.' Now, there wasn't anyone in sight except those four tankers. They were a good 50 yards away from me. I thought, I'm hearing things, so I went a little step and a sterner voice said, 'Don't go!' So I thought,

Lieutenant General George S. Patton and Lieutenant General Omar Bradley meet with General Bernard Law Montgomery after the arrival in France of Patton's Third Army. Patton's signature white-handled revolver hangs from his belt.

okay, and I went and got in my slit trench, and just as I got in my slit trench a German shell hit this pile of ammunition and blew those four guys to eternity. It would have been me too. And I spoke to the pastor about it and he said, 'God spoke to you.' I said, 'Well why me, I mean, what's so special about me, why should he speak to me, not to them?'"

A panzer and a machine gun from an SS unit poised for battle in July 1944. U. S. 1st Infantry Division machine gunner Ernest "Andy" Andrews comments on the enemy he faced. "My perception of the German soldiers is that...first of all we ran into some very young soldiers, 17 years old. But as we got into combat we discovered the German soldier was a tremendously effective fighter. Not the people that they had forced into their armed services from other countries. But the Germans were good fighters."

Cannonades and local attacks continued throughout the night and into the next two days. Although some villages took a week to clear out, by July 22 *Operation Goodwood* was over.

The stubborn resistance of the German armor and guns caused the British to fall short of their objectives on July 18 although the II Canadian Corps reached most of theirs. By the end of the day the Second Army line bulged out to the east short of Troarn then ran west to Vaucelles.

Of the Allied air resources used in the operation, the *Typhoon* fighter-bombers had the most impact on the raging tank battle. They were able to slow down the tanks in the German counterattacks coming over Bourguébus Ridge onto the plain. The Germans also revived their sagging air effort. Junkers 88s bombed Orne bridges and positions within the new Second Army-held territory east of the river on the night of July 18. The next two

A group of young German prisoners in camouflage and Totenkopf caps. At Caen Hitlerjugend (Hitler Youth), made up of 17 and 18-year-olds who grew up as devout Nazis, fought with the 12th SS Panzer Division against the Canadians.

days, those British units continuing to assault the ridge were strafed by Messerschmitt Bf 109 fighters. But the most significant air attack was one on the evening of July 17 by a solo Spitfire. The fighter strafed the staff car of Erwin Rommel, badly wounded the Field Marshal and left the German army in Normandy without an overall commander. At least three Allied pilots (a Canadian, a Brit and an Australian) have claimed credit for the Spitfire strafing attack that knocked Germany's most famous commander out of the war.

The controversy surrounding the offensive was whether or not Montgomery had oversold *Goodwood* as a drive to Falaise, for which it fell far short. Only one reconnaissance unit got to the other side of Bourguébus Ridge for a look down the Caen/Falaise Road. For the amount of ground taken, which did completely secure Caen in the process, Second Army lost a horrific number of men and tanks in the fight. Eisenhower and Churchill came to visit Montgomery personally on July 20 and 21 to express their concerns. Monty reminded them of the value the Second Army achieved in keeping German armor away from the U. S. First Army advance in the west, but repercussions were coming. The Canadians were formed into a new First Canadian Army to head the drive for Falaise. Montgomery's days as overall Allied ground commander were now numbered as Eisenhower

A stacked echelon of P-51 Mustang fighters returns from an uneventful bomber escort mission. The emergence of the long-range P-51 as both an escort and tactical fighter gave the Allies complete domination of air-to-air combat in Europe until the too little, too late introduction of the Luftwaffe ME-262 jet.

resolved to eventually assume that role (which Ike did in September, adding this responsibility to his SHAEF command). But as July wound down attention shifted to the western part of Normandy and the plans of the U. S. First Army.

PATTON'S THIRD ARMY ARRIVES IN FRANCE

At about the same time that Lieutenant General George S. Patton's Third Army was beginning to be formed with the arrival in Normandy of the XII, XV and XX Corps, Lieutenant General Omar Bradley's First Army was beginning the much delayed *Operation Cobra* to open the door for the planned sweep through Brittany and beyond. With St.-Lô finally being wrested from a stubborn enemy, the front was cleared for Bradley's broad advance. The advance was led by VII Corps with Major General

J. Lawton "Lightning Joe" Collins in overall command. Major General Troy H. Middleton's VIII Corps was to follow closely behind to the west to take the town of Coutances and follow down along the coast, while Major General Charles Corlett's XIX Corps and Gerow's V Corps protected the line to the east and extended communications to the Commonwealth positions. The main objective initially was the city of Avranches, which sat on the west flank of the German Seventh Army. Taking that city would enable First Army to turn the flank of the German defenders and break out into Brittany.

Opposing this assault were the 2nd SS and Panzer Lehr Divisions and infantry units that had managed to remain somewhat intact after the previous fighting in the hedgerows – about 5,000 troops on the front line, 30,000 total including support. With the Americans on the verge of escaping the hedgerow country – which was advantageous to either side when dug in on defense – they would now also be facing the larger German Panther and Tiger tanks which could not operate in the bocage. Field Marshal Kluge – in command of Army Group B as well as OB West since Rommel's wounding and return to Germany – a few days into *Cobra* ordered two divisions from Panzer Group West to the new front facing First Army. The Americans were also improving their leadership and fighting skills as far as the coordination of infantry and armor – something that would continue to be as important in the coming operation as it was to grind through the last of the hedgerows.

Lieutenant Frank Towers and the rest of the 120th Infantry Regiment would be in the lead of the advance. But first, he and the other ground units stood by as the air forces took to the skies to lay down a path of devastation, to be followed by rolling artillery barrages, much as the Second Army had done to begin *Operation Goodwood.*

"We were faced with the major breakthrough that was called *Operation Cobra.* This was an operation where we were to crack the German defenses in this area. General Patton and his newly-formed Third Army, made up mostly of armor, was to go through the hole that we cracked in the line, proceed southward to Brest [Brittany] and to capture that particular area. In order to facilitate *Operation Cobra* we had to coordinate with the air to do a certain amount of carpet bombing to our immediate front and the 24th of July was the date set and 11:00 o'clock in the morning was the hour set for the bombing and the attack.

"The main line of departure was the St.-Lô/Périer Road, which was a major road, well-defined and obvious from the air. In order to facilitate the air corps' view of the road we were asked to put red smoke from artillery shells up on that road to more clearly define the area where they were to bomb. We did that; the artillery fired smoke shells which landed basically on the St.-Lô Road. At the same time, just as a safety factor, our troops withdrew about a half-mile. A half-mile is a long way to withdraw for a safety factor and we were aware of that.

"We felt that we were virtually safe that far back and we left the safety of our foxholes to move back a half-mile and we didn't bother to dig any more foxholes. However, just before 11:00 o'clock we heard the drone of planes coming, we looked back over our shoulder and we could see this massive black wave of planes coming. As they approached our area they were down fairly low, about 1,500 feet, and we could see the belly of the planes. We could see the bomb bays open in preparation for dropping the bombs and we could also see the bombs starting to fall from the planes. Having been through this in previous days, on a much smaller scale, we were able to judge when the bomb bays opened and the bombs began to fall…we had a pretty good idea where they were going to fall. We always felt reasonably safe, but this morning the bomb bays opened up a bit too early, per our calculations, and the bombs began falling down…we could see them.

"Well, unfortunately for us, as the artillery put the smoke down on the road Mother Nature didn't cooperate and she generated a small, slight breeze from the south which drifted the red smoke slowly back and was on top of our troops. When the air saw that red line, they said, 'Aha! There's that red smoke line we're supposed to bomb on,' and they let it go.

"The consequences were that we had over 300 men killed [and] wounded and it disrupted the whole *Operation Cobra.* The planned attack had to be called off because we were in such disarray and had lost so many men we just couldn't have a coordinated attack. As quickly as possible we got replacements for these men, replacement for the equipment that was lost, and the plan was revised to do the same thing the next day, on the 25th of July.

"Again, the same plan, the red smoke went out on the St.-Lô/Pérrier Road, the air force came up behind us and opened the bomb bay doors. Mother Nature not cooperating again she drifted that red smoke right on top of us the second day in a row. Consequently the air force came over and saw the red smoke down in the line and dropped their bombs just where they were supposed to. Again, we had large numbers of casualties [111 killed, 490 wounded], among them was Lieutenant General Leslie McNair [an observer to the action], who was the highest-ranking [American] officer to be killed in the entire World War II.

"At that point it was decided that since we had notified the German troops in the forward area that we were coming, we had to go forward with the attack regardless of the losses we had and the disarray we were in and the lack of equipment. So we just tried to do the best we could with what we had. The attack went forward…very fortunately for us…unknown to us at the time this was a very thinly-held part of the line and we broke through it easily. Fortunately for the Germans they did not receive the major part of the bombing which was intended to be for them, we got it instead."

The twin bombing disasters of July 24 and 25, due mainly to the air forces' insistence on bombing *perpendicular* to the front line instead

Men of the 28th Infantry Regiment, part of the 8th Infantry Division, march past a line of destroyed enemy vehicles in Bréhal, France on their way to Avranches on July 31.

of *parallel* to it, as Ike and Bradley had wanted, would change the way strategic bombing was handled by SHAEF later in the war. Albert Piper was on the front also with his artillery headquarters unit.

"The one that killed [General] McNair was only 2,000 to 3,000 yards from us. We were supposed to go through and relieve 'em, the 9th Infantry Division. Now McNair got killed. You remember [William] Westmoreland? Well Westmoreland at that time was only a major…he was either a major or a lieutenant colonel. He had left to get something, see, and then he came back [after the bombing]."

"I remember July the 25th 'cause it was my birthday," says Pete Chavez of the 65th Armored Field Artillery Battalion. "And that day the Americans sent bombers, they were all over the place. Heavy bombers, medium bombers, fighter-bombers. And I'll tell you what, I'm not tryin' to stretch it, but the ground was really shakin' you know. When we got there, there was craters all over the place and there was them Germans come outta there just kinda groggy but some of 'em made it through that thing. And I don't see how in the world anybody could escape that. And we broke through that evening. And from there on, we kept going pretty good."

As Towers and Chavez stated, the offensive took off rather rapidly except in places where small pockets of resistance occurred. By July 30 American armored brigades crossed the See River and entered Avranches from the north, where they tangled with panzer units heading the same direction, trying to escape entrapment by the quickly advancing U. S. VIII Corps. By the last day of July, Major General John S. "P" Wood's 4th Armored Division had also secured the bridge over the Selune at Pontaubault, the

last water obstacle north of Brittany. These pushes on July 30-31 were directed by Patton, even though he did not officially take command until August 1. But they were an indication of his aggressive combat style.

The success of *Cobra* prompted reflection on both sides. Hitler, while continuing his dissatisfaction with his army officers in France, also sacked many of them. The Germans in Normandy, however, were fighting as well as anyone could expect under the circumstances. Hitler finally gave up on the idea of a second Allied invasion at Pas de Calais, ordering all remaining units in that region and the south of France to be available for containing the Normandy breakout. He did not, however, authorize the building of fixed fortifications along the Seine. Eisenhower used the momentum of *Operation Cobra* to establish the U. S. 12th Army Group under Bradley. General Bradley's command included the First Army, placed under his former assistant Lieutenant General Courtney H. Hodges, and the Third Army under Patton.

Most of the hard-driving VIII Corps was shifted to the Third Army, leaving the First Army with the veteran V, VII and XIX Corps until fresh forces arrived from England. As new units arrived, many divisions were brought down to the opening at Avranches and fed through to the

Top: M5A1 Stuart light tanks of a reconnaissance platoon roll along one of the main highways between Normandy and Brittany near Avranches, the principal city at the juncture of the two provinces that, when taken, opened the door for the Third Army breakout. Bottom: Troops of the 357th Infantry Regiment, 90th Infantry Division, walk beside a column of Sherman tanks from the 4th Armored Division in Coutances on July 29. Like others in the VIII Corps, these forces were headed south out of the hedgerow country of Normandy toward the coastal plains of Brittany.

south side as quickly as possible where they were sent out on one of many roads to organize. Among the arriving units was the 80th Infantry Division of which Gilbert Zamorano of Colton, California was a member. Zamorano remembers his initiation into infantry combat in France and some of the tips he and his comrades learned quickly in the field.

"We landed in France. To me, it was just a lot of apple orchards. We started eating apples! But the enemy was right there already. I remember when the hedgerows were part of our defenses, but sometimes you have to cross like a building or a fence made out of rock…they had a lot of rock and on the top they had glass…they had broken bottles and when you went in like that to grab, you were out of action, right? And we finally learned not to go over it, to go around it, but sometimes it took a long time to go around it. At night, you know, even in the daytime, the machine guns were firing, and we could see the tracers going, so we said we'll go in the middle, but then they had other machine guns cross firing like that, and they caught us right in the middle, so we got to…we couldn't cross that way. But, then we started being more careful, and then when we went into the

hedgerows, they had a wire from here to there. We would start running and that grenade would blow up. They had booby traps, they had everything."

Led by the armor of Middleton's VIII Corps and aided by the French Resistance, Patton's army moved quickly around the perimeter of Brittany, bypassing German strongholds such as Lorient and St.-Nazaire which held on for many months. Even Brest, the region's largest city and port, did not surrender until September. The rapid Allied progress and changing strategy minimized Brest's importance as a port of entry for invading forces.

Like a ball passing through the curved interior of a jai alai glove, Patton's army seemed to accelerate rapidly as it changed direction and headed east to Le Mans, Nantes and the north side of the Loire River valley. If it wasn't becoming obvious to the Führer that France was slipping from Nazi hands, it was to most of his commanders. Rommel had seen the signs in mid-July, and used the prediction to bolster the resolve of those plotting against Hitler. The Seventh Army commander, General Paul Hausser, could see it, although Kluge was still hopeful of containing the Allies. They continued to solve their tactical problems while in his East Prussia command

An M-18 Hellcat tank destroyer at work on the streets of Brest. Most of the VIII Corps bypassed the stronghold and fighting continued there until September 18.

post Hitler vetoed the idea for a withdrawal behind the Seine River in favor of a bold stroke that he hoped would cut Patton off from the rest of the Allied forces.

The Führer called for eight of nine panzer divisions then in Northern France to be drawn together for a counterattack on the American First Army. The location was sound; it was at the hub of the wheel or the jamb of the door where the Allied line swung from an east-west direction to the southwest, opening the path for the breakout. The idea was to drive northwest to Avranches and then, in Hitler's plan, cut all the way up the Cotentin Peninsula. Field Marshal Kluge was less ambitious, only looking as far as Avranches as a means to shore up his defensive position. He also was unable or unwilling to commit more that four panzer divisions to the counterattack, and with time short, Hitler went along with the idea. Although Kluge minimized preparation in order to keep the assault a secret, once again ULTRA intercepts and espionage revealed the German plan – and that it would be aimed directly at the U. S. 30th Infantry Division in their position around the town of Mortain.

Troops from Company K, 120th Infantry Regiment move through a destroyed village on July 27. They and the rest of the 30th Infantry Division advanced three miles that day to cut the St.-Lô/Coutances highway, an important achievement in the first seventy-two hours of Operation Cobra.

"Immediately following *Operation Cobra*," recalls Towers, "We were scheduled to go into a rest and reorganization period, and get replacements in for the men we had lost in that operation, but the higher command had other plans for us. We moved about 50 miles to the south to the town of Mortain where the 1st Division had been for a few days. They wanted to relieve the 1st Division in order for them to go with Patton. Arriving at Mortain they [the men of the 1st] were happy to see us, of course, and they told us they had been patrolling out to their front about one mile and had encountered no enemy. Basically they said there was nothing out there at the front and have a good time while you're here. We relieved them during the day of the 5th of August and by 8:00 o'clock in the evening we had completed the exchange of man for man in all the positions they had. We didn't take any further defensive measures and just prepared for a restful night and would start off the next day sending out our own patrols."

In support of the 30th Infantry Division were field artillery and tank destroyers, including the 823rd Tank Destroyer Battalion in which Staff

Sergeant George Wichterich of New Orleans led a platoon of 3-inch anti-tank guns.

"We went into an area along Omaha Beach, D plus 4. We were attached at that time to the 29th Infantry [Division]. About two weeks later, the 30th [Division] came ashore, and they switched us over to the 30th. From there…there's an area called St.-Jean-de-Daye…a little town in hedgerow country with apple orchards all along. We went from there all the way to a town called Mortain. Mortain was where the Germans were trying to cut off Patton. You've heard of Patton's breakthrough, 'Make way for Patton and his killers.'

"We started out with these tow[ed anti-tank] guns. We kept them all the way through the hedgerow and all the way to the [Battle of the] Bulge. There were 36 guns, 12 guns per company and we had 4 guns to a platoon. There were 50 men to a platoon at that time. You had a 10-man gun crew, plus 2 or 3 machine [gun] squads. When you saw a German tank coming out of the fog in the morning with an 88[mm cannon] sticking out the front end, you didn't know what to do. You were afraid to let them get too close because they could wipe your gun out before you could even fire it. At a couple hundred yards they could be pretty accurate. It was very good."

"At the east edge of Mortain," continues Tower. "There is a large hill, Hill 314. From the top of that hill we had an observation over the entire road network from 20-30 miles around. So it was very imperative that we retain control of that hill. In order to do so the 2nd Battalion of the 120th [Infantry] Regiment was put up on that hill and they were to hold that hill at all cost. At midnight this night [August 6-7] three panzer divisions and one infantry division attacked Hill 314. They also knew that they had to control that hill in order to have control going to the west.

"The operation was to cut through our lines and go to Avranches on the west coast of France. This would have cut off Patton's Third Army from any contact with our First Army. If cut off, he would not have been able to make any effort to assist us, and at that point we could have very well been driven back to Omaha Beach and back into the sea. So it was imperative that the hill be held and after five days of tremendous fighting [and] air bombardments, that hill was held and the German attack was stopped."

Buster Simmons was at Mortain, as the 105th Medical Detachment was still attached to the 30th Division.

"I have to say that Mortain, France down below St.-Lô was the toughest battle we were in…for the medical detachment as well as others. We had the 2nd Battalion surrounded on a hill there, and they were surrounded for about a week…and the Germans threw everything in the book at us up there. And the medical detachment lost an entire battalion aid station there, 22 men, two officers, a chaplain, and his assistant were captured there.

"I wondered at the time what the heck the Germans wanted to go in there and capture 22 non-combatants for. I never did learn until after the war was over what their objective was. They had lost a hospital in Cherbourg, with its entire personnel, and they had gone out to capture a medical unit because they wanted to use that as a bartering chip, make a trade. Well, we didn't play that game, so we kept their hospital and they kept our aid station. Those guys lived a rough life, the guys who were taken prisoner, and all across Europe we were about 24 hours behind them, every day. We had some good men in that outfit too."

Although the 120th Infantry Regiment bore the brunt of the original attack, including the 2nd Battalion that needed air drops of food and medicine but provided an invaluable observation post for the whole division, the 119th and 117th Infantry Regiments of the 30th Division and the 39th Infantry Regiment of the 9th Infantry Division were also engaged at Mortain. Mike Pachuta was a platoon sergeant in the 119th Infantry Regiment, 3rd Battalion, Company G.

"We were moving into Normandy…D-Day plus 3 was when my outfit went in. From Normandy we fought our way all the way

The Battle of Mortain was fought because it was at the center of the First Army line when the long anticipated Wehrmacht counterattack began in Normandy. Under the command of Waffen SS General Paul Hausser, four panzer divisions struck regiments of the 30th Infantry Division that had just arrived in the area. However, the soldiers of the 30th, aided by other infantry and armored units as well as Combat Command B (CCB) of the 3rd Armored Division, stalled the German offensive until the overall situation required the Germans to withdraw.

up to St.-Lô, then to Mortain. At Mortain I was wounded, facial wounds from a mortar shell. I was out of commission for four months which I spent in the hospital in England, the 140th General Hospital, and I spent a month in rehabilitation.

"I remember everything about it, from the time I was wounded, well even before I was wounded. Well, when I was hit I realized, because I heard the mortar shell coming down. They say you never hear the one that hits you, but I did, I heard it.

"One piece of shrapnel hit here. It knocked out six

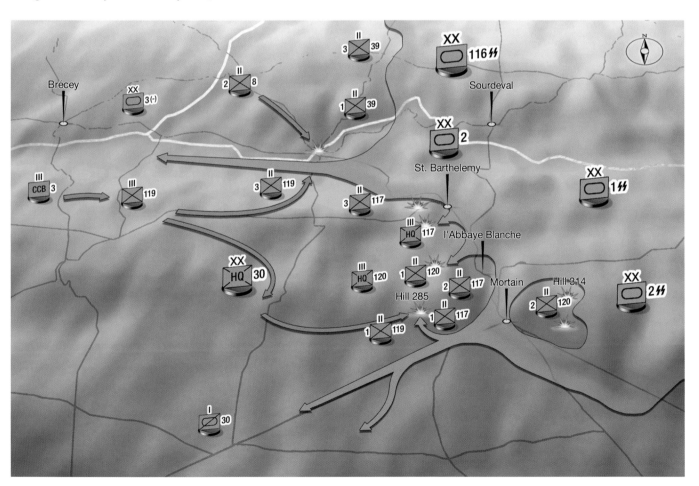

teeth, broke my jaw and lodged back into my palate, another piece went into my shoulder. Another piece hit my helmet right above this eye, and cut a big gash into my helmet. I gathered myself up, went back into the dugout where part of my platoon was. They wanted to get a medic for me but I knew we didn't have any medics up there so I took care of myself. I put sulphur powders in that hole, because I tried to talk and just talked right out that hole, so I quit talking.

"I walked back down through Mortain and someone came out of a building and got me by the arm and led me in, it was an aid station. A doctor looked at it and said, 'There ain't nothing I can do for you.' There was a mattress laying down and I went over and laid on it and went to sleep because I was out of it.

"Along about two or three that morning they had to get an armored ambulance in there to get

A view along the road leading east from L'Abbaye Blanche, a center of fighting in the Battle of Mortain toward the Neufbourg - Mortain train station. Most of the vehicles seen here were knocked out by a 57mm gun commanded by Sergeant Miller Rhyne of the 120th AT Company.

me out. The Germans were up here, so they got armor and took me over to another aid station, a MASH [Mobile Army Surgical Hospital] unit, like you're in a big tent. They patched me up, sewed me up, and eventually I got back to the Channel. I was loaded on [an] LST with German prisoners that had been wounded, other GI's that had been wounded...a whole boatload going across the English Channel. They was feeding me glucose, a gallon jug was hanging up here. The German prisoners had great big slices of bread and big sandwiches. Man, they scarfed the sandwiches down and I got so mad because I couldn't eat [laughter]."

By the afternoon of the attack's second day, Kluge had had enough. Not only was the U. S. First Army resisting his advance, but his tanks were under relentless attack from the air. Allied communication had improved to the point of allowing tank commanders to talk to the tactical fighter-bombers flying above them. Hitler, naturally, wanted the offensive to stay the course and berated Kluge for not doing so – Hitler would replace him shortly. Nevertheless, Kluge changed the route of the counteroffensive slightly and ordered a resumption of the attack on August 9 with a combat group under General Heinrich Eberbach, commander of Panzer Group West, who a few weeks earlier was commanding the panzers against Montgomery's British-Canadian assault. But the real alarm was in what was going on to the south and east of the Mortain battlefield.

The XV and XX Corps of the Third Army never made the trip into the Breton Peninsula. Instead, Patton ordered them directly south to the area north of the Loire River where they covered great distances and moved into the formerly German-occupied cities of Le Mans, Nantes and Rennes. Eisenhower and Montgomery then concurred with Bradley's idea to turn these corps northward toward the Allied line and squeeze off the over-extended German Seventh Army. Bradley was confident that the First Army could contain the German counteroffensive without Third Army's help. At the same time, the First Canadian Army would press toward Falaise while the British Second Army applied pressure along the line.

Fred Purdy and his Signal Corps outfit were about to become more than mere spectators to the action. They would finally receive their specialized communications equipment for field encoding transmissions and join Major General Walton H. "Johnnie" Walker's fast-moving XX Corps through the rolling hills north of the Loire River.

"We saw a lot of combat stuff in Normandy," says Fred Purdy. "I went every day for a long time with Irwin Shaw [U. S. Army warrant officer who later became an esteemed novelist and playwright] and we went all over the front. The next major thing that happened in Normandy on July 24th, I believe it is, we had received communication equipment. It was mounted on a truck in the field. I was in the First Army at the time, and then we joined the Third Army. Patton's Army had just been organized. And so Patton made the first breakthrough and breakout.

"We went down to Avranches…Avranches to Rennes, which is a pretty good sized city, first city I had seen. The Germans put up a pretty good defense there at Rennes. From Rennes we went to Le Mans, and Patton's Army was split up pretty much between Brittany, down below Le Mans, and up toward where they had the Germans and the Falaise Pocket. And that was one of the most big killing grounds of any place in the whole war. We had the Germans trapped between the British and Americans and Canadians, and there was a Polish armored division and a French armored division. And we…we didn't go up toward Argentan where they had them trapped. We left Le Mans…was there for a few days…and we left and went to our next stop…was Chartres. A pretty good size city before you get to Paris."

THE FALAISE GAP BECOMES A POCKET

After the British attempt to penetrate the German defense line between Caen and Falaise stalled in *Operation Goodwood*, a few inconclusive advances had been made on the left flank. On August 8, with the progress being made by the American units on the right flank, the revived offensive toward Falaise began. In the lead of the First Canadian Army were the 2nd Canadian and British 51st Infantry Divisions, departing just before midnight, August 8, in what was termed *Operation Totalize*. Another saturation bombardment from the air and a ground barrage led the way. Other units would follow to exploit the breakout.

Although the first phase of the attack was deemed a success, a few hours after daylight the 4th Canadian Armored Division and 1st Polish Armored Division (composed of Polish exiles and organized in Britain), encountered problems. There were traffic jams that delayed the tanks and armored vehicles in passing through the front lines. A follow-up air bombing in this operation also went awry, causing 355 casualties among the armored troops. Then they were hit by panzers standing in their path. The advance stagnated.

Receipt of this news confirmed Hitler's resolve to continue the offensive toward Avranches. But that was a trap that hastened the Wehrmacht's demise in northwest France. The First Army continued to contain the counteroffensive. The Third Army was moving east. The Canadian offensive restarted and continued on the road to Falaise. Along the way an increasing number of isolated German soldiers and units were surrendering to the relentless drives of the better manned and equipped Allied units.

Sergeant Leonard Roger Gariépy, a tank commander in the Canadian 6th Armored Regiment

Though this image was the result of a photo opportunity, it recreated a scene of Polish officers meeting their American counterparts after elements of the 10th Polish Dragoons met a company of the 359th Infantry Regiment on August 19 in closing the Falaise Gap.

(1st Hussars), in advancing toward Falaise became separated from the rest of his troop. He hooked up with tanks from C Squadron because he had malfunctioning communication equipment and overheated machine guns from a previous fight. But problems with his tank caused him to continue to fall behind.

"I eventually met Lieutenant Everett of C Squadron and told him of my reduced efficiency and suggested that I should conform to his troop. With him I crossed the river Laize on a 'Bailey' bridge. Then we continued our advance to the high ground south of Rouves. Reaching the apex we swung left [east] and continued. There was much firing because a big number of the enemy could be seen ahead. My last Browning [machine gun] finally gave up and could not be used any longer. I continued advancing using AP [Armor Piercing] and HE [High Explosive shells]. There was a big number of heavy caliber enemy guns on our front and the 75[mm] demanded priority. My solenoid firing mechanism also gave out then, so I waited for an opportunity of a depression in the ground to take cover and do something about my deplorable condition.

"Coming near a copse [of trees] I was going to halt when I observed a few enemies at the end of the copse. I charged them and being very close, they took fright and came out with the now familiar 'Kamerad.' The first individual being a major or the equivalent I shouted to him to come forward and I dismounted to search him personally while my crew covered me with the 75 mm. The enemy officer was about to burn some papers which I gave to Bde I.O. [Brigade Intelligence Officer] on my return. There were sixteen men there when I arrived and I asked if there were any more he said 'Yes, in the copse further.'

"I climbed back in the tank and while my co-driver was covering the prisoners with his Sten [submachine gun] I told the officer to order the remainder out or I would blast the copse. He gave a command but only two came out and he had shouted very loud. I did not seem satisfied for he shouted again, this time he said, 'All surrender' in German and to add, I fired one round of HE with the mechanical trigger. The remainder came out, twenty-four men, four of whom were lieutenants. I noticed the majority wore spurs and smelled of stable strongly so I investigated the copse and saw eight guns…75s and 88s…with limber lined up ready to be towed in a line facing our advance. After cleaning the copse of men the number of prisoners was growing all the time, they were coming from everywhere.

While linking up to surround the German Seventh Army in the Falaise-Argentan area, British Second Army Lieutenant Harold Ashby (left) exchanges information with Major Harold Delp of the U.S. Army. Critics charge that General Montgomery's positioning of his British divisions allowed more Germans to escape the Falaise Pocket.

"I had 110 [enemy prisoners] around my tank in no time so I got the senior officer by my side, ordered him to line them up in fours immediately before my tank, which they did promptly. I then told him to have them drop the rest of their equipment, and they did also. I explained to him that they would march in front of my tank in a column of four and if anyone made a move suspicious to my crew they would fire and shoot the lot. I then ordered the column to march and we moved towards Mézière which I knew was occupied by our infantry. On the cross-country march I stayed in the open as much as possible because I did not want my people to fire on me. All the way along we were joined by small isolated groups of more prisoners and when I neared Mézière the count had gone over 200."

Gariépy continued to move to the rear, seeking a POW cage where he could turn over his prisoners to the appropriate authorities, but not finding a place for them. Along the way, the POWs in his charge had grown to 325 men.

"I marched the column all the way with my tank covering them from the rear, and me leading on foot with the senior officer by my side. We reached Cauvicourt at darkness much to my relief. There I handed my prisoners to an interrogation officer. He then informed me to stand by because he wanted me to escort them further. I explained to him that it was impossible for me to do so because it's extremely hard to escort POWs with a tank alone. He said he sympathized with me but it could not be helped.

"After seeing my men I took it upon myself to refuse. We had had nothing to eat since early morning, we fought at a disadvantage from 1200 to 1600 hours, herded a few hundred prisoners for six miles. My men were tired so I ordered to pull in a yard under cover, took leave on the 'QT' from the interrogation officer and made the crew take a well earned rest."

The 325 German soldiers and eight pieces of captured artillery finally arrived at a place where they could be processed. Gariépy and the rest of the 6th Armored Regiment continued the push down the road to Falaise while to the south, American forces where standing down when they wanted to be pursuing an enemy they appeared to have on the run.

The XV Corps of Patton's Third Army reached Argentan on August 13, southeast of Falaise, where a brief fight with Panzer Lehr Division led to the German panzers disengaging. The XV Corps commander, Major General Wade H. "Ham" Haislip, and Patton wanted the armored units to continue north to seal the pocket formed by Allied forces pressing from the west, north and south on the German defenders gathering near Falaise. But General Bradley put the brakes on the XV Corps' advance. Part of Bradley's reason was to avoid XV Corps becoming too separated from the rest of 12th Army Group and thereby risking an isolated attack by the caged animal that was then the German Seventh Army. The other reason was that Montgomery, still in charge of the ground war, had

drawn a line on the map where he wanted the American forces to stop and the Commonwealth forces to begin.

Despite this lost opportunity to cut off and trap the entire German army, a great number of Wehrmacht soldiers were captured or killed in the Falaise Pocket in the middle of August. If Montgomery had thrown more support behind the Canadian offensive, he still might have closed the Falaise Pocket without the Americans crossing into his sector. However, German units and remnants of units were escaping and heading east across the Seine.

Hitler, on August 16, finally realized that the army must escape if it was to survive. When he sacked Günther von Kluge he replaced him with a favored commander. Field Marshal Walter Model came from the Eastern Front to take over in the West. However, by the time the change of command occurred on August 19, there was little Model could do other than supervise the withdrawal east begun by Kluge. The Führer continued what he had been doing since Mortain – micromanaging the details of troop movements from his headquarters hundreds of miles to the east.

The loss of life in men and horses on the German side at Falaise was unfathomable, but war is a unique kind of tragedy that brings out rare

Top: Covering this field are the abandoned helmets of German soldiers who surrendered en masse here on August 23 as Allied units closed the Falaise pocket around them.
Bottom: Two Sherman tanks of the Sherbrooke Fusiliers add firepower to the attack on the High School for Girls in central Falaise where several dozen soldiers of the 12th SS Panzer Division are holed up. The picture was taken along Rue des Prémontrés at the intersection of Rue Saint-Jean on August 17.

emotions in otherwise reasonable men. Illustrative of this were the feelings of William Funkhouser, a 1st Infantry Division veteran of the entire Normandy Campaign: "It wasn't the man, it wasn't the enemy...it was 'one.' Now I know you can't understand that, but there wasn't any personality involved. Whenever they could they'd bring us a hot meal up, and I remember sitting one day, leaning back against this building eating and there were two or three dead Germans laying around over there. That didn't bother me one way or the other. Now Americans I could never look at their face...a dead American. I'd avoid looking at their faces if I walked by them on the road. But the Germans, it just didn't seem to matter. I can't explain it."

The Allied commanders, and General Eisenhower in particular, were then faced with how to exploit the situation in France. It wasn't the complete collapse that COSSAC and SHAEF outlined in contingency plans. Although 50,000 Germans were taken prisoner in the Falaise Pocket and more than 10,000 were killed, individual soldiers, panzers and organized units were escaping eastward to continue the battle for France, probably behind the Seine River barrier. Eisenhower now needed to satisfy the political issues, as well as the military and logistical needs of Allied forces whose leaders had divergent ideas in defeating the enemy. Among these considerations was the situation about to come to life on France's Mediterranean coast as *Operation Anvil* was poised to add even more Allied forces to those stamping out the Nazi presence in the country.

Lined up on August 20 in front of a wrecked German tank and displaying a captured swastika flag is a group of GIs who were left behind to "mop-up" in Chambois, France, the last Wehrmacht stronghold in the Falaise Gap area.

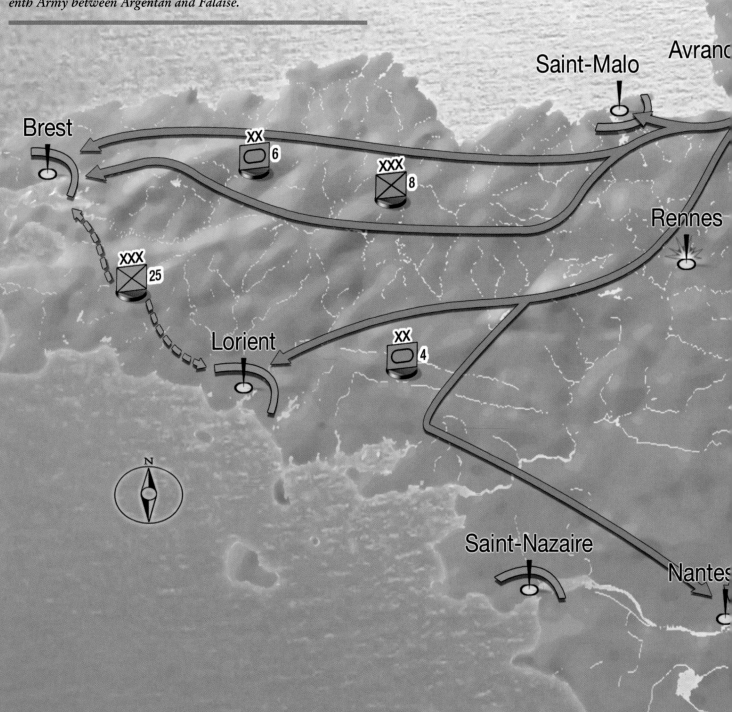

The area of France controlled by the Allies went from the constrained confines of Normandy, where for two months progress was measured in yards, to more than a third of the country being overrun within a few weeks in August 1944. The most dramatic movements were made by Lt. Gen. George S. Patton's Third Army that ranged from Brittany and the Loire River valley to the Seine River and Paris. The First and Second Armies caught up with the Third along the Seine after trapping a large portion of the German Seventh Army between Argentan and Falaise.

Saint-Malo

Avranc

Brest

XX
6

XXX
8

Rennes

XXX
25

Lorient

XX
4

N

Saint-Nazaire

Nantes

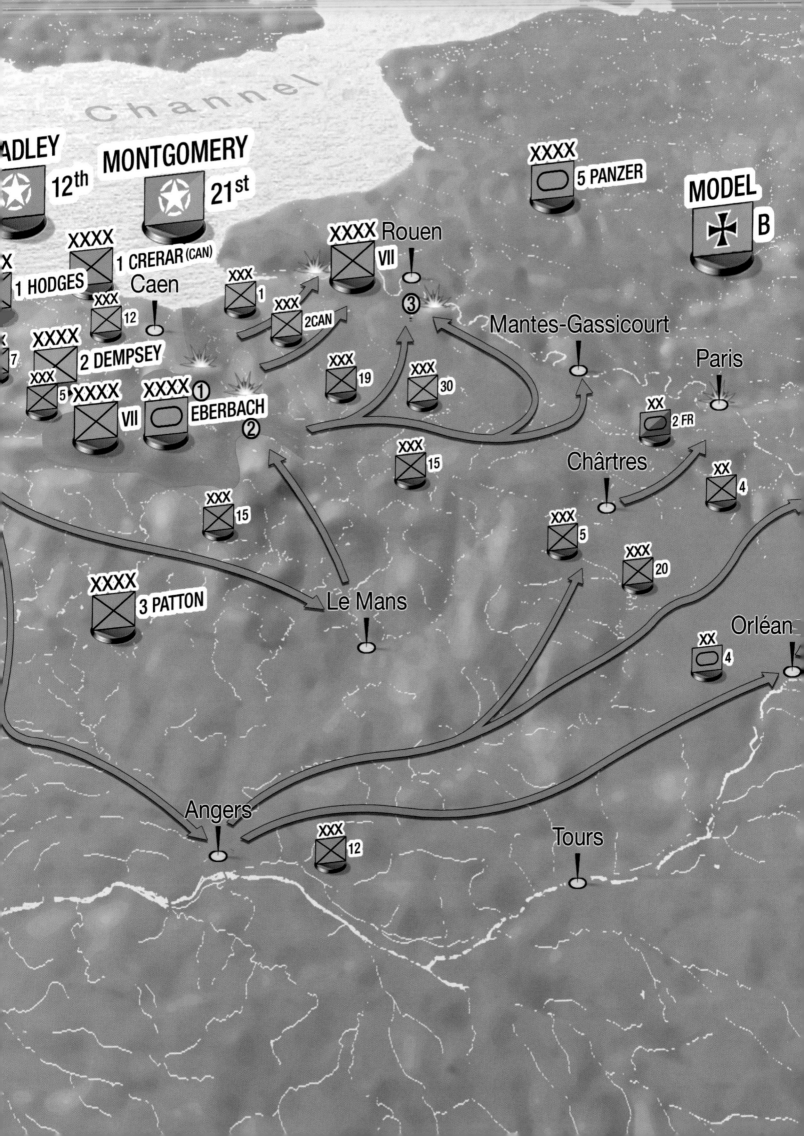

The Plot To Assassinate Hitler

On July 20, 1944 an exploding bomb hidden in an officer's briefcase in Hitler's East Prussian command post nearly brought an abrupt end to the Nazi dictator's life. Although there had been many attempts on Hitler's life during his political career (at least 40 are documented between 1930-44), this assassination plot was conceived and launched by German military officers serving in high positions in army leadership. It very nearly succeeded, and Hitler wreaked terrible retribution on the plotters and anyone even remotely suspected of being involved.

In the OKW headquarters called "Wolf's Lair" near Rastenburg in East Prussia, a trusted staff officer, Lieutenant Colonel Claus Schenk Graf von Stauffenberg, placed the bomb-laden briefcase under a large conference table during an afternoon meeting. Stauffenberg excused himself to make a phone call and left the room. The briefcase exploded, stunning the Führer but not seriously injuring him.

Left: Adolf Hitler and Benito Mussolini inspect damage to the conference room at Führerhauptquartier Wolfsschanze (Führer headquarters or "Wolf's Lair") near Rastenburg, East Prussia after the July 20, 1944 assassination attempt on Hitler. Right: Lieutenant Colonel Claus Schenk Graf von Stauffenberg.

"During the time of our retreat from France, a German officer, Colonel Graf von Stauffenberg tried to assassinate Hitler on July 20, 1944," explains Fritz Baresel. "He failed and was executed on the same day. This failed attempt to eliminate Hitler brought some changes. The whole Army was ordered to salute by raising the right arm in the Hitler salute and never use the traditional soldier's salute anymore. Many officers lost their lives in the months following the assassination attempt, even Field Marshal Rommel, one of the best commanding officers in WWII."

This assassination attempt was the culmination of a campaign which began in 1938 as officials inside and outside the military could not accept a Germany with Hitler and the Nazis in charge. It was a popular pastime inside gatherings of German bureaucrats and intellectuals as well as selected officer messes to talk of ways to bring down Hitler. Even some Abwehr (German Military Intelligence) officials were involved. The highest ranking officers in the resistance were General Ludwig Beck, former Chief of Staff of OKH, Admiral Wilhelm Canaris, the head of the Abwehr and Field Marshal Erwin von Witzleben, former commander of the German First Army. They recruited prominent civilians as well but there was little beyond talk to come from these early meetings.

In 1942 Colonel Henning von Tresckow jump-started the resistance movement by developing a network of far-ranging contacts with reserve army units from the Bendlerblock, an army office building in central Berlin. In this he was aided by two high-ranking army staff officers. In looking to stage a coup and change of government after Hitler's death, Tresckow and his associates used a contingency plan called *Operation Valkyrie*, originally a contingency plan to mobilize the Replacement Army (Ersatzheer – the home guard) in case of an uprising by the millions in Germany's foreign forced labor pool or to put down urban riots caused by Allied bombing. Although capture and trial of Hitler, rather than assassination, was discussed, it was decided that soldiers could only act against their oaths of allegiance to the Führer if he was dead. The new movement attracted more interest among Germany's army and navy officer corps, civilian officials and opposition politicians. Excluded from the revolution circle were Communists and most Nazis, although two SS men were involved. Outside of Germany, knowledge of the conspiracy was extremely rare. And still no assassination attempts were made.

Enter Stauffenberg, an aristocratic field officer who distinguished himself in Tunisia but who was also horribly injured in an air attack there. After he returned to his home in Germany to recover, Stauffenberg, like a growing number of officers, saw that the course of the war waged by Hitler was leading Germany into a devastating defeat. He was recruited into the inner circle of conspirators in 1943.

Over the period of a year from March 1943, Tresckow and the other conspiracy leaders on four occasions tried to get one of the military in the group close enough to Hitler to assassinate him in what would most likely be a suicide bomb or grenade attack. All four failed. As the war went against the Nazis, Hitler stopped most public appearances, rarely visited Berlin and was surrounded by more and more security men.

In order for the post-assassination coup to be successful by implementing *Valkyrie*, the head of the Replacement Army, General Friedrich Fromm, needed to be involved or be taken out of the picture. Fromm had known about the conspiracy for some time and seemed to go along. An indication of this was Stauffenberg's appointment as Fromm's Chief of Staff, working out of the Bendlerblock. More importantly, Stauffenberg would be in a position to attend military meetings at the OKW headquarters as Fromm's representative – meetings in which Hitler would be present.

In the summer of 1944, the tide of war was turning against Germany on three fronts and officers like Erwin Rommel foresaw Germany's eventual defeat. Rommel felt Hitler should be arrested and tried as a criminal rather than be killed; he allowed men around him who were involved in the conspiracy to prepare for the coup even though Rommel himself took no direct action in it.

Also in the summer of 1944, the conspirators felt the Gestapo secret police were closing in on them rapidly. Some, like Tresckow, began to see themselves as martyrs, sending a message to the world that there were honest, rational people inside Germany opposed to the Nazi's war even if the coup failed. More officials were recruited, including the military head in Paris who would direct the disarming of loyal Nazi troops in France. Field Marshal Günther von Kluge was recruited to reach out to the Allies after Rommel's July 17 brush with death sent him back home to Ulm, Germany.

New assassination attempts were planned. After another conspirator, General Helmuth Stieff lost his nerve, Stauffenberg began carrying briefcase bombs to the "Wolf's Lair." On July 11, Heinrich Himmler, head of the SS, wasn't at the meeting so the attempt was aborted. By July 15 the conspirators decided Himmler's presence wasn't required; but that day the Führer wasn't present. Finally by July 20, everything was in place. Hitler and nineteen officers, including OKW chiefs Keitel and Jodl were present.

Stauffenberg armed the plastic explosives bomb in a bathroom by setting a delayed chemically-activated detonator. He placed the briefcase bomb under the table near Hitler. After he excused himself from the meeting another officer, Colonel Heinz Brandt, unwittingly moved the briefcase with his foot. This act shielded Hitler from the brunt of the blast, but killed Brandt, two other officers and the meeting stenographer.

Adolf Hitler welcomes dignitaries to Wolf's Lair including Claus von Stauffenberg (left), and his boss General Colonel Friedrich Fromm on July 15. On the right edge of the photograph is Field Marshal Wilhelm Keitel, chief of the OKW.

By this time, Stauffenberg was making his way to a plane to fly back to Berlin. Another officer had phoned the Bendlerblock to announce that Hitler was dead and the officers there began to implement *Valkyrie*. In Paris, the military governor of occupied France, Carl Heinrich von Stülpnagel, disarmed the SS and others loyal to Hitler and captured most of their leaders. He informed Kluge to contact the Al-

lies. In other cities throughout the Reich similar actions occurred.

However almost as it occurred, the coup started to unravel. Reports began to circulate that Hitler had survived, and by the time Stauffenberg reached Bendlerblock Fromm had confirmed this with Keitel. There was a struggle in the Bendlerblock and elsewhere between revolutionist and loyalist officers. By 2300 on July 20 the loyalists were getting control of the situation. Fromm attempted to cover his involvement by arresting Stauffenberg and three others at Bendlerblock after a brief shootout. After an impromptu court martial the four officers were executed just after midnight in the Bendlerblock courtyard. When Fromm went to Propaganda Minister Joseph Goebbels to report that he had suppressed the coup, Goebbels' only reply was, "You've been in a damn hurry to get your witnesses below ground."

A sweeping investigation followed and many of the conspirators who did not take their own lives like Beck and Tresckow were tried and executed or sent to concentration camps. Some 5,000 were arrested and 200, including Stülpnagel and later Fromm, were executed. Some of the victims were not conspirators at all, just people whom the Gestapo wanted to get out of the way for other reasons. Industrial head and Hitler confidant Albert Speer was implicated but found innocent. Kluge was allowed to continue to lead German forces in France for almost a month. However, once he was relieved of command, he feared being tried in a "People's Court" for his involvement and took a cyanide pill on the trip back to Germany.

Erwin Rommel was implicated by a member of Stülpnagel's staff under torture. Hitler knew he could not bring charges of treason against one of Germany's most beloved military leaders. Two of Hitler's generals visited Rommel's home on October 14, 1944 and offered him a choice: Rommel could commit suicide that day and he would receive a funeral and pension fitting his stature; or he would be tried by the "People's Court" in which case his family and staff would be executed with him. Rommel chose the former. He was given a full military funeral with honors and a declaration of a national day of mourning by Hitler after his death (reported as being due to complications from his injuries in the strafing attack).

When General Eisenhower arrived at General Montgomery's headquarters on July 20 after the failure of *Operation Goodwood*, he was temporarily distracted from confronting Monty over the misrepresentation of *Goodwood's* goals by reports that Hitler was dead. When the truth came out shortly thereafter, Eisenhower returned to the business at hand – defeating Hitler and Germany by military means.

During the trial of the July 20 Plot *conspirators at the Elssholzstraße (People's Court) in Berlin, Else Bergenthal, former housekeeper of Colonel General Ludwig Beck, gives a Nazi salute to People's Court President Roland Freisler after her questioning on August 7, 1944.*

GENIA
LILY
L'incomparable danseuse
de l'A.B.C.
L'inénarrable Comique
LYDIA
La remarquable
mains à mains
FARINA
Le réputé ZAZOU
ET
Compositeur Henri

CHAPTER 5

THE ALLIED INVASION OF SOUTHERN FRANCE

ANVIL BECOMES DRAGOON

As Allied forces moved away from the Normandy invasion beaches after the capture of Cherbourg at the end of June, 1944 and after the opening phase of *Operation Goodwood* in mid-July, the role of the British and American navies in the Channel changed. Gone were the big warships – back to England or other ports for resupply and rejuvenation. What remained of naval combat vessels in the English Channel and the Bay of the Seine were smaller warships, mine sweepers and patrol craft to protect the continuous flow of men and materiel across the Channel.

The German Kriegsmarine and Luftwaffe made attempts to disrupt this flow, but few of these attacks resulted in significant losses for the Allies. The most effective of the enemy attacks were aerial torpedo drops by JU-88s. German

mines – those previously undiscovered and some new sea mines sown by the enemy - continued to cause problems, but constant minesweeper vigilance kept the transports and supply ships safe as long as they stayed on course and away from the enemy guns still active in the Pas de Calais. However, many of the ships involved in *Operation Overlord* would soon be summoned to the south to reinforce the tiny U. S. Eighth Fleet in the Mediterranean.

The ships would support *Operation Anvil* – a code name changed to *Operation Dragoon* in the summer of 1944 because it was feared that German agents may have discerned the target of the stale code name. Yet the more rapidly planning proceeded for this invasion of southern France, the less British Prime Minister Winston Churchill liked it. When meaningful progress finally came in Italy and northern France in late July, Churchill again schemed for a change in Allied Mediterranean strategy. He had new ideas for a Balkan campaign – this time to land in the Adriatic and push through northern

Left: Looking like a scene staged for a movie, this female FFI fighter carrying a machine gun and wearing a French military helmet seeks cover beside a signpost during the Paris uprising. **Right:** *Lieutenant General Alexander M. "Sandy" Patch, commander of the U. S. Seventh Army.*

Yugoslavia and over the mountains to Austria. When that idea was thrown overboard he suggested landing on the French Atlantic coast. To these and all other attempts to change the mission he was given an emphatic "No" by SHAEF, by General Eisenhower personally most of the time, for many reasons. With the Allied front pushing across Northern France, consuming resources at an alarming rate, at the top of that list of reasons was capturing Marseille (Marseilles) and its huge port on the Mediterranean coast.

In March 1944, Lieutenant General Alexander M. "Sandy" Patch came from duty in the Pacific to lead the new U. S. Seventh Army based in Algiers. The combined staff planning the operations of Allied forces in *Dragoon*, serving under Allied Commander in Chief, Mediter-

British soldiers land during an exercise in Algeria. Early training of units expected to land in the invasion of Southern France, including French soldiers, occurred here.

ranean, General Sir Henry M. "Jumbo" Wilson, had an important additional consideration for the southern France invasion: American and British units executing the *Dragoon* operation would be joined by the French II Corps led by Général d'Armée Jean de Lattre de Tassigny. The French would capture Toulon and Marseille and then lead the drive up the central Rhône River valley to the Belfort Gap. Landing site selection was quickly decided – of the possible beaches, only those east of Toulon, along the French Riviera, were within range of Allied fighters and were suitable for landing large troop formations. U. S. Navy Vice Admiral H. Kent Hewitt commanded the Western Naval Task Force whose job it was to put the troops ashore and support the *Dragoon* landing.

Veteran U. S. Army units, the 3rd, 36th and 45th In-

fantry Divisions, were pulled from service in the Italian Campaign to form the VI Corps under Major General Lucien K. Truscott. The corps would form the assault troops for the landing with two French divisions coming in on D plus 1. Airborne and commando forces were also assigned roles in the operation. For several months the troops for the invasion had been training; the Americans in Italy with their assault naval complement and the French in Algiers. These exercises were operated on the *Overlord* model, complete with full-scale dress rehearsals. Also, since April, Allied strategic bombers, including B-24s from the Fifteenth Army Air Force, had been bombing targets along a wide stretch of the Mediterranean coast. The XII Tactical Air Command added medium bombers to the operation.

A Supermarine Spitfire Mark IX of RAF Squadron 242 taxies past parked aircraft to a refueling depot at Calenzana, Corsica, after covering the invasion beaches during Operation Dragoon.

Some American fighter wings were moved to the island of Corsica to be closer to the landing area. As at Normandy, air operations were disguised so the actual landing beaches were kept secret. The strategic bombing missions hit Toulon harbor, bridges and rail lines while the tactical sorties bombed casemated guns, strong points and radar installations on the coastline.

The German high command was concerned about the situation in southern France in addition to its many other worries. The Nineteenth Army in Army Group G was responsible for this area. There were 30,000 men in the immediate vicinity, perhaps 200,000 to draw on in the region. Atlantic Wall style fortifications were built to protect ports, along with strong points and beach obstacles. Most of the infantry

were static divisions. However there were not enough of these to man the fortifications adequately and there were no panzer units stationed along the French Riviera before the invasion. While Allied bombing patterns and deceptive intelligence kept the Germans guessing as to where the invasion might occur – either on the French coast or on the northern Italian coast behind the front lines – by the beginning of August they had just about pinpointed the date and location of the *Dragoon* landings. Hitler, as usual, did not want his commanders to give up any ground at all in southern France. In any case, Hitler wanted to avoid a "walkover" in which the Germans could be manhandled by just the Free French forces without tying up other Allied units in the region. However, there was little the Germans could do to stop the invasion because their forces everywhere in France continued to suffer from a lack of ships, planes, equipment and manpower. About all that could be done was to send the 11th Panzer Division west from the First Army guarding France's Atlantic coast.

THE MEDITERRANEAN LANDINGS

By August 5, 1944, *Operation Dragoon* was moving forward at full speed, despite Churchill's obstinate opposition. The British Prime Minister failed in every effort to have Eisenhower change his mind, including threatening to resign. Churchill didn't resign, but punned that he was "dragooned' into the operation. Soon, the last of the Dragoon pre-D-Day air attacks were completed, assault troops were loaded and shortly convoys cast off from a number of ports in Italy and North Africa. Something new was added to *Operation Dragoon* that wasn't a part of the Normandy invasion – aircraft carriers. Nine escort carriers of the British, American and New Zealand navies carried squadrons of Grumman F6F Hellcat and Seafire (Royal Navy version of the Spitfire) fighters to spot for naval artillery fire and to cover the drive inland.

USS *Bayfield* was among the many ships dispatched from England to take part in *Dragoon* because the attack transport remained the flagship of one of the assault force commanders, Rear Admiral Don P. Moon. Unfortunately, at least two tragedies struck the *Bayfield* as the campaign began. First, Admiral Moon, a perfectionist who took his job perhaps too seriously, was suffering from physical and stress-induced fatigue during preparations for the Provence landings. He was worried that everything was not in order and though he seemed satisfied with Admiral Hewitt's assurance on August 4, the following morning Moon took his own life. Then, a few days before the invasion, *Bayfield* received a direct hit from a bomb dropped on her deck by a German plane. The bomb hit the LVCP for which Coast Guardsman Tommy Harbour was the mechanic.

"Harold Schultz [my seaman] was hit in southern France, and Jones [John W. Jones] was hit there when a shell hit in our LCVP No. 4, and shot a hole in the side of it big as your fist, see. I had just moved outta the way…it was 'General Quarters' and an air raid. I was gettin' ready to go over and lay a smoke screen, and I

Top: Two GIs who had just landed at St.-Raphaël on August 15 stop to examine a buried Panzer II turret, part of the German beach defense. **Bottom:** *U. S. Army soldiers landing during* Operation Dragoon. *Among them was Charles Serio, a forward observer for the 995th Field Artillery Battalion: "We come in behind 'em and we landed at St. Tropez Bay, which was one of them beaches where you go down for the summer. They didn't have enough soldiers there for any kind of resistance."*

moved outta the position where we was standin' and a shell hit there…woulda got me in the back if I had a stayed there a few seconds longer. And it got Jones…got Harold [both wounded]."

Harbour joined the crew of another LCVP for the landing at St.-Raphaël in the Camel Beach sector, where the eastern landing zones were located.

"Well, we hit southern France," Harbour recalled. "I'll tell you what, we took on seasoned troops is what they called 'em. Now they brought them from the mountains above Rome, down through Naples and put 'em on the *Bayfield*, and we took 'em down to St.-Raphaël and landed 'em down there."

More than 800 ships participated in the August 15 landing operation. The Mediterranean coast of Provence rises rapidly into high mountain ranges. It was important to gain the high ground quickly, so an air drop of American and British paratroopers preceded the invasion by a few hours. This 1st Airborne Task Force was commanded by General Robert T. Frederick. The drop went smoothly with few losses. One stick came down in the middle of a German corps headquarters and there was a dis-

ruption of corps' command and control as a result. The airborne troops fought off enemy attacks and one unit made contact with the 45th Infantry Division on D-Day. Just after the start of the amphibious landings, glider troops landed successfully.

As at Normandy, the invasion was preceded by air and naval bombardment although all occurred in daylight. In addition, many diversions were timed to confuse the Germans about the exact landing sites and also to surprise some of the village garrisons. Dummy parachutists, complete with uniforms and booby traps in their torsos, were dropped between Marseille and Toulon, while other air and sea deceptions were employed to fool German defenders. However, German commanders were not tricked into shifting resources to the west.

The assault carriers of Operation Dragoon's *TF-88 steam in formation off the French Mediterranean coast. HMS* Attacker *and HMS* Khedive *are behind HMS* Pursuer, *with three Wildcat fighters visible on the flight deck.*

Another diversion was conducted on the opposite end of the French Riviera just east of Cannes to cut off enemy reinforcements from the east. A Special Operations Group of PT and gunboats landed French naval commandos to block the coast road east of the invasion site. This operation, called *Rosie*, was under the command of American acting icon

Lieutenant Commander Douglas E. Fairbanks, Jr., USNR who was in the thick of it while commanding the operation. The U. S. 1st Special Service Force, aka the "Devil's Brigade," secured the Hyeres Islands on the left flank of the American landing zone. They were one of the groups of French, American and Commonwealth commandos that landed on islands and coastal areas west of the

U.S. Navy Lt. Cmdr. Douglas Fairbanks Jr., the American actor who commanded the naval portion of the August 15 commando raid near Cannes, meets King George VI during a naval review earlier in the European war.

in this popular resort region. By the end of the day they hooked up with commandos, paratroopers and members of the Forces Françaises de l'Intérieur (FFI) who were and would continue to be very active in this campaign.

In the Camel Beach area the terrain was more challenging with short beaches backed up by cliffs. But St.-Raphaël was a vital objective.

main landing zones to capture strategic roads and enemy batteries. Their work was extremely successful as they surprised most of the defenders and took numerous prisoners. Most of the actual fighting during this *Romeo* operation was at sea when some of the escort ships tangled with German patrol boats.

By the time the first assault troops landed in the three zones, Alpha, Delta and Camel Beaches, at 0800 August 15 there existed an almost anti-climactic feel to their assault – so much had been accomplished by the commando, airborne and bombing operations by that time. The misty morning did not deter the Allies from providing excellent covering fire and at Alpha and Delta Beaches there was almost no resistance and few casualties (except to mines). Combat teams from the 3rd and 45th Infantry Divisions moved inland quickly and captured St. Tropez and other towns

There was a small airfield there, the railroad ran nearby and a road left the town to travel through a gorge to the interior. Because the Camel Red Beach area in front of St.-Raphaël was mined and the town was full of strong points, the landing there was postponed until the afternoon. Landings on Camel Green and Camel Blue Beaches went off on schedule in the morning.

"It just so happened that No. 4 boat, at No. 2 hatch, was settin' out from the bow of the ship to where we could go down quicker than anybody else," says Harbour. "We could unhook the ring, and we could swerve…that boat was a runnin' when we hit the water, and we'd run the same speed as the ship. I had the smoke pot goin' by the time we hit the water. And we really did puff the smoke. Wind wasn't blowin' hard or anything. I could really lay a good one like we did in southern France.

"[The troops]…they were seasoned all right, because they run the Germans 60 miles the first day. That's what come on the movie on the ship. Somebody was filmin' it. And at nighttime, after chow, you could go up, and they'd show the movie and show what was goin' on at different places, different things, you know. So, anyhow, we took some soldiers back to Naples. The *Bayfield* had a good doctor and crew on there because we took on wounded in Normandy, Utah Beach and in St.-Raphaël. And we didn't take on near as many in southern France, St.-Raphaël, 'cause [a] big hospital ship come in there. Anchored right out from us there."

The Camel Green and Camel Blue Beaches landings went smoothly. There were trenches and defense positions on Camel Blue but the defenders, including sixty Poles, did not have their hearts in the fight and quickly surrendered. Most casualties came during unloading operations later in the day when a Luftwaffe air at-

tack damaged two LSTs. Despite a lot of naval support fire, Camel Red Beach was still saturated with sea mines the sweepers could not reach and the gunfire failed to detonate many of the land mines on the beach. The Camel Red Beach assault force was landed at Camel Green and St.-Raphaël was taken from the landward side early on August 16.

Bud Taylor continued to serve the 5-inch guns on USS *Thompson* when the destroyer was summoned to join the naval force for Operation *Dragoon*. The destroyer was part of a separate convoy control group that Admiral Hewitt had designated to guard follow-up landings. A large number of French Navy ships were in the Western Naval Task Force, most of them in this convoy, adding a Gallic presence to the sea as well as the land elements of *Dragoon*.

U. S. Army soldiers examine the bodies of four Germans killed during the preparatory bombardment of St.-Raphaël during Operation Dragoon.

"We left [after] 40 days there [off Normandy]," says Taylor. "We went to the Mediterranean

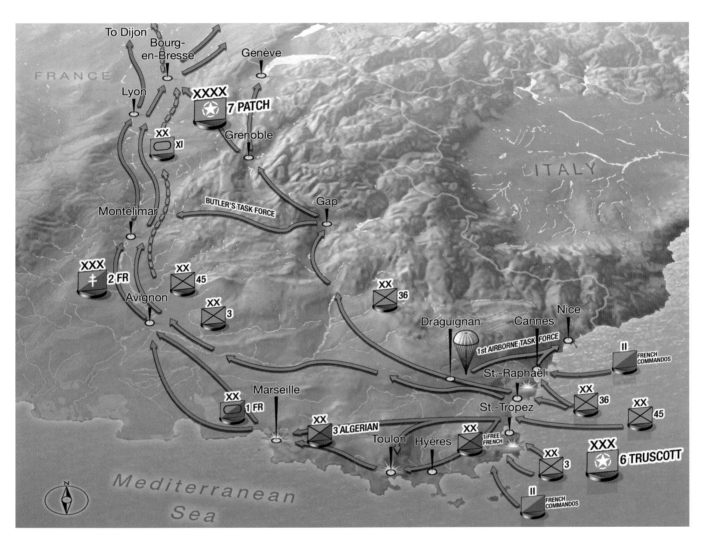

and was in North Africa. We came up and around and made [the] southern France invasion. We had a little island off of France, I forget the name of the town on the island out there [Ile du Levant]. It was assigned to us. They said they had an emergency, 18-inch gun out there or something like that. So we sorta dreaded that, an 18-inch gun, that's pretty good. We didn't see it anyway, we were just there. We didn't fire a shot. We were just there to put the troops ashore."

After landing on the beaches of the French Riviera, Americans of the assault force cleared the immediate area and prepared for the French II Corps to land. The French then attacked to the west and drove the Germans from the key coastal cities of Toulon and Marseille while the Americans moved inland through the mountains of Aix-en-Provence. They also sent a task force east to the Italian border. Eventually both French and American forces moved north along the Rhône River to a juncture with U. S. Third Army forces.

THE ALLIED PUSH NORTHWARD THROUGH CENTRAL FRANCE

The *Operation Dragoon* assault troop landings and the initial push off the beaches were executed beyond expectations of all concerned. Certainly much was learned from the Normandy experience; but other factors, such as using all combat veteran assault troops and decreased enemy resistance, played a part in *Dragoon*'s early success. The opposition of the

British Prime Minister to the operation was a fact only known to the high command. On the afternoon of the invasion, Churchill, on board a British ship, was visible to the landing troops, cigar in hand, flashing his signature "V for Victory" sign. Later he would congratulate Eisenhower on the operation's successful beginning.

Naval operations continued to the west and for "psychological" rather than military reasons General Patch wanted Cannes and Nice taken. The famous resort city of Cannes, after an intimidating naval bombardment, fell on August 24 to the American 1st Airborne Task Force. Neutral Monaco was bypassed and Nice fell on August 30 to the airborne task force. By September 9 the entire French Riviera was secured to the Italian border, toward which German Nineteenth Army survivors were retreating.

To the west, more coastal objectives were being pursued. The VI Corps moved inland through the Provence passes where German defenders were executing a fighting withdrawal. Meanwhile, the French II Corps moved due west to take the important ports of Marseille and Toulon. The big warships continued to pound coastal strong points around Toulon and on the coast approaching Marseille. There the Allied ships also encountered German naval ships and a U-boat attempting to escape Toulon harbor. All of these small engagements worked out in favor of the Allies and German naval personnel ended up in prison compounds with their army brethren.

The French II Corps liberated both Toulon and Marseille on August 28 and then proceeded up

Minister of War André Diethelm and General Jean de Lattre de Tassigny (in the light military shirt) review French II Corps soldiers in Marseille following its August 28 liberation.

the west bank of the Rhône River to secure a potential supply line for the forces moving across France. A French reconnaissance patrol made contact with General George S. Patton's Third Army near Dijon on September 12. At the same time, the 3rd and 45th Infantry Divisions were pushing northward while an independent task force that Truscott formed from various units was swinging to the northeast in order to encircle German defenders.

John Ervin from New Jersey attended ROTC classes while a student at Rutgers University and became an officer. He was a veteran of the campaigns in Sicily and Italy and in southern France was a captain leading a 4.2-inch mortar company,

American soldiers head inland from the beach. U. S. Army Lieutenant John Ervin remembers the reception they received: "The people were so happy that we were there and had liberated them that they gave us fresh fruit and vegetables as we traveled along. My three years of French in high school did come in very handy on many occasions."

part of the 3rd Chemical Mortar Battalion.

"I went into southern France...H plus an hour. My platoons went in H plus thirty minutes. They were supporting a battalion and I was liaison with the regiment. It was with the 3rd Division, with the 15th Infantry Regiment. There was no firing and we moved in quickly. Now, you have to remember, the invasion of southern France was August the 15th.

"The landing in Normandy was on June the 6th. They were stymied, but they broke out from St.-Lô, if I remember correctly, about two days [actually about three weeks] before we invaded southern France. With that breakout, then, the

Germans were interested in saving all of their troops, and they had troops down in the southwestern portion of France as well as in the western portion of France. We landed in the southeastern portion of France, east of the Rhône River. Our job was to get over to the Rhône River and make a beachhead available, so that the French divisions could come in and go over to Toulouse, I guess it was, and go up the west side of the Rhône River, and we went up, the American troops went up, the east side of the Rhône River. It was going very quickly, simply because the Germans were trying to preserve their army and it was withdrawing."

The American units were advancing faster than were their supplies, particularly artillery am-

Five Germans taken prisoner during the invasion, in-structed to keep their hands around the exposed cover ribs of this GMC truck, await movement to a POW holding area.

munition, and the Germans were withdrawing even faster. As a result, a number of German Army Group G units escaped the jaws of the French and American advance, much as their comrades did at Falaise. But they left behind 57,000 POWs, tons of equipment and another strategic region lost to the Allies.

As the Allied armies moved north in central France they encountered more and more FFI members who revealed themselves to the arriving soldiers. These Resistance members had been op-erating throughout the long period of the Nazi-collaborationist Vichy government control and, like the Resistance members in northern France, they received help from British and American special operations branches. John Dowling, Jr., another New Jersey native, served in a special section of the USAAF from a highly classified base in England.

"They moved us up to the Midlands and assigned our outfit to the OSS, Office of Strategic Services, which had to do with sabotage work behind enemy lines, and there were two bases in England that did that. One base was our base at Alconbury and another base that the British just called 'Base X.' We were involved for about a year and a half in working with the French underground, supplying people behind enemy lines for sabotage ventures, and, when a man was behind enemy lines, he had to be supplied with equipment, bombs, ammunition, guns, everything, and so we would drop supplies to him on predetermined, pre-designated signals.

"The people that did this work were called 'Joes.' The man going behind enemy lines, he didn't want anybody to know who he was, and so, everybody was 'Joe.' There was a hole cut in the bottom of this great big B-24 airplane and it was covered with just a plain piece of plywood, and that we called the 'Joe Hole.' We would get to where the person was to do his sabotage, blow up a bridge, blow up an ammunition dump, or something like that, and would take that [plywood] off, and he would fall out the 'Joe Hole' and parachute to the ground. Now, mind you that this is done from the big B-24 bomber flying at high speed, flying at low altitude, and flying in the dead of night. One airplane to a target, no protection, no guns, no armor plate, just an airplane flying as fast as it goes. So, it was quite hazardous to drop people out in that fashion.

"We would drop the 'Joe' and his equipment but we could never drop enough, because the airplane was flying so fast that we covered too much territory, and you wouldn't dare make a

second run, because then the people would know. So you had to come back another time to surprise them. We would come back again, and drop whatever he would need, and we flew all over France, Belgium, Holland, up into Norway.

"The men, surprisingly enough, many of the men were prisoners out of jails in the United States, and they traded their freedom for a chance to serve the country in this fashion, and so a lot of those people that dropped out volunteered for this kind of work. Most of them were from the United States, although many were from the country where we dropped. You'd take a guy from France who [had] escaped the country, and he would volunteer, or we'd get word to him, and he would come back to do a certain job, but most of them were Yankees, Americans, at least that we had.

"[One thing] that always intrigued me was that just before they were to take off on a mission, most of the Joes would go to the edge of the taxiway and pick up some mud or dirt and rub it all around their teeth. They said they did that in order to make their mouth look dirty because…if they got picked up immediately…if anyone saw that they had clean, shiny teeth, they would know that they were just not a native walking down the street.

"You'd go to the mess hall at six o'clock in the morning, and you'd see a guy sitting in the mess hall that you'd dropped out a couple of weeks ago, and he would have to be picked up by a man in an airplane. We had people with real small, fast airplanes that could land on a very small field, and they would locate such a field, and he would land and wouldn't even stop the airplane, and the man would run out of the woods and jump in the airplane and come home. In the morning, he'd be sitting there eating his corn flakes and eggs and you'd wonder how he got back."

Mike Pachuta, seen here as a tech sergeant in his European service, grew up in West Virginia in a family of Czech immigrants and spoke the language.

Pioneering combat zone nurses including Muriel Kappler ironically crossed the Altantic on the *Susan B. Anthony*.

Edward Keffer, seen here at Camp Blanding, Florida, was a staff sergeant at the time he began impressing Glen Robinson with his steady leadership. Keffer's daughter, Barbara, is art director of this book.

Glen E. Robinson was a replacement soldier going overseas the first time when he was assigned to the 314th Infantry Regiment. After the war, he turned his experiences into an autobiographical manuscript *Once A Soldier*.

After surviving Nazi occupation, Allied liberation and being reunited with her POW father, who was a great influence on her, Yvette Lamacq Alaniz left Verdun, France in a few years' time to marry an American army officer.

In Eastern France Jean Rene Champion is pictured standing in the turret of the tank he commanded, called the "Mort-Homme" after a World War I battle.

Gilbert Zamorano was a diminutive package of energy who left Colton High School right after the Pearl Harbor bombing to join the California National Guard. By the middle of 1944 he was fighting the Germans in France.

Leonard Roger Gariépy was a sergeant and tank commander whose Canadian M-4 landed as a DD tank at Juno beach. He continued to serve in the 6th Canadian Armoured Regiment through the campaigns in France.

What About The French?

With horrific memories of World War I carnage still fresh in their minds, the population of France looked on four years of Nazi occupation with different attitudes. Politically, the country was separated into two parts; the north being under the control of German occupation forces, the south under the Nazi-collaborationist Vichy regime headed by Marshal Philippe Pétain with German forces present. The allegiance of the population was not split on the same boundary line across the center of the country. As life went on in the war years, the population did what occupied populations do – they adapted.

The polar opposite of the Fascist governments of the European Axis, the Communists, had their own plans for postwar France if the Allied liberation campaign was successful. Their ideological differences prevented them from being included in internal and external efforts to form espionage, sabotage and military cells to resist Germany, her allies and the Vichy government. Others in the French population cooperated with or joined the Nazi occupiers, for economic, if not ideological reasons.

For those whose nationalism or anti-Nazi/anti-Vichy sentiments led them to action, their resistance could be classified as passive or active. Those who passively resisted did so by work slowdowns, strikes or allowing resistance activities to happen around them. Many French train workers engaged in work slowdowns, particularly when the Allies landed in the country. Robert Chapius was a Frenchmen who dabbled in passive resistance while working in Vichy France maintaining lines for French Telecom.

"On the first of July 1944, I began my active service in the French 'Long Lines.' It was for me a very exciting period, but very hectic! The French long-distance cables had to be restored by the French Long-Lines teams when they were not directly in the battlefields, according to an agreement between German and French offices. There was sabotage of the cables by the French Resistance. Cables were also destroyed by bombing of Allied planes of roads and railway tracks. Sometimes, when we had finished restoring the cable, small armed groups of the Resistance would arrive and we would tell them, 'OK, let us restore it. When we finish, one day later, you can come back and cut the cables again.'

"At the end of July, after my first term with the cable teams, I went to Lyons to be at its main repeater station. That was a very bad journey from Paris to Lyons...it took two and a half days by train. The train stopped whenever the planes came. Then we scattered into the countryside, then we returned to the train. Then I remember in Dijon we were parked quite a long time. I saw a train of people going to deportation [French civilians or Jews being sent to camps in Germany]. What could we do?

"I went for liaison to Vichy, which was then one of the headquarters of French Telecom, and said, 'What shall we do when the Allied troops come?' I received a very diplomatic note...this was at the time of Vichy government...telling me, 'You restore the cables so we

This young woman pays the penalty for having had personal relations with the Germans. French civilians shave her head as punishment in the Montélimar area of Southern France on August 20, 1944.

can get the connections from Lyons to Paris.'

"I went to a subsidiary repeater station. Then a German team of Alpine Jägers came through the repeater station and asked, 'What are you doing here?' That morning the Resistance had come and, after firing, left some cartridges on the ground. Well, by chance I could speak a little German and got out of a very unpleasant situation."

Those who engaged in acts of resistance themselves, as individuals or in organized cells, were part of the Resistance. The FFI had a difficult beginning but, with the help of British and American agents, by the summer of 1944 it was a moderate to serious cause of disruption for German occupation forces and military units. Noted French chemist and scientific corporation executive Jacques-Emile Dubois was a member of the FFI in the Lyon (Lyons) area of central France, which was an objective of French troops that landed in *Operation Dragoon*.

"I joined the Resistance from the very day I arrived in Grenoble and was active in it from 1941 to 1945. One of the challenges of the Resistance was the variety of underground movements and the potential friction between them. Beyond typical resistance activities, one of my roles became to act as liaison between the different movements. November 1943 in Grenoble would come to be called by some the 'Saint-Bartholemy of Grenoble,' because of the way the Gestapo cracked

Violette Szabo was an Anglo-French store clerk who volunteered as an SOE operative after her husband was killed fighting in North Africa. She parachuted into Limoges, France in June 1944 to strengthen the local Resistance movement.

down on the Resistance there at that time.

"They targeted and either gunned down or tortured all the intellectuals and thought leaders heading up various underground 'reseaux' [networks, as they were called] in an attempt to decapitate the movement and kill all support for it. That came to life in a particularly stark way for me. Professor [Jean] Bistesi, my electrochemistry professor, headed the regional section of *Combat*, a famous national underground movement in which I was active. I was working in the lab directly under his on 29 November, when I heard a slight thud above my head. You had to be constantly on the alert for anything unusual in those times, and react swiftly. On instinct, I took off my lab coat and left the building at once, stopping only to warn someone I thought would be in danger on the floor below mine. Five minutes later, the entire building was cordoned off by the Gestapo. The thud I had heard was that of Professor Bistesi's body falling to the ground when they shot him with a silencer.

"My Resistance activities forced me to interrupt my studies for a couple of prolonged bouts, but each time I returned to my work. At one point, I was turned in by an informer, arrested, and interrogated by the Gestapo. My apartment was one of our unofficial Resistance hideouts and had luckily just been emptied of a store of weapons the previous day. The Gestapo took me back to it and kept it and me under surveillance for a while, hoping to catch other Resistance members. Luckily, I had identified the spy responsible for my arrest and had been able to send out a warning just in time, so that no one suspicious ever came. My cover story was a good one, my knowledge of German probably helped and, tired of finding nothing, the Gestapo and the Italian police finally gave up on me."

Madame Yvette Alaniz was a young girl living in the significant French and German occupation city of Verdun when the war began. Her father was a local government official who was drafted into the French army when war broke out and became a POW for four years. Yvette lived with her mother and sister in the main government building where her father had worked. The building was used as a German military government and

Gestapo headquarters during the occupation. Her mother aided French resisters although she was not an FFI member herself. Yvette remembers how the local people, when the Americans liberated Verdun, treated those who collaborated with the Germans.

"The women...also was prostitution, who knows what it was, parties and stuff. But it was men there too that was collaborators. Oh yeah. The women, and we knew them because you could see them in the street with the Germans...and they shave their hair. They all got them together one Sunday, in public, and they put them in a place somewhere, and they shave all their hair. They [the local people] didn't have no pity, believe me. Well, it happened and I was very happy myself that they did that. And then after that, we knew...they were walking in the street, shaved."

A U. S. Army Air Force B-24 conducts an aerial resupply for partisans in a part of France still occupied in late summer, 1944.

CHAPTER 6

THE LIBERATION OF PARIS
PATTON'S RUN TO THE SEINE

n mid-August 1944, as the Falaise Pocket was being sealed, George Patton's armor was running their gas gauges toward empty through the fields and villages of northwest France. Two divisions of Major General Wade Haislip's XV Corps, which participated in closing the Falaise Gap by taking Argentan, did not tarry there. The V and VII Corps took their place on the south lip of the pocket and the XV Corps units moved eastward. On August 19 at Mantes-Gassicourt the corps' advance units discovered a foot bridge over the Seine River and then a larger bridge nearby. The XV Corps established the first Allied bridgehead over the Seine River on August 20. This aggressive drive and rapid progress pleased 12th Army Group chief Bradley, who ordered it, and Eisenhower, who realized the need to capitalize on the momentum of the Normandy breakout and extend the drive to and beyond the Seine. A planned three-month pause in the campaign to rest, refit and build support installations was thrown out the window.

"It was, I guess, about the 14th of August," recalls J. J. Witmeyer. "A couple of months after the invasion and General Patton came up behind from about 50, 60 feet with an entourage…he said something like, 'Let's go. Oh, Boy!' I was put on security, with my 30 men or so, for a heavy artillery unit. And that was the first time I'd been in the dugout where they had range finders and everything. And this was a black outfit and their motto was 'Rommel Count Your Men.' They had come from Africa, and they were on the bank of the Seine. We crossed the Seine River that night and we were the first troops to cross the Seine, and there was a scheduled paratrooper drop but they didn't have to drop because we were already there.

Left: Soldiers of the 4th U.S. Infantry Division admire the Eiffel Tower in Paris after the French capital had been liberated on August 25, 1944. Right: U. S. Army infantry and tanks move forward under heavy enemy fire at Fontainebleau, France during their approach to the Seine River south of Paris, on August 23.

"And we didn't lose a man until we got to the other side. And that's the first time I ever thought of blood and guts, you know, they'd say 'His [Patton's] guts and our blood.' This year when I went back…unusual circumstance there…the town was named Mantes-Gassicourt and now it's named Mantes [la Jolie], and Mantes has the heaviest population of any city in France of Muslims."

Patton's tanks were moving so fast that keeping them fueled was the only real concern. The airborne operation mentioned by Witmeyer was a planned drop between Paris and Orleans. It was cancelled so the mission's C-47 cargo planes could carry gasoline to thirsty tanks at Le Mans. Orleans was quickly overrun by Third Army armor on August 17. Major General John S. Wood's 4th Armored Division was just passing through Orleans on its way to extending the XII Corps' reach to Troyes, more than 100 miles southeast of Paris, on August 25. At the same time, the XX

Corps of Patton's Third Army reached Fontainebleau on August 20.

The German units that were not trapped in the Falaise Pocket were reorganized by Field Marshal Walter Model east of the Dives River. With the American bridgehead established, German panzer units could no longer form a viable defense behind the Seine. The German Seventh Army under General Heinrich Eberbach (who took over from Paul Hausser, wounded in the retreat from Falaise) fought a delaying action to prevent Allied forces from crossing the Seine northwest of Paris. But by August 26 Seventh Army could not hold back the advancing Allied front and joined the German army's other retreating ele-

American soldiers of the 11th Infantry Division follow an M-10 tank destroyer on Valvins Avenue, which leads from Fontainebleau to the Seine River.

ments. Fritz Baresel's reconnaissance unit pulled back from the front, but they weren't out of danger.

"Our reconnaissance vehicle was almost hit directly by a bomb, it really shook us up. The air pressure was so strong that our turret shifted and we couldn't move it in any direction, making the cannon useless. We were ordered to drive to the nearest repair company, but every time we finally found the repair company they in turn were ready to move further east. This way I retreated from the front line through France. We even stopped in Paris and we came across some supply depots with precious food, alcoholic beverages and cigarettes shortly before they were blown up and we filled our armed reconnaissance vehicle to the top with those items so much in demand at the end of the war."

German forces in most of France were either under siege, cut off, or rapidly on the move east. Back to the west in Brittany, St.-Malo fell to Major General Troy Middleton's VIII Corps units on August 17, and Brest was finally captured after a long and costly siege on September 19; yet, the Allied need for these two ports was largely negated when the front moved rapidly east. Sixteen-year-old Wilhelm Gerstner from Moersch, near the French border, was drafted into the Luftwaffe infantry on June 1, 1944. After training in Germany, he was sent to Nimes, northeast of Marseille.

An M-4 Sherman tank crosses the Seine River on a pontoon bridge recently constructed by U. S. Army engineers.

"The Allies advanced toward southern France so we left Nimes. We didn't fight any battles but we retreated back and back. We had horses to help transport some of our equipment. They pulled our field kitchen and I saw them moving field artillery. All the German units in southern France were trying to escape to the north. Eventually I was separated from my company and couldn't find it. The American and British airplanes were attacking us all day. All day! That's why we couldn't go out on any streets until it was dark.

"We would be retreating at night and the terrorists [French partisans] would shoot at us from houses or from anywhere else. We never knew where the shots came from. It was very hard to get the partisans. The terrorists would also shoot any of us who surrendered to them. The French were worse than the Americans because Germany occupied France for four years. Things like that happen in war. Normally prisoners were taken alive by the soldiers on both sides.

"There wasn't a panic to escape from France, but everyone wanted to go home. We wanted to end the war. I know that when the Americans advanced many German units didn't even

The bodies of German soldiers along with vehicles meant to get them out of the Falaise Pocket instead stand silent on a road in the Falaise-Argentan area.

shoot at them. They just surrendered. I was taken prisoner by the American army. I was standing at one of our field kitchens waiting to get something to eat in a village. Then we saw some American tanks three or four blocks away from us. They came up on us too quickly and we didn't know they were there until it was too late. Some of us ran away but I gave myself up with a couple of hundred others."

Three days later, Gerstner escaped from a U. S. Seventh Army POW holding compound with several comrades. Near the Swiss border one of the group was stopped by an SS field policeman while attempting to cross the Rhine. Gerstner and the others intervened and talked themselves out of the SS officer's accusations that they were deserting, which would have resulted in their being shot on the spot. They were instead sent to Colmar, Germany for reassignment.

THE FIRST ARMY ADVANCE

On the evening of August 19 the Falaise Pocket was sealed at Chambois. That freed the U. S. First Army to advance west. Lieutenant Frank Towers, 120th Infantry Regiment, was in the First Army's drive east once the Falaise

Pocket collapsed and the trapped German soldiers were taken prisoner.

"From that point onward we raced to the east and started what was called the 'Rat Race.' We were moving forward at a very rapid rate, 25-30 miles a day, which was a great contrast to our previous advances at Normandy where we were advancing one field at a time, 100 yards a day or 200 yards a day. This continued on across northern France, across the Seine River, north of Paris, and as we moved on east day by day we were going longer distances and actually in one day we covered over 180 kilometers [112 miles]. This was [one of] the longest distances that any attack was made against an opposing army in all of world history."

"Well, we moved very much by truck," remembers Charles Shay. "They [the armor] moved very fast. They were able to occupy...once the resistance had been broken, they were able to move inland very fast and we were moved by truck from the positions where we had to resupply ourselves, get the replacements for the people that we had lost, and we continued...we even moved to Paris on trucks."

General Eisenhower was satisfied with the progress of destroying as many German units as possible west of the Seine and he planned to launch a two-prong attack to the German Ruhr and Saar industrial areas (even though there was unhappiness and squabbling among British and American subordinates over the details of this plan). Ike was also happy to bypass Paris to the north and south and avoid the prospect of urban combat to take France's largest city (two million inhabitants). The liberation of the city would mean fighting in the streets and the *rues* of Paris were numerous.

Most likely, such combat would have meant that the city would endure some of the intense bombing that shattered Caen and other Norman cites, potentially damaging or destroying such iconic Parisian landmarks as the Eiffel Tower and Notre Dame. Once the city was taken or partially occupied, the population would be depending on the Allied forces to solve the food shortages present and that could eat up seven divisions' worth of supplies. Eisenhower decided that the Parisians could endure a few more weeks of occupation until the Germans were forced out of the city. That was a good plan in theory, but as the residents of St.-Nazaire in Brittany could testify, it did not always work out in practice.

Soldiers of the 1st Battalion, 119th Infantry Regiment, advance during an attack on the village of Romagny. The 119th, along with the other regiments of the 30th Infantry Division, moved rapidly eastward as part of the First Army advance once the Falaise Pocket was secured.

MOVEMENTS OF THE BRITISH SECOND AND FIRST CANADIAN ARMIES

The 21st Army Group under Field Marshal Montgomery (promoted to that rank on September 1, 1944), for the moment made up of General Miles Dempsey's British Second Army and Canadian Lieutenant General Harry Crerar's First Canadian Army, advanced northeast toward the Seine River between Paris and the coast. Due to logistical problems General Dempsey was unable to organize two divisions to campaign down the left bank of the Seine. Bradley therefore received permission from the Second Army commander and Montgomery to have American units move across the British front. Elements of the XIX and XV Corps turned to the north and headed for Elbeuf, south of Rouen, where they fought a spirited two-day battle on August 24 with Eberbach's Seventh Army. Bad weather prevented Allied bombers from destroying enemy units and equipment during the fight, and the Germans used everything that could float to get the remnants of their force over the river.

The retreat of the German force at Elbeuf and elsewhere along the river put the military force occupying Paris in a precarious position. By design, the Commonwealth forces left that situation in the hands of their American allies while they headed northeast toward the Low Countries. The First Canadian Army cap-

Left: A Sherman tank of the Sherbrooke Fusiliers Regiment, 2nd Canadian Armoured Brigade covers infantrymen fighting in Rue des Ursulines at Falaise, August 17. **Right:** Lieutenant General Henry Crerar commanded the First Canadian Army and led their push to and beyond the Seine River in August after the Canadians began operating separately from the British Second Army.

tured Le Havre on September 3. The Commonwealth forces were constantly on the lookout for German rocket sites in order to shut down the V-1 and V-2 terror weapons operations from France. However, the Germans operated many of the V-2 rockets from portable launchers that were transported by trucks and were able to pack up their operations and move ahead of the Allied advance. The Canadians also returned to and captured Dieppe, site of that unsuccessful landing two years earlier.

Lieutenant Garth Webb and his four-gun "Charley Troop" (Troop C) advanced with the rest of the 14th Royal Canadian Artillery in the 3rd Division. As they advanced east of the Falaise Gap with the 21st Army Group, they would occasionally be called upon to

Left: A Crusader gun tractor MKI equipped with a booster-type "fording kit" pulls a 17-pounder anti-tank gun through Bayeux Creully. Right: A French World War I veteran waves a French flag in a salute to passing vehicles of the South Saskatchewan Regiment of the 2nd Canadian Infantry Division.

unlimber their 25-pounder field cannons which they used after landing in the M-7 "Priest" self-propelled guns on D-Day. Webb explains that although their use was often routine, it was necessary to a successful infantry advance.

"At the guns we don't actually see the engagement, but we're very conscious because we get warning and we get our guns organized so we're able to support the infantry. And when an attack goes in there's a schedule of firing. It would probably cover an hour and go out every five or ten minutes. We'd change the range so we would be firing ahead of the infantry…when they went into an attack.

"We engaged…off and on our gun position engaged close enough that we could shell troops. And we had casualties in the

gun position as well as the forward observation [teams]. I guess you'd say we had occasional casualties...so there were changes from time to time. But by and large we all considered that there was no doubt but what 'Charley' Troop was the best in the war. We were all trained; we got a call to go and pick up a gun position...we could do it faster, more efficiently than anybody else in our opinion. We were the best."

THE PARIS UPRISING

While Ike was deciding what to do about Paris, the citizens of the French capital made the decision for him. On August 19, Resistance members, bol-

Bottom: Members of the FFI, mostly policemen, fire across the Pont Neuf Bridge to the Ile de la Cite during the Paris uprising. Right: Two Paris policemen in civilian clothes fire from a window of the Prefecture de Police during the Paris uprising. The wall above their heads was taken out by a tank round.

stered by the presence of massed Allied troops nearby, began fighting German occupation troops in the center of the city and the uprising spread. The German military governor arranged for a cease-fire until August 23 while he withdrew his forces from west Paris, along with allowing food supplies to come in. However, violence broke out again as FFI leaders could not control the armed French civilians in the city. Feeling betrayed, the Germans vowed to defeat the insurrection and by August 21 they were gaining the upper hand. The French Resistance leaders then came to the Allies for help. The Supreme Commander hoped the French leaders in Paris would gain control of the situation but eventually he reluctantly turned to General Charles de Gaulle for help.

In the meantime, Fred Purdy, who often seemed to find himself in opportune situations while traveling with his Signal Corps outfit, had a preview of the Paris situation firsthand while Germans were still occupying the city.

"We went south of Paris to Étampes. We went into some chateaus at Étampes and there had been a German air base nearby and a lot of their equipment was still there in these chateaus. We did not stay in the chateaus. We were out on the grounds and this Jeep pulled up, and it was a full bird colonel in the Jeep, and he had on the emblems of a chaplain. He asked could he have some of our coffee we were making. We said 'sure.' Well, we got to talking and he said, 'I'd like to get a couple of you guys that's armed to go up into Paris with me.' We said, 'Well, colonel, it hadn't been took yet.' This was in August…about the 23rd. He said, 'Fellas, don't worry. I have lived in Paris. I've been in the army in World War I.' He was about fifty somethin' years old. And he said, 'I know Paris, I know people there, I know their streets. I'll keep us out of any of the fighting going on. We'll just go around it.'

"Well, you know, we guys…we've never been to anything like that. We volunteered and [after receiving permission from their commanding officer, Lt. Earl Hicks] said we'd go with him. So, we got in the Jeep…we left in the morning. We went up and went in near the Port de Orléans…that's the main road down to Orléans in middle France. We didn't go in on the main road. We went in on some other road. The fighting that was going on was between the FFI…that's the French Forces of the Interior…and the Germans that were still there. Most of them shooting out of buildings…the Germans up in buildings shooting down at the FFI, and they were behind vehicles and things

down on the streets. We went on up to across the Seine River from the big cathedral of Notre Dame. Couldn't cross on the other side because there was too much fighting going on on the Rue de Rivoli, which was…German headquarters was on the Rue de Rivoli to the Place [de la] Concorde.

"The colonel stopped and said, 'Fellas, I'm gonna let y'all out here. You'll be all right 'til I can come back. I'll be back in a few hours. I've got some business…some people I want to see.' Frankly, I think he had a woman. [Laugh] I don't know that, but the talk he talked when he got back, we thought he did. Anyway, he left and we stayed there and was liberating the women. We were the first Allied soldiers these people had seen."

Purdy's little patrol was picked up by the colonel and returned to base that night, but a much larger group of Allies was about to head into the city. General de Gaulle, in France and enroute to the front, wrote Eisenhower on August 21 that French troops would take the responsibility of entering Paris and restoring order. His reasons were absolutely selfish – he feared that the Parisians involved in the revolt, left to their own devices, would split into factions and many of those factions did not recognize de Gaulle's provisional government.

Moving with the American Third Army was the French 2nd Armored Division under the command of Général de Division Jacque Philippe Leclerc. Also known as the Leclerc Division, the unit contained a number of Free French, including Jean Rene Champion.

"I was a tank driver. I had two tanks shot out from under me. These were, in fact, Sherman tanks. I guess the Free French forces at that time were being withheld from combat outside of France and being kept primarily to take part in the liberation of France. And so I eventually, with the Free French forces under General de Gaulle, we landed in Normandy.

"We saw General de Gaulle many times. I remember, for example, de Gaulle was shaking hands with me…he had us review a number of times before we got involved, not only before but including when we got involved in combat. And I remember having a brief conversation with him, and he asked me…he had heard that I had lived in the United States…and he and I chatted briefly, you know maybe two minutes, as he walked by and reviewed the troops. We greatly admired de Gaulle.

"It was a wonderful, exhilarating adventure. I did not have any particular patriotic feeling in favor of France because I had lived most of my life in the United States. But what I do remember, all of us in the Free French 2nd Armored Division were volunteers and we came from all over the world. And our special mission in France was the liberation of Paris. But of course, the Germans who were occupying France didn't just step aside on the roadside and wave to us as we went by. They fought back and we fought day by day, and eventually reached Paris and eventually succeeded in liberating Paris."

*Above: General Charles de Gaulle is shown here during a Bastille Day review in Algiers, July 14, 1943. **Bottom**: High ranking German officers seized by Free French troops in Paris huddle on August 26 in the Hotel Majestic, which was headquarters for the Wehrmacht during the Nazi occupation.*

Twice Leclerc had requested to enter Paris and twice he had been turned down by American commanders. On August 22, reports were that the fighting was subsiding and Eisenhower finally ordered Leclerc into the city. However the division was 100 miles away when they moved out on August 23 and although other units gave them right of way on the roads, the French people didn't necessarily do the same. The celebration started early as the French armored column slowed down to exchange pleasantries and accept gifts from the people lining the road. General Bradley was quite concerned about the slow pace of the French 2nd Armored Division and so he ordered the veteran U. S. 4th Infantry Division to enter Paris as well. That got the Leclerc column moving. By noon on August 25 both French and American troops had reached the center of Paris. Unfortunately for him, Rene Champion was tardy in reaching the victory celebration when his tank was hit by enemy gunfire upon entering the city.

Général de Division Jacque Philippe Leclerc, commander of the French 2nd Armored Division, visits his men as his division awaits movement orders prior to being sent into Paris.

"The first tank [shot out from under me] was in Paris. It was on fire and I managed to get out of that without... I and my tank crew... we managed to get out without being injured. My tank was called the Mort-Homme. In French that means 'dead man.' That probably strikes you as a strange name but our tanks in the Leclerc Division were all named after famous French battles throughout the history of France and Mort-Homme was a World War I battle that France was involved in."

PARIS CELEBRATES LIBERATION

The Germans in Paris surrendered the same day, August 25. De Gaulle entered the city and installed his government as the legitimate French government, backed by the Allied military presence of course. The next day De Gaulle relit the flame at the Tomb of the Unknown Soldier and led a procession down the Champs-Élysées in which

French troops paraded in front of the city's joyous citizens.

Many GIs outside the 4th and 28th Infantry Divisions nearly or completely missed their chance to see Paris during this historic time. But that didn't mean they missed the celebration entirely.

"We went through the outskirts of Paris by truck," Shay remembers. "Well, they were very jubilant, the French. They were throwing flowers at us and offering us bread and wine…if we had the opportunity to stop and go down…and this continued on through France."

"We went through Paris," says wireman Douglas Jenney. "They drew my name and I was eligible to go to Paris one time. I didn't have any money but the boys said they'd all chip in so I would have enough money to go to Paris. I had an allotment taken out of my pay…I was only a private…so my mother would have money. She didn't have any income to get along on. They talk about hard times now, but it's nothing compared to what it was back then."

Some, like Joe Sorrentino, arrived a little later.

"On the way our truck broke convoy. We hadda see Paris. I was amazed, I couldn't believe what I was seein'. I never believed in my life I was gonna' see the Eiffel Tower. But here we were, right underneath the Eiffel Tower and the people were jumpin' all over us, kissin' us. This was about a week after it was liberated…they're still celebratin', givin' us wine and stuff like that. So we left there, everybody in the truck was drunk. Believe me. I was one of 'em."

A halftrack of the French 2nd Armored Division moves through a street in Paris. Jean Rene Champion and others in the division fought the withdrawing German army as they entered the city.

Muriel Kappler also made it to Paris. Her field hospital had been tracking along with the Third Army across France.

"We were in a town called Liberté, it was like a suburb of Paris. So we went through the streets and had all the people, you know, throwing flowers. And then…Hal Boyle, Kansas City news reporter…his Jeep turned over outside of our unit so he came in for X-rays, and I happened to be in the X-ray tent.

"So he asked if I wanted to be the first nurse in Paris, and first [American] woman I guess. And so I asked my C.O. and he said, 'Get going, I don't know a thing about it.' He couldn't give us permission, 'cause Paris was off limits. And we went out for dinner, which we hadn't…I remember we had steak and cantaloupe which we hadn't [had]…you know, our food, we had been on K-rations and C-rations."

Even though there was still more of France to traverse, and more of the German army and other military units to face, the liberation of Paris symbolically represented the liberation of France from Nazi control. General Eisenhower was pleased to report to the Combined Chiefs of Staff on August 25 the results of less than three months of campaigning from the beaches of Normandy to the streets of Paris. And even though exhaustive planning and nearly mistake-free leadership had been hallmarks of the operation so far, Eisenhower was quick to point out that the greatest reason for success was the fighting qualities of the Allied soldiers, sailors and airmen who landed, fought and sometimes died in France.

Parisians line the Champs-Élysées as tanks and halftracks of the French 2nd Armored Division pass before the Arc de Triomphe during the Victory Parade of August 26.

American troops of the 28th Infantry Division march down the Avenue des Champs-Élysées on August 29. Eisenhower ordered the parade both to get the division quickly through the city and to show Parisians that their liberation was an Allied, not just a French effort.

Driving For The Line

Though the liberation of Paris was only a symbol of the transformation of France from Nazi occupation to a free nation again, to many American and Commonwealth troops it also meant the end of the war was in sight. A common idea was that with the German line breaking in front of the Seine and the U. S. Seventh and French First armies pushing north through France's heartland the door to Germany seemed to be open. It was not going to be that easy, however, and Eisenhower cautioned reporters and others sharing a premature euphoria that Adolf Hitler knew he would be hanged if captured and so he had nothing to lose by continuing to fight. The first "casualty" of the incredibly rapid Allied advance was General

Left: A convoy of U. S. Army trucks taking a road in Normandy under the supervision of an MP. In the foreground is a Chevrolet G-7113 tractor with trailer and 3.5 ton stake platform. These trucks are traveling on an early segment of the Red Ball Express Highway. Right: Corporal Charles H. Johnson of the 783rd MP Battalion moves traffic along the Red Ball Express Highway in Alençon Province on September 5, 1944.

Patton's armored column. As it exceeded the speed limit driving toward the old World War I battlefields and Maginot Line in eastern France, it outran its supplies.

In Eisenhower's compromise position on strategy, worked out with a small bit of deference to Montgomery's "Single Thrust" plan of one large army moving toward the Ruhr Valley, Patton's Third Army was behind the First Army in the allocation of gasoline supplies. Though Patton's armor had captured Reims on August 29 and his advance units were crossing the Meuse River the following day, Patton was informed that his allocation of fuel was about to run out. He was forced to apply the brakes to the advance and was not happy when he returned to SHAEF headquarters to confer with Eisenhower, Bradley and other American commanders on September 1, the date Eisenhower assumed direct command of all Allied ground forces.

Many stopgap measures had been taken to keep the Third Army tanks moving. However, there were some better solutions in the works to alleviate the problem. The first "Pluto" undersea oil pipeline from England to Normandy was opened on August 12. It was a small flexible pipe designed by British petroleum engineers and laid on the ocean floor. A ship's anchor fouled the first line shortly after it went into service, but a second line was quickly laid and seventeen "Pluto" lines were eventually opened. Allied support units were doing their best to make sure that Third Army, along with the rest of the American 12th and British 21st Army Groups, did not outrun their supply lines. Truck transportation units assisted by MPs cleared a system of roads through northern France dubbed the "Red Ball Express Highway."

Raul Garcia, a native of Northern California, was in the 100th Infantry Division when they started their service in France on the "Red Ball Express."

"So we ended up in Southampton and I wasn't there very long, about a week and a half, and they got a group of us, different parts of the division, and they [made] like small companies and sent us over into France. They called that 'Red Ball,' which [was] a trucking outfit, and we was hauling equipment to the front lines. They put me in charge of about five, ten trucks, drivers, assistant drivers. There was quite a few of them, you know, we drove day and night."

Trucks averaged 20 hours a day on the road, stopping only for fuel, repairs and to change drivers. Along the way, anti-aircraft artillery guarded the route. And wherever those guns were positioned the barrage balloons could be found as well.

"Wherever the guns would move, we would move," says William Dabney. "And of course, the 'Red Ball.' This was transportation that was carryin' ammunition and food up to the front line. So they would pass right through us and

going up, going right up to the front lines to take food and supplies to the infantry and all those that was on the front line."

The Germans were also suffering fuel shortages, the result of relentless Allied bombing combined with the necessity of over-straining scarce resources. German forces were quickly being backed to their own border, but the fight wasn't out of them yet. There were a few ideas that Adolf Hitler had left in his bag of tricks in order to slow down the Allied advance when it reached the borders of the Low Countries, as well as the West Wall defensive complex separating France and Germany. The ground forces under Field Marshal Walter Model would take up strategic positions to protect the vital industrial areas of the Rhine and Ruhr river valleys. Response to the next series of Allied movements, beginning in September, would determine how well their advance could be halted or slowed down. The German high command hoped that Model's forces could delay the eastward movement of the front long enough for the manufacture of greater quantities of Germany's best weapons and the employment of technology such as jet aircraft and improved rocket engines.

General Eisenhower, aware of the potential for Germany to still find ways to disrupt the Allied advance, had to carefully navigate through the military and political challenges ahead. Successful planning and execution of every aspect of the continuing campaign by the combined Allied armies he had come to rely on would be necessary to fulfill the orders he received when he assumed SHAEF command.

A joyous couple embraces to celebrate the liberation of Paris.

STAFF

Bill Breidenstine
Publisher & Marketing

J-C Suares
Creative Director

Barbara Justice
Art Director

Jerry Morelock, PhD
Editor

David T. Zabecki, PhD
Foreword and
Additional Editing

Gregory Proch
Map Designer

Zachary Bathon
Photography Editor

Sharon Gytri
Research and Clearance

Jennifer Liese
Interview Coordinator

Karen Morris
Publicity

Virginia Wilson
Administrative Assistant

Bonnie Thompson
Proofreader

Patricia Grove
Transcriber

Tara Pelander
Transcriber

Lexi Pappas
Transcriber

ACKNOWLEDGEMENTS

*The author wishes to acknowledge
the contributions of the following
people and organizations:*

Mike Faley, Anne Montague,
Ronald A. Abboud, Kevin Eyre,
Ken Davy, Frank C. Everards,
Aaron Elson, Sheldon Hochheiser,
James Ellis, Marie-Eve Vaillancourt-
Deleris, Nathalie Worthington,
David Allender, Stephanie George,
David Caruso, Jessica Herdina,
Andrew Brozyna, Gerald Swick,
Noemy Wertz, Ellis Oxley, Russell
Horton, Jim Adams, Shaun
Illingworth, Sandra Stewart Holyoak,
Peter John, Andrew Whitemarsh,
The National World War II Museum,
Wisconsin Veterans Museum

Memoirs of Ernst Goth as transcribed
by grandson, Martin-Robert Galle,
courtesy of D-DAY, NORMANDY
AND BEYOND
www.normandy1944.info; *9 Lives:
An Oral History,* interview of Patsy
Giacchi in New Jersey, 4-25-1998
and interview of Vincent "Mike"
McKinney in New Mexico, 2-5-1990
courtesy of TANKBOOKS.COM
www.tankbooks.com; interview of
Dr. Eugene Eckstam in October
1994 courtesy of WISCONSIN
PUBLIC TELEVISION:
WISCONSIN IN STORIES
http://wpt.org/WisconsinStories;
Bowman Diary by Marvin Bowman,
Ed Wolf Crew Diary by Ed Wolf,
William R. Fogel's Journal by
William R. Fogle, courtesy of 100th
BOMB GROUP FOUNDATION
www.100thbg.com

Interviews of Robert Balkom,
Eugene Cook, Henry A. French,
Joseph Horn, James M. Roberts, and
Albert Skourpa were conducted by
the U.S. Army's 44th, 53rd, 99th and
305th Military History Detachments,
which were attached to the U.S. Army
in Europe's Task Force Normandy
60 to support the 60th anniversary
observances of the D-Day landings
in June of 2004. The interviews were
conducted in Normandy, France.

*D-Day Easy Red Beach on Nor-
mandy* – memoir written on April
14, 1994 by Joseph Vaghi courtesy
of 6th NAVAL BEACH BATTAL-
ION www.6thbeachbattalion.org;
interview of Joseph H. Gibbons
used with permission of the Department of the Navy, courtesy of
NAVAL HISTORY CENTER; in-
terviews of R. G. Lloyd and P. W.
Stansfield from Warren Tute

Collection, England, courtesy of
PORTSMOUTH D-DAY MUSEUM
www.ddaymuseum.co.uk; interview
of Howard Proud in Riverside,
California, 3-12-2003 courtesy of
RIVERSIDE PUBLIC LIBRARY:
RIVERSIDE VETERAN'S HIS-
TORY PROJECT
www.riversideca.gov/library

*2nd Battalion The King's Shropshire
Light Infantry; D-Day 6th June 1944
-9 July 1944 Normandy, A Personal
Account* by Major Harry G. Jones at
Shropshire Regimental Museum,
Shrewsbury Castle; interview of Les
Davis in England, November 1999,
interview of Lionel Knight, Imperial
War Museum, London, interview of
Bob Littlar in England, November
12, 1999 and interview of John R.
Roberts, England, 11-3-99 all cour-
tesy of WAR CHRONICLE
www.warchronicle.com

Interviews of Jack Armitage, Dr.
Bruce MacKenzie and Joe Womers-
ley courtesy of THE MEMORY
PROJECT: DOMINION INSTI-
TUTE, Toronto, Ontario, Canada
www.thememoryproject.com;
memoir of Leonard Gariépy cour-
tesy of THE JUNO BEACH CEN-
TRE: CANADA IN WWII
www.junobeach.org; interviews of
Ernest Andrews, 10-31-2006 and
William Funkhouser, 10-1-2006
courtesy of VIRGINIA MILITARY
INSTITUTE: JOHN A. ADAMS
CENTER FOR MILITARY HIS-
TORY & STRATEGIC ANAYLSIS
www.vmi.edu

Interviews of John Dowling, Jr.,
5-17-1997 and Dr. John Ervin on
7-24-2009 courtesy of RUTGERS
ORAL HISTORY ARCHIVES
www.oralhistory.rutgers.edu; interview of Robert Chapius, 8-24-1993
courtesy of IEEE HISTORY CEN-
TER www.ieee.org/history_center;
interview of Jacques-Emile DuBois,
in Paris, France, 2-21-2001 courtesy
of CHEMICAL HERITAGE
FOUNDATION
www.chemheritage.org; interview of
Wilhelm Gerstner, O.H. 2483, 10-
25-1994 courtesy of CALIFORNIA
STATE UNIVERSITY, FULLER-
TON: CENTER FOR ORAL
AND PUBLIC HISTORY
http://coph.fullerton.edu

Excerpts taken with permission from:
Baresel Family History – Fritz Baresel;
Once a Soldier - Glen E. Robinson;
My Life – Dr. John Ervin

ABOUT THE INTERVIEWED VETERANS

As of the publication of the second volume of *War Stories: World War II Firsthand*, I have personally interviewed 300 men and women for this project. The interviews will continue until the series is completed, and the important work of preserving these veterans' experiences is done. I am grateful to the veterans, who often allowed me into their homes and shared their experiences and mementos with me; and also to the family, friends and organizations who have allowed me to gain access to these individuals. I am also deeply in debt to those organizations and individuals who have provided oral histories of veterans whom I could not interview myself.

I cannot express my appreciation enough for the opportunity to learn from these veterans about how they handled war and military service. Regrettably, since this project began some of those veterans interviewed have passed on. More will continue to do so every month as they reach well into their golden years. And while they cannot be expected to retain every detail of the war, or even of the campaigns they fought in, there is no substitute for what their memories bring to this project.

BIBLIOGRAPHY

Books

Ambrose, Stephen E.,
D-Day, June 6, 1944:
The Climactic Battle of World War II,
New York, Simon & Schuster, Inc., 1994

Brokaw, Tom,
The Greatest Generation,
New York, Random House, Inc., 1998

Goodenough, Simon,
War Maps,
London,
Macdonald & Co. Ltd., 1982

Griess, Thomas E.,
Series Editor
The Second World War:
Europe and the Mediterranean:
The West Point Military History Series,
Wayne, N. J., Avery Publishing
Group, Inc., 1989

Harrison, Gordon A.,
The European Theater of Operations:
Cross-Channel Attack,
Honolulu, Hawaii, University Press
of the Pacific, 2002

Jackson, Robert,
Tanks and Armored Fighting
Vehicles Visual Encyclopedia,
London, Amber Books Ltd., 2009

Morison, Samuel Eliot,
History of United States Naval
Operations in World War II:
Vol. XI, The Invasion of France
and Germany 1944-1942,
Boston, Little, Brown &
Company, 1947

Reardon, Mark J.,
Victory at Mortain, Stopping Hitler's
Panzer Counteroffensive,
Lawrence, Kansas, University Press
of Kansas, 2002

Trew, Simon and Stephen Badsey,
Battle for Caen,
Phoenix Mill, Gloucestershire, England, Sutton Publishing, Ltd., 2004

War Department Historical Division,
Omaha Beachhead,
Washington, D. C., Center of
Military History, CMH Pub 100-11, 1945, 1994

War Department Historical Division,
Utah Beach to Cherbourg,
Washington, D. C., Center of
Military History, CMH Pub 100-12, 1948, 2002

Willmott, H. P., Robin Cross and
Charles Messenger,
World War II,
New York,
DK Publications, 2004

More information on the War Stories: World War II Firsthand series, the individual books and their subjects can be found at:
www.WWIIWarStories.com

A sample of websites relevant to this volume:

www.exercisetiger.org
www.omaha-beach.org
www.519thportbn.com
http://people.mnhs.org
http://seekingmichigan.cdmhost.com
www.ucg.mil/history
www.history.navy.mil
www.history.army.mil
www.nationalww2museum.org

IMAGE CREDITS

Veterans and United States government sources graciously provided the vast majority of images in this book. The items are listed by page number and sometimes position (t-top, m-middle, b-bottom, l-left, c-center, r-right).

The National Archives and Records Administration Collections:
2; 11; 12; 14; 15; 16; 17; 18-19; 20; 21; 25; 27; 28-29; 31(tl); 31(tr); 31(m); 34; 35; 37; 40; 42-43; 45; 46; 47; 48; 49; 52; 53; 56; 59; 60; 62; 63; 65; 68; 71; 72-73; 74; 77; 78; 79; 80-81; 82; 85(t); 85(b); 86; 87; 88; 89; 90; 91; 101; 105; 106; 108-109; 110-111; 113; 116; 117; 120; 121; 123; 126; 129; 130; 132-133; 135; 137; 140; 141; 148; 151; 152; 155; 158; 161; 162-163; 166; 168-169; 170-171; 173; 174; 176; 178; 179; 181; 182; 185(t); 185(b); 187; 189; 190; 192(tl); 192(tr); 192(b); 193; 195; 196-197; 199; 200; 202; 204; 207; 208; 209; 210-211; 212(t); 213(t); 213(b); 214-215; 220-221; 223; 224; 228; 229; 231; 232; 234-235; 237(t); 237(b); 238; 239; 242; 244; 245; 247(t); 247(b); 248-249; 250-251; 258; 259; 260; 263(t); 263(b); 266; 268-269; 270; 271; 274; 277; 278; 279; 280; 281; 282; 283; 284(r); 286; 287; 289(t); 289(b); 291; 292-293; 294-295; 296; 297; 299.

Imperial War Museum, London:
13; 22(t), EA 33078; 39, CS 354; 145, BU 1181; 149, B 5251; 218(l), A 23960; 218(r), CL 217; 219, B 6794; 226, B 7510; 261, CL 880; 264, A 25184; 276, HU 16541.

Ullstein Bild/The Granger Collection, N.Y.:
160(bl); 216; 230; 252; 253; 255; 256-257.

U. S. Army Center of Military History:
112, National Guard Heritage Series; 160(t); 160(br); 190, U.S. Army Painting; 206, U.S. Army Painting.

U. S. Naval History & Heritage Command:
54; 55; 103; 265.

Images from other sources:
7, The Library of Congress - Serial and Government Publications Division; 8, Defense Department Photograph by Cherie A. Thurlby; 9, © Robert Capa/International Center of Photography/Magnum Photos; 22 (b), Keystone/Getty Images; 23, Keystone-France/Gamma-Keystone via Getty Images; 30, 31(b) and 205, Rommel Family Archives; 50 and 94, Courtesy of the 100th Bomb Group Foundation, 100thbg.com; 67(tl), Jackie Volkl; 67(tc) Joseph Sorrentino; 67(tr) Fritz Baresel; 67(mc) Marianna Webber; 67(mr) Robert Wolff; 67(br) Charles Serio; 67(bc) Ernest Andrews; 76 and 83, *Armchair General* archives; 97, Original Painting by Ronald Wong GAvA, ASAA; 157(tl) Courtesy of the University of South Florida Tampa Library Special Collections; 157(tr) James Weller; 157(ml) Ken Bell and Juno Beach Centre; 157(mr) Albert Piper; 157(bl) Thomas McKinney; 157(bc) William Funkhouser; 157(br) Ernst Floeter; 165, Ullstein Bild - SZ Photo; 175, LAPI/Roger Viollet/Getty Images; 273(tl) Mike Pachuta; 273(tc) Muriel Kappler; 273(tr) Barbara Justice; 273(ml) Sharon Robinson; 273(mr) Jean Rene Champion; 273(bl) Yvette Alaniz; 273(bc) Gilbert Zamorano; 273(br) Juno Beach Centre; 284(l), 285(l), 285(r) and 290, Library and Archives of Canada.

Endpapers:
Veterans supplied their own images unless otherwise noted. Jay Wertz: (left side) 2,3-6,9,10,12-14,16, (right side) 4,6,8,10,15; Marianna Webber: (left side) 1; Sharon Gytri: (left side) 7; Juno Beach Centre: (left side) 8; Mike Faley: (right side) 2; Thomas McKinney: (right side) 3; Michelle Hyatt: (right side) 5,14.

INDEX

A

Aircraft, 58, 97, 143, 165, 172; B-17s, 48, 51-4, 94-5; B-24s, 49, 95, 261, 272; B-26, 54, 209; C-47s, 77-8, 102; HE 115, 184; P-38s, 97, 100, 162; P-47, 96, 191, 209; P-51 Mustang, 97, 211, 232; Spitfire, 97, 231, 262

Alaniz, Yvette, *273, 277*

Allied Forces, 24, 34-5, 47, 51-2, 54-5, 57-8, 123, 126, 184, 188, 191, 198, 238-9, 241, 254, 259-60, 265, 268, 271, 288; advance to Seine, 279-84; airborne operation for D-Day, 77-100; breakout from Normandy, 203-32; continuing through France, 297-8; Dieppe Raid, 22-3; Falaise Pocket, 243-50; fighting in the hedgerows, 159-77; finishing D-Day, 150-6; Gold, Juno & Sword Beaches, 143-50; ideas for the cross-Channel Invasion, 13-22; liberation of Paris, 290-4; naval operation for D-Day, 100-7; Omaha Beach, 107-31; Operation Dragoon, 259-67; preparations for cross-Channel invasion, 35-66; taking Cherbourg, 178-91

Amfreville, 82, 84, 153-4
Andrews, Ernest, 230
Armitage, Jack, 227-30
Arnold, Roy, 53
Avranches, 232, 234, 236, 239-40, 243-4

B

Baker, James, 196-8
Balkom, Robert, 208-9
Barrage balloons, 101-2, 165-6, 298
Baresel, Fritz, 32-3, *67*, 93, 95, 162, 203-4, 253, 281
Battery Hamburg, 188-9, 191
Baumgarten, Hal, 39, 63, 100, 102, 106-7, 113-16, 119-20, 121-2, 125, 127-8
Bayeux, 144, 149, 151, 159-60, 164, 174, 203
Blakey, Tom, 46, 60-1, 66, 77, 84, 86, 88, 150, 153-4, 167, 169, 178-9
Bourguébus Ridge, 225-6, 230-1
Bowman, Marvin, 96
Bradley, Omar N., 47, 153, 206, 208 234, 236, 243; advance to Seine, 284; breakout from Normandy, 209-32; building the bridgehead, 159; confers with Eisenhower, 297
Bradshaw, at Exercise Tiger, 71, 74-5
Brittany, 23, 92, 164, 174, 177, 184, 188, 232-3, 236, 238, 243, 250, 281, 283
Buschmeier, Frank, 52-3

C

Caen, 26, 93, 97-8, 126, 144, 149, 151, 159, 164, 172, 174-5, 203, 216-19, 221-2, 225, 227, 231, 243, 245, 283; on D-Day, 95-151

Calais, Pas de, 52, 58, 79, 93, 177, 236, 259
Campisano, Michael, 142
Canada, Army: 2nd Infantry Division, 23, 285; 3rd Infantry Division, 144, 217, 222; 6th Armored Regiment, 244; 14th Royal Canadian Artillery, 148; Armoured Brigades, 244, 284; First Canadian Army, 231, 243, 284; II Canadian Corps, 226; Royal Canadian Artillery, 148, 285
Canada, Royal Canadian Air Force, 97
Canadians (*see also* Allied Forces), 183, 209, 217, 231, 243-4; advance to Seine River, 284-6; Commonwealth Beaches on D-Day, 144-50; on D-Day, 97-100; Dieppe losses, 23, 32; fighting in breakout from Normandy, 222; near Caen, 172
Cannes, 264-5, 268
Carentan, 82-3, 87, 136, 151, 159, 167, 169, 172, 174, 184, 206, 214
Caumont Gap, 172, 174-7
Champion, Jean Rene, 45-6, *273*, 288-9, 290
Chapius, Robert, 275-6
Chavez, Pete, 44, 136-7, 167, 236
Cherbourg, 24, 82, 93, 142, 159, 161, 164, 174-5, 177-8, 182, 184, 186, 188-91, 195, 203, 205-7, 240, 259
Churchill, Winston, 13, 15, 20, 29, 45, 268; at Big Three Allied summit, 26; concerns about landing craft, 24; disagreement about Operation Dragoon, 259, 262; disagreement with Montgomery, 231; inspects ruins of Caen, 221
Cole, Robert G., 91, 167
Colleville, 26, 35, 108, 117, 124-6, 131, 159, 161
Collins, Joseph Lawton, 140, 159, 186, 188, 232
Commonwealth forces, 44, 222, 225, 246, 284-5, 297
Connor, Charles, 121, 125
Cook, Eugene, 90-1
Corlett, Charles, 232
COSSAC, 22, 24, 248
Cota, Norman D., 125
Cotentin Peninsula, 31, 82, 91, 93, 100, 102, 108, 132, 153, 156, 159, 161, 164, 177-9, 182, 191, 196, 203, 205, 239
Cullen, Curtis, 166

D

Dabney, William, 165-6, 298
Davis, Les, 145-8
Dawson, Joseph P., 124
De Gaulle, Charles, 45, 286, 288-90
DeGlopper, Charles, 156
Dempsey, Miles, 218, 221
Derby, Woodrow, 55-7, 103-4, 188
Devers, Jacob L., 49
Dieppe Raid, 22-5, 32

Ditmar, Robert, 121
Dollmann, Friedrich, *160,* 164, 173, 184; death, 205
Dönitz, Karl, 31
Dowling, John, 271
Doyle, John, 74
Dubois, Jacques-Emile, 275-7

E

Eaker, Ira C., 49
Eckhardt, Hans, 32
Eckstam, Eugene, 70
Eisenhower, Dwight D., 20-2, 29-30, 59-60, 65, 113, 116, 159, 164, 204, 209, 232, 234, 236, 243, 248, 256, 262, 268, 279, 294; assumes direct command of Allied ground forces, 297; breakout from Normandy, 225; choosing date for D-Day, 66; with Churchill and Montgomery, 231; goes behind German lines, 211; liberation of Paris, 283 -292; Marshall Memorandum, 17
England, 13, 20, 24-5, 29, 36, 38-9, 41, 43-8, 50-3, 55, 57, 60-2, 64, 69, 82, 92, 97, 100, 116, 118, 151, 164-5, 176, 184, 188, 196, 198-9, 201, 203, 206, 208, 216, 236, 241, 259, 262, 272, 298
Ervin, John W., 270
Exercise Tiger, 57, 65, 69, 75, 134

F

Fairbanks, Douglas Jr., 265
Falaise Pocket, 96, 225, 231, 243-4, 246, 248, 250, 271, 279-80, 282-5
Farley, Mary Josephine, *36*
Floeter, Ernst, 82-3, *157,* 182-4
Fogle, William R., 95-6
French: 2nd Armored Division, 292; de Gaulle installs his government, 290; the Free French forces, 45, 262, 288; the II Corps, 260-7; Leclerc Division enters Paris, 290; liberation of Paris, 290-4; resistance, 275-7; treatment of collaborators, 277; uprising in Paris, 286-9; First Army, 297
French, Henry A., 124-5
French Navy, 266
French Resistance (FFI), 58, 78, 91, 93, 95, 162, 199, 238, 265, 270-1, 275-7, 282, 286, 288
Fromm, Friedrich, 254-5
Funkhouser, William, *157,* 248

G

Garcia, Raul, 298
Gariépy, Leonard, 244-6, *273*
Gavin, James M., 84, 92, 150, 153-4, 156
German Schutzstaffel (SS), 254, 282
German Army: 3rd Parachute Division,

174-5; 30th Mobile (bicycle) Regiment, 159; 77th Division, 164, 184; 91st Air Landing Division, 82, 136, 143, 153, 178, 182, 184; 314th Infantry Regiment, 189; 325th Division, 164; 352nd Division, 159, 166, 173, 184; 441 Ost [East] Battalion, 144, 148; 709th Division, 188; 726th Regiment, 160; 914th Regiment, 126, 160; 916th Grenadiers Regiment, 83, 125, 144, 159; 1057th Regiment, 179, 182; 1058th Regiment, 161, 167; Fifteenth Army, 93, 184, 205; II Parachute Corps, 164, 167, 206; LXXXIV Corps, 83, 151, 160, 186; LXXXVI Corps, 186, 225, 227; Nineteenth Army, 261; Seventh Army, 79, 160, 164, 174, 232, 238, 243, 246, 250, 259-60, 280, 284

German Army Panzer Divisions, 33-4, 93, 148, 151, 160, 162, 164, 167, 169, 172, 174-5, 184, 203, 217, 219, 222, 225, 227, 230-3, 236, 239-40, 243-4, 246, 248, 262; 2nd, 175; 12th SS, 217, 246; 17th SS Grenadier, 167; 21st, 93, 148, 164, 203; Lehr, 32, 93, 162, 164, 174, 203-4, 218, 232, 246

German Luftwaffe, 19, 47-8, 51, 78, 100, 102, 162, 164, 184, 186, 188, 219, 232, 266; 16th Luftwaffe Field Division, 219; planes on D-Day, 100

German Navy: E-boats or S-Boats, 69-70, 74; Kriegsmarine, 23, 34, 57, 78; U-boats, 20, 31, 34, 57, 100, 172, 204, 268

Germany, 15, 17, 23-4, 46-7, 49, 51, 54, 57-8, 65-6, 75, 84, 86, 88, 91, 204-6, 212, 275, 277, 279, 281-5, 288-90, 297-8; assassination attempt on Hitler, 253-9; breakout from Normandy, 222-48; building the bridgehead, 159-62; defenses before D-Day, 30-5; defenses in Normandy, 184-203; defenses on D-Day, 92-153; Exercise Tiger, 69-71; fighting in Cherbourg, 180-4; fighting in Paris, 286-90; fighting in the hedgerows, 161, 164-78; plot to assassinate Hitler, 253-6; in Southern France, 262-71

Gerolstein, Paul, 74-5
Gerow, Leonard T., 108, 204
Gerstner, Wilhelm, 282
Giacchi, Patsy, 70-71, 75
Gibbons, John, 51-4
Gibbons, Joseph H., 122
Gibbons, Sam, 88, 92, *157*
Gliders, 47, 64, 66, 77, 83-4, 88, 92-3, 96, 100, 104, 143, 153-6, 161, 166-7, 178, 181
Goth, Ernst, 35, 83, 159
Great Britain (*see also* Allied Forces), 13, 15, 36, 38, 44, 46-9, 57, 64, 77, 93, 98, 172, 174-5, 221-2, 225-8, 230, "Blitz" on London, 16, 203; breakout from Normandy, 203, 219, 227; at D-Day on Common-

wealth beaches, 143-50; Dieppe Raid, 22-4; Falaise Pocket, 243-4; fighting in the hedgerows, 159-60, 164, 198; invasion of Southern France, 259-67; liberation of Paris, 282-98; planning for cross-channel invasion, 20-6; working with French Underground, 272

Great Britain Army: 1st Battalion of Black Watch in Scotland, 149; 3rd Infantry Division, 144, 164, 222; 6th Airborne Division, 47, 77, 93, 164, 225; 7th Armoured Division, 174-5; 21st Army, 298; 47th Royal Marine Commando, 159; 50th Division, 144, 159-60; 51st British (Highland) Infantry Division, 227-8; I Corps, 226; King's Shropshire Lt. Infantry, 44, 144, 222, 225, 227; Oxfordshire and Buckinghamshire Light Infantry, 93; Second Army, 143-4, 174, 217-18, 221, 230-1, 233, 243, 284; Staffordshire Yeomanry, 144-5, 148, 222, 226-7; VIII Corps, 203, 206, 226-7, 232, 236, 238; XXX Corps, 203

Great Britain RAF, 44, 218; 2nd Tactical Air Force, 95, 97, 162; Bomber Command, 96; Third Air Fleet, 186
Great Britain Royal Navy, 57, 125, 217, 226, 262
Great Britain Royal Navy vessels: HMS *Apollo*, 164; HMS *Azalea*, 70; HMS *Black Prince*, 102; HMS *Glasgow*, 190; HMS *Pursuer*, 264; HMS *Rodney*, 218-19

H

Haigler, Frank, 104
Haislip, Wade, 246, 279
Hall, John L., 55
Harbour, Tommy, 41, 44, 69, 116-17, 262, 264-5
Hausser, Paul, 238, 280
Heydte, F.A.F. von der, 167
Hitler, Adolf, 13, 15, 30-4, 52, 58, 79, 93, 160, 164, 177, 188, 205-6, 217, 225, 236, 238-9, 241-4, 246, 262, 297-8; meets with Rommel & Rundstedt near Paris, 184; ordered harbor destroyed at Cherbourg, 191; plot to assassinate Hitler, 253-6
Hobson, Sam, 36, 212
Hodges Courtney H., 236
Holland, 30, 49, 272
Horn, Joseph, 136-7

I

Intelligence, 16, 32, 58, 78, 96, 112-13, 174, 218, 225, 239, 262; Enigma encoder/decoder, 13, 57; OSS, 60, 272; ULTRA intercept helped Allies at Breakout from Normandy, 204
Italy, 25, 30, 34, 259, 261, 270, 277

J

Johnson, Charles H., 297
Johnson, Leon W., 49
Jones, Harry G., 144-5
Jones, John W., 262

K

Kappler, Muriel, 200-1, *273*, 291-2
Keffer, Edward P., 207, *273*
Kellem, Frederick A., 86
King George VI, 96, *265*
Kirk, Alan G., 55, 57
Kluge, Günther von, 233, 238-9, 242-3, 246, 254-6; takes over command of OB West, 206
Knight, Lionel, 227
Krause, Edward C., 92, 153

L

La Fière Bridge, Battle for, 150, 153-69
Landing craft, 20, 24, 26, 41, 46, 55, 60, 104, 111, 113-4, 119, 122, 129, 137, 141, 143-5, 148, 184, 198; LCIs (Infantry), 69, 101, 105-6, 123-4, 130, 164; LCTs (Tanks), 25, 57, 74, 102, 107, 112, 116, 122, 137, 148, 184; LCVPs (Vehicle and Personnel), 24-5, 45-6, 71, 104, 106, 108, 116, 118, 134-5, 140, 262, 264
Leclerc, Jacque Philippe, 288, 290
Libaudais, James, 46-7, 92-3
Littlar, Bob, 44-5, 225
Lloyd, R.G., 147

M

MacKenzie, Bruce, 97, 100
Marcks, Erich, 160
Marr, John M., 82, 84, 154-6
Marshall, S.L.A., 156
McCandless, Dean, 77-8, 86-7, 150-1, 153, 181-2
McKinney, Vincent, 118, *157*
McNair, Leslie J., 208, 234, 236
Middleton, Troy H., 232, 238
Mines, 35, 86, 92, 125, 127, 142, 165, 180, 259, 265
Montgomery, Bernard L., 59-60, 66, 173, 203, 216-18, 221, 225, 228, 243, 246, 284, 297; meets with Eisenhower & Churchill, 231; Operation Goodwood, 222
Moreno, Patty, 70
Morgan, Frederick E., 22
Mortain, 239-43, 246
Mountbatten, Louis, 23
Mulberries, 25-6, 41, 57, 164, 172, 186, 188
Mussolini, Benito, 34, *253*

N

Nazis, 32, 45, 57-8, 238, 248, 253-4, 275, 289, 297
New Zealand Navy, 262
Normandy, 26, 35-6, 172-3, 176, 180, 184, 186, 195, 198, 200, 261, 264, 266, 270, 283, 289, 297-8; breakout from, 203-50; invasion, 55-167, 222, 248, 262
Norway, destroyer sunk at Sword Beach, 143

O

Omaha Beach, 35, 45, 55, 132, 139, 142-3, 159, 164-6, 170, 172, 186, 188, 198-9, 201, 212, 214, 216, 240; D-Day landing, 106-31
Operations: *Anvil*, 248; *Bolero*, 20, 39; *Charnwood*, 217-18, 222; *Cobra*, 209, 211, 232-3, 236, 239; *Dragoon*, 259-62, 266-7, 276; *Goodwood*, 217, 222, 225-6, 230, 233, 243, 256, 259; *Neptune*, 65-6, 98, 100, 103; *Overlord*, 24, 26, 36, 43-7, 54-5, 63, 75, 98, 132, 159, 172, 179, 190, 200, 259

P

Pachuta, Mike, 241, *273*
Paratroopers, 46, 64, 77-150, 161, 167, 169, 178-9, 181
Paris, 34, 45, 93, 184, 203, 222, 243, 254-5, 275-6, 279-81, 283-4, 288-9; liberation of, 289-90, 292, 297-8; uprising, 286-9
Patch, Alexander M., 259-60
Patton, George S., 60, 164, 208, 228, 233, 236, 238-40, 246, 279; arrives in France, 232; breakout from Normandy, 243; commands fake First Army, 58; Eastern France, 297; push to the Seine, 250
Périers Ridge, 144-5, 147, 149
Piper, Albert, 64-5, 105-6, 118, 123, 127, 157, 236
Polish forces, 244, 266
Proud, Howard, 191
Purdy, Fred, 38, 62, 142-3, 243-4, 288

Q

Queen Mary, 36, 38-9, 43, 196
Queen Elizabeth, 36, 38-9
Quesada, Elwood L., 209, 211

R

Raff, Edson D., 143
Ramsay, Bertram H., 60
Ridgway, Matthew B., 77, 86
Roberts, James Milnor, 23, 129, 131, 225
Roberts, J.H., 23
Roberts, John R., 44, 222, 225-6

Robeson, Clarence, 121
Robinson, Glen E., 207, *273*
Rommel, Erwin, 30-1, 34-5, 95, 164, 167, 173-4, 177, 181, 206, 219, 231, 238; in Germany on D-Day, 79; Hitler visits him near Paris, 184; with Rundstedt private meeting with Hitler July 1st, 205; support of assassination attempt on Hitler, 253-4, 256; wounded and left Normandy, 231
Roosevelt, President Franklin D., 13, 15-16, 20, 26, 29
Roosevelt, Theodore Jr., 136
Rosie the Riveters, 26, 36
Rundstedt, Gerd von, 30, 32, 93, 164, 177, 205; command replaced, 206; meets with Rommel and Hitler June 17th, 184
Russians, 32-4, 116

S

Sabotage, 78, 93, 272, 275
Schlieben, Karl-Wilhelm von, 192, 205; appealed to Hitler for reinforcements to defend Cherbourg, 188; surrenders at Cherbourg, 191
Schweppenburg, Leo Geyr von, 34, 160, 164, 174-5; relieved of command, 206; returned to command Panzer Group West, 203
Scotland, 36, 38-9, 41, 44, 51, 196
Serio, Charles, 67, 262
SHAEF, 29, 51, 54, 65-6, 78, 92, 142, 166, 218, 232, 236, 248, 260, 297-8
Shaw, Irwin, 243
Shay, Charles Norman, 36, 38, 45, 61, 104-5, 118-19, 121-2, 128, 131, 195-6, 283, 290
Simmons, Buster, 38, 44, 61-2, 172, 209, 209-11, 240
Skorupa, Albert, 134
Slapton Sands, 61, 64, 67, 69, 71, 73-5
Sorrentino, Joe, 62-3, 65, 67, 212-16, 272, 291
Southern France, invasion of, 259-62, 264-6, 270, 275, 282
Spaatz, Carl, 49
St.-Côme-du-Mont, 87, 161, 167
St.-Lô, 164, 175-7, 203, 208-9, 211-12, 214, 216, 226, 232-3, 270
St.-Nazaire, 23, 204, 238, 283
Stalin, Joseph, 26, 29
Stansfield, Capt. P.W., 145
Stauffenberg, Claus Schenk Graf von, *253,* 254-5
Ste.-Mère-Église, 77, 83-4, 86, 87-92, 136, 142-3, 150-1, 153-4, 161, 167, 169, 178, 184, 200, 214
Steele, John M., 91
Sutton, Eddie, 38, 199-201

T

Taylor, Bud, 102-3, 125, 266-7
Taylor, Maxwell D., 78, 88, 90, 125, 161, 167, 266
Tedder, Arthur, 59
Towers, Frank, 176, 233-4, 236, 239-40, 282
Troyer, David, 65, 69, 74-5, 134-6

U

United Nations, 16, 29, 45
United States, (*see also* Allied Forces), 3, 17, 26, 38, 41, 45, 61, 272, 283, 286, 289 ; arrival in France of Patton's Third Army, 232-43; Exercise Tiger, 69-75; Omaha Beach, 107-31; push of First Army to Paris, 282-3; push of Patton to Seine, 279-82; Utah Beach, 132-43
United States Army: 2nd Ranger Battalion, 45, 112; 4th Armored Division, 236; 4th Engineer Battalion, 142; 6th Airborne Division, 46, 93, 132, 181-2, 186, 188; 12th Army, 236, 298; 21st Army Group, 203, 221-2; 82nd Airborne Division, 46, 78, 82, 84, 86-8, 92, 98, 143, 150, 153, 156, 161, 167, 177, 179, 182; 101st Airborne Division, 77-9, 82-3, 86-7, 141, 161, 166-7, 169, 175, 177; 531st Engineer Shore Regiment, 134; 823rd Tank Destroyer Battalion, 239; African-American barrage balloon battalions, 165-6; Armored Field Artillery Battalions, 44, 107, 112, 136, 167, 236; First Army, 153, 161, 164-5, 167, 172-3, 177, 199, 201, 211, 226, 231-3, 236, 239-44, 262, 282-3, 286, 297; Quartermaster Corps, 62, 65, 75, 134, 212; Second Army, 218, 230-1, 233; Seventh Army, 297; Signal Corps, 38, 62, 77, 142, 243, 288; Tank Battalions, 112, 116, 136, 161, 166, 211; Third Army, 172, 177, 203-4, 208, 228, 232-3, 236, 240-1, 243-4, 246, 250, 267, 270, 280, 288, 291, 297-8
United States Army, Signal Corps, 38, 62, 77, 142, 243
United States Army, Third Army, 208, 236
United States Army Air Force: 100th Bomb Group, 49, 51, 95, 97; Eighth Air Force, 48-9, 51, 61, 95-6; Ninth Air Force, 51-2, 95, 132, 162, 209, 211; VIII Bomber Command, 48
United States Army Corps: V, 108, 131-2, 159-60, 172, 175, 177, 203, 208, 236; VI, 261, 268; VII, 82, 132, 140, 159-61, 175, 177-8, 181-2, 184, 186, 189, 203, 232, 236, 279, 281; VIII, 182, 206, 232, 236, 238, 281; XII, 232; XIX, 177, 232, 236
United States Army Infantry: 1st Division, 64, 104, 159, 173-5, 230, 239; 2nd Division, 172-5, 177; 4th Division, 44, 69, 132, 139, 184, 186, 188, 195; 8th Regiment, 132, 136, 161, 178, 195; 9th Division, 181-2, 186, 188; 12th Regiment, 178; 16th Regiment, 107-8, 116, 118, 123, 125-6; 18th Regiment, 159; 22nd Regiment, 132, 178; 26th Regiment, 131, 159; 28th Division, 294; 29th Division, 63, 100, 108, 112, 166, 172-3, 175-7, 212, 240; 30th Division, 36, 175-6, 209, 211, 216, 239-40; 38th

Regiment, 177; 77th Division, 181; 79th Division, 186, 188, 191, 206; 90th Division, 132, 179-82, 236; 115th Regiment, 131, 159-60; 116th Regiment, 106, 112, 116, 118-19, 122, 125-6, 160, 166; 118th Regiment, 212; 120th Regiment, 38, 172, 176-7, 233, 239; 175th Regiment, 159, 161, 166-7; 314th Regiment, 191; 357th Regiment, 179, 236; 358th Regiment, 179, 181; Glider, 47, 84, 143, 153, 155-6, 161, 166, 178, 181; PIR (Parachute Infantry Regiment), 60, 77-9, 82-3, 87-9, 91-2, 141, 150, 153-4, 156, 161, 167, 178, 181
United States Coast Guard, 25, 41, 55, 106-7 *see also* Harbour, Tommy
United States Marines, 39, 41
United States medical teams, 38, 44, 61, 69, 75, 92, 104, 119, 132, 139, 172, 180, 184, 186, 188, 195-9, 200-1, 207, 209, 240, 242; 42nd Medical Battalion field hospital, 200; 105th Medical Detachment, 209
United States Navy: 6th Naval Beach Battalion, 123; sinking of USS *Osprey,* 100; underwater demolition team, 123
United States Navy vessels, 54; Liberty ships, 41; USS *Arkansas,* 55, 112, 124, 162, 188; USS *Augusta,* 112, 126; USS *Bayfield,* 69, 103, 107, 117, 262; USS *Nevada,* 55, 102-5, 188-9; USS *Pennsylvania,* 102; USS *Quincy,* 102, 190; USS *Texas,* 55, 102, 112, 124, 188-9; USS *Thompson,* 64, 102, 125, 190, 266; USS *Tuscaloosa,* 102
Utah Beach, 55, 65, 69, 79, 82, 84, 93, 96, 101, 104, 107, 132, 134-7, 139-43, 150, 153, 161, 178, 200, 212, 266

V

V-1 flying bombs, *203,* 205-6
V-2 rockets, 205-6
Vaghi, Joseph, 123-4
Vian, Philip, 55
Volkl, Jackie, 36, 64, *67*

W

WAC (Women's Army Corps), 36
Wade Haislip, 246, 279
Webb, Garth, 148, *157,* 245, 285-6
Webber, Al, 41, 44, 67, 179-81, 183-4
Weller, Jim, 44, 64, 107, 112, 129, *157*
Wichterich, George, 239
Witmeyer, J.J., 38, 140-2, 186-7, 190-1, 206-8, 279-80
Wolf, Ed, 96
Wolff, Robert, 48-9, *67*
Womersley, Joe, 149-50
Wood, John S., 236

Z

Zamorano, Gilbert, 238, *273*

FROM TOP LEFT TO RIGHT

1. Alan Webber
2. Charles Norman Shay
3. James Libaudais
4. James Weller
5. Yvette Alaniz
6. Tommy Harbour
7. Howard Proud
8. Garth Webb
9. Dean McCandless
10. Frank Haigler
11. David Troyer
12. J. J. Witmeyer
13. Fritz Baresel
14. John Marr
15. Robert Wolff
16. Joseph Sorrentino